EUROPEAN FINANCIAL CONTROL IN THE OTTOMAN EMPIRE

EUROPEAN FINANCIAL CONTROL IN THE OTTOMAN EMPIRE

A STUDY OF THE ESTABLISHMENT, ACTIVITIES, AND SIGNIFICANCE OF THE ADMINISTRATION OF THE OTTOMAN PUBLIC DEBT

BY

DONALD C. BLAISDELL, PH.D.

INSTRUCTOR IN GOVERNMENT IN COLUMBIA UNIVERSITY

Submitted in Partial Fulfillment of the Requirements for the degree of Doctor of Philosophy, in the Faculty of Political Science, Columbia University

NEW YORK

1929

CONTENTS

INTRODUCTION

International debts are seldom devoid of political, emotional, and psychological complications. And when the debtor is a "backward" country a veritable host of difficulties arises to plague all parties concerned. These facts have been so long patent to Europeans that they have become axioms of statecraft and a factor in that sense of inevitability, resignation, and destiny which has been characteristic of the expansion of western civilization. Americans, on the other hand, are just beginning to learn in the hard school of experience that although the flag need not follow the dollar, all sorts of other things do; news despatches and diplomatic correspondence reaching the United States from such divergent sources as France, Germany, Great Britain, Mexico, China, Nicaragua, and the Dominican Republic indicate that not all gold sheds rays of sunshine pure and serene. The student of American foreign affairs during the past quarter-century has become increasingly concerned with such prosaic matters as loans, refunding agreements, supervision by experts of the budgets of foreign countries, and varying degrees of political and military intervention which sometimes follow in the wake of these. No one is more keenly alert in this respect than the departments of State, Commerce, and the Treasury at Washington.

Dr. Blaisdell's history of the Ottoman Public Debt should therefore attract the attention of all students of international relations, whether or not they have heretofore concerned themselves with Turkish affairs. Americans will doubtless continue their instruction in the costly school of trial-and-error, but there is no reason why they should not acquire a modicum of knowledge from the experience of others. The Near East has long been a laboratory for students of world politics. In the tangled affairs of the Near East there are few institutions of greater significance than the Ottoman Public Debt Administration; it is therefore a matter of prime importance that an objective account of European control of Ottoman finances should be made available. In the diversified but pertinent material which is here presented the reader may learn a great deal concerning the affairs of the former Ottoman Empire, the policies of the several Great Powers in the Near East before and since the Great War, the relative merits of financial tutelage of a "backward" country, and the political implications of foreign investments.

It is a merit of Dr. Blaisdell's book that it is no mere chronicle of events but a serious attempt, as well, to view them in perspective and against the background of world affairs. There will be some, to be sure, who will object to linking the Ottoman Public Debt Administration with European imperialism inasmuch as it was apparently non-political in origin, personnel, and operation. This is a largely a matter of terminology. But Dr. Blaisdell's thesis in this respect is strongly buttressed by the treaty which the Allies dictated at Sèvres and which the Turks subsequently refused to ratify; here are revealed to public gaze for the first time a number of suppressed desires the existence of which had long been suspected. Dr. Blaisdell has rightly assigned to the Public Debt Administration a large place in the economic history of the Balkans, Asia Minor, and the Arab provinces of the Sultans. He has emphasized the highly important fact that the personnel (Christian and Moslem) of the Administration set a high standard of official integrity in the midst of an imperial system which otherwise was shot through with corruption. Nevertheless, the Turkish nationalist movement swept the Public Debt—along with the Capitulations and other instrumentalities of foreign intervention—into the large and impressive scrap-heap of the former Empire. Why? Because nationalism chafes under restraints imposed from without; wherever a vigorous nationalist movement asserts itself, foreign tutelage is its own Nemesis. Liberty, said the Turks, is more to be desired than efficiency; in this sentiment they appear to be joined by the Chinese and other peoples with whom Americans have a variety of economic contacts. This point of view must be recognized, however much it may be held in contempt.

Dr. Blaisdell's study, therefore, can be cordially commended to all who profess an interest in world affairs and, more especially, to those whose particular concern is the Near East.

EDWARD MEAD EARLE

PREFACE

Imperialism seems always to be with us, yet to some it must seem bold to present another book on imperialism in the Near East. Were this a conventional treatment of the age-old eastern question its justification might be doubtful. So far as I am aware, however, it is the initial attempt to interpret European interests in the Ottoman Empire from the standpoint of economic control.

The writing of such a book was first suggested to me in the winter of 1925-26. I had just returned to the United States from a three years' sojourn in the Near East and, under such circumstances, the suggestion was an attractive one. The fact that I had been privileged to witness at first-hand some of the historic events of 1922 and 1923 in the Near East made me desirous of uncovering the foundation of the interests which brought the Entente powers and the Turkish Nationalist Government to the brink of war.

With the appearance in 1923 of Professor Earle's book on the Bagdad railway that enterprise emerged from the obscurity of diplomacy and international rivalry and stood forth as one of the forces which contributed to the Great War. French interests in the Near East were of such long standing as to have impressed the features of the "civilizing mission" upon the entire eastern Mediterranean area. Only the dramatic character of the rise and success of Turkish nationalism and the turning of the tables against the Allies at Lausanne drew public attention from the Treaty of Sèvres and the nature of that settlement. Yet in large measure the provisions of that treaty were drawn up on the basis of the material interests of the Allies in Turkey. But, almost unknown to the world at large, these interests as well as those of Germany and Austria (which became the spoils of war), had been safeguarded for years by a European-controlled institution—the Administration of the Ottoman Public Debt.

The problem was apparent, but the method of solving it appeared only at a later date. Obviously, such material as was available in America would have proved insufficient for a successful inquiry into this question. The availability of one source in particular—the archives in Constantinople of the Public Debt itself—became essential. Columbia University made it possible for me to go to Constantinople, and Sir Adam Block, at that time British member and president of the Council, granted permission for research in those archives. Equally important was his action in 1928 when he gave his permission for excerpts from the Council minutes, heretofore confidential, to be incorporated into this work. To Columbia University and to Sir Adam I am glad to acknowledge my debt of gratitude.

For having provided me with important but somewhat less essential information, I am indebted to others in Constantinople. Hussein Djahid Bey, war-time president of the Council, Mouslihéddine Adil Bey, counsel for the Turkish Government at Lausanne, and Ahmed Emin Bey, were generous of their time and patience in answering many questions. M. Lescaillet and M. Dochoda of the Public Debt Secretariat facilitated the task of research in Constantinople.

In Berlin I was provided with significant material by Dr. Weigelt of the *Deutsche Bank,* Dr. Breslauer of the House of S. Bleichröder, Dr. Ziemcke, of the German Foreign Office, and Dr. Boetzkes of the German Bank for Industrial Obligations. Likewise M. Eugène Borel of Geneva, and Sir Vincent Caillard of London, explained important aspects of the problem. Many details were furnished by officials of the Paris branch of the Imperial Ottoman Bank, by officers of the London Corporation of Foreign Bondholders, and by M. Raymond Maurel, director-general of the Public Debt Administration.

The manuscript has been read by my professors in Columbia University, Edward M. Earle, Parker T. Moon, and Joseph P. Chamberlain, all of whom made valuable suggestions and criticisms. To my father I am glad to express my appreciation of his generous expenditure of time and energy in assisting in the revision of the text. By the patient performance of many a tedious task of searching and checking my wife has contributed not a little to the volume. Indeed, it stands as a tribute to her forbearance.

A book on such a subject must of necessity evoke criticism and difference of opinion. For the interpretation of facts and for the expression of opinion I accept full responsibility.

D. C. B.

Columbia University,
May, 1929.

Chapter I

THE PROBLEM OUTLINED

This book tells a tale of the East, not Kipling's East, but the Near East, the cross-roads of civilizations. It is the story of European economic penetration into the Ottoman Empire. Its central theme is the establishment, activities, and significance of the organization known as the "Administration of the Ottoman Public Debt." This prosaic title masked an institution the extent of whose activities ranged from northern Africa to the frontiers of Persia, and from the Danube to the Red Sea. Its rights in the Ottoman Empire rested on an agreement the existence of which was defended by the foreign offices of Europe. The opinions of its executive committee were eagerly sought in the chancelleries of western Europe, while in post-war days members of its Council aided in the drafting of two peace settlements.

The Council of the Ottoman Debt an Outpost of European Capitalism

In 1875 the Ottoman Government defaulted the charges on a foreign debt of two hundred million pounds sterling. Six years later a contract was concluded between the Sublime Porte,[1] as the Ottoman Government was called, and representatives of its foreign and domestic creditors for the resumption of payments on Ottoman bonds. This agreement, called the Decree of Mouharrem (from the Turkish month in which it was drafted), instituted European control of a part of the imperial revenues. Thus came into existence the international body called the Administration of the Ottoman Public Debt. In 1881 the revenue-collecting agents of this organization numbered over three thousand. Its executive committee, called the "Council," the "Public Debt," or merely the "Debt," was composed of six delegates representing the British

[1] Strictly speaking the title "Sublime Porte" applied to the Ministry of Foreign Affairs. In the public mind, however, and, indeed, throughout Europe in both official and unofficial circles, the term was used to designate the Ottoman Government. Such is the use of the phrase in this work.

and Dutch, the French, the German, the Italian, the Austro-Hungarian, and the Ottoman holders of Turkish securities, and a seventh delegate representing a series of priority bonds, held largely by the Imperial Ottoman Bank.[2]

The activities of this Administration were far-reaching in their direct and indirect results. As the guardian of the loans included in the Decree of Mouharrem (1881), the Council was the organ erected to safeguard the investments in Ottoman securities made prior to this date by European capitalistic society. Over one hundred millions sterling invested in these bonds represented the earnings and savings of tens of thousands of Europeans. In the middle of the nineteenth century Englishman and Frenchman had been attracted to Ottoman bonds by the prospects of a liberal return on their money, particularly as these bonds were sanctioned, in their opinion, by a favorable attitude of their governments.

Later on, when doubts were afloat concerning Turkish good faith, possessors of ready capital were encouraged to lend yet more money to Turkey by the establishment of the Imperial Ottoman Bank which, despite its name, was the child of French and English capital. This institution, through the many prospectuses issued under its ægis, stressed the gratifying extent of Turkish resources. Ottoman revenues had begun to rise; but so had the foreign indebtedness. Foreign ambassadors to the Sublime Porte agreed with Sultan Abdul Aziz (1861-76) that he should expand his navy. Thus he indulged in a pet extravagance, the purchase of iron-clads. The charges on the external and internal debts increased; another loan and yet another was necessary. Wily representatives of Paris and London banking houses persuaded Turkish officials that the best way to pay off a rapidly mounting debt was to increase it by floating another loan. Finally, in 1875, the process broke down under its own weight. A weak Grand Vizier and an unscrupulous, but powerful, Russian Ambassador brought about the default which caused the temporary ruin of Turkish credit.

---

[2] The official title of this organization was *L'Administration de la Dette Publique Ottomane,* which meant both the Council of Administration and the revenue-collecting machinery under its control. In these pages the various abbreviations—Council, Public Debt, or merely Debt,—refer to the Council of Administration as the executive organ of the institution, while the administrative agencies, as distinct from the executive committee, will be designated by the initials, P. D. A.

As European integrity and administrative skill were manifestly necessary, Sultan Abdul Hamid II (1876-1909) ceded to his creditors sufficiently wide powers and adequate revenues to insure interest and sinking fund charges. But he did not part with enough to impair seriously his financial sovereignty. To manage this foreign debt, consolidated in 1881 by the Decree of Mouharrem, was the primary function of the Council. In this capacity it was eminently successful; by 1903 nearly a quarter of the bonds had been redeemed. Details of its activities in this connection are elaborated in later chapters.

An Instrument of Imperialism

After the erection in 1882 of the Administration of the Ottoman Public Debt European capital, temporarily diverted from Turkey by the default in 1875, once more sought profitable employment in the Near East. But financiers in Europe were loath to place their faith solely in the Ottoman Government. The P. D. A., directed by a European-constituted council, was recognized as a more stable guarantee of efficient and trustworthy stewardship of capital than existed in the Ottoman Government. Bankers thus sought to enlist in their enterprises the coöperation of the Council.

In 1888 the Ottoman Government granted to the *Deutsche Bank,* of Berlin, a concession for the extension to Angora of the sixty-mile railway running south from Haidar Pasha (Constantinople). The Debt accepted the responsibility of collecting for the Bank certain imperial revenues which, by the concession, had been assigned to guarantee a minimum annual return from the railway. In later years a similar obligation was undertaken towards other progeny of the *Deutsche Bank,* such as further extensions of the Anatolian Railway and the Bagdad Railway. This function was assumed also for the benefit of the French-constructed Smyrna-Cassaba and Salonica Junction-Constantinople lines, and the network of French railways in Syria, which enterprises were the offspring of the Imperial Ottoman Bank, the creation of English and French capital with the latter dominant. Thus the Council was impartial in its willingness to undertake the administration of railway guarantees. Loans to the Ottoman

Government which were engineered by the Ottoman Bank and by the *Deutsche Bank* were also secured, for the most part, by revenues administered by the Public Debt. In the promotion of railways and in the floating of loans to the Ottoman Government, these two banks, as well as the Imperial Government itself, found a willing and worthy partner in the Council.

In coöperating with the Ottoman Bank and the *Deutsche Bank* and with their railways and industrial enterprises, the Debt functioned as the colleague of modern European capitalistic society intent on the economic exploitation of the Ottoman Empire. Probably, however, the Administration of the Public Debt was not an aggressive element. Its rôle was that of a well-ordered, capable, and powerful minor partner of the more energetic instruments of western economic penetration. The Council could not be called inactive, however. Its position in the Empire was firmly established, even though it rested on inchoate, but potential, legal and diplomatic sanctions. If no disputes arose with the Government to impede its forward march, the Council dispatched its business with serenity and efficiency. But when the established rights of an institution towards which it had assumed obligations were threatened, the Council transformed itself into a zealous and active partisan of the interests in danger. This quality of flexibility enabled the Public Debt to serve not only its own interests, but also to defend the wider group of projects with which it became associated.

In this capacity the Public Debt was a partner in imperialistic enterprise. That certain interests in western Europe were actuated by such motives in the Ottoman Empire is all but universally conceded.

Germany was frankly interested in the Near East. Was not the Bagdad Railway a ribbon of steel binding together all the economic, political, and cultural aims of the Kaiser's Government in the Empire of the Sultans? True, at an early date in its development it had been envisaged as a purely business enterprise with international backing. But certainly with the definitive concession of 1903, which granted to Germany the right to extend the Anatolian Railway to the Persian Gulf, concomitant political dangers were beginning to appear in the background. Some maintain that the inception of the idea was surrounded with political considerations.[3] In any event, the bargains of 1913-14 among Great Britain, Germany, France and Turkey recognized the project as a German imperialist enterprise. The Public Debt and its interested coöperation were indispensable to the success of the Bagdad Railway.

What were the foundations of French claims to a privileged position in Syria? Here, too, the network of railways constructed with French capital, the financial success of which depended on the strict discharge of obligations assumed by the Public Debt Council, was the most significant element. The French-constructed ports of Beirut, Smyrna, and Constantinople, the French-financed Smyrna-Cassaba Railway, the French-directed public utilities in Constantinople, Beirut, and Salonica, the French-exploited mines in northern Anatolia and commercial establishments in many Turkish cities; and finally the bulk of the Ottoman Government bonds held by French citizens,—all these "private" interests must have been the basis for the statement that "a financial protectorate has superseded the religious protectorate which has for so long guaranteed French influence in the Orient."[4] Of the capital which constituted the basis for this "financial protectorate," the overwhelming majority was invested on security guaranteed by the intervention of the Public Debt.

An Agent of the European Powers

In 1907 the Public Debt began the discharge of a function which made it the ally of the powers of Europe in their relations with the Empire of Abdul Hamid. At that time, because the British Foreign Secretary, Sir Edward Grey, was convinced that the Council was the only available organ that could function in the matter as the "agent" of the powers, the Public Debt agreed to supervise the collection of a three percent customs surtax, levied in order to meet Macedonian budget deficits. The powers, whose consent was necessary to any upward revision of Turkish import duties, agreed to this surtax on the condition that the proceeds

---

[3] As, for example, the British capitalist and promoter, Sir Vincent Caillard, who, in an interview with the author, stated that in 1888 Dr. von Siemens made the statement that he intended to build the Bagdad railway whether it paid or not.

[4] See *infra*, Chapter IX, note 13.

therefrom be applied to the improvement of conditions in Macedonia. The dissatisfaction of Sir Edward because the Public Debt Council was not originally named as the "effective guarantee" of the employment of this revenue in Macedonia, was removed in the definitive 1907 customs convention between the Ottoman Government and the powers of Europe.

Thus the Debt, in functioning under the terms of this convention, showed its willingness to participate in a political program, as well as to undertake the discharge of obligations of an economic character.

A Benefit to Turkey

Finally, the existence of the Administration of the Ottoman Public Debt created conditions which benefited both the Imperial Government and the population of the Empire. The able management of the Council exerted a salutary influence on imperial finances. The Government was enabled to borrow in the money markets of Europe on much more favorable terms than had been possible prior to 1881. After that date the usual interest rate on Ottoman Government bonds was three or four percent, and the issue prices of these loans were ordinarily eighty or ninety percent of par. The average issue price of the loans negotiated before the institution of the Administration was in the neighborhood of sixty percent, with an interest rate of five or six percent.

Theoretically the Administration was a department of the Ottoman Government; practically it functioned as a largely independent section of the Ministry of Finance. Thus, by the integrity and efficiency of its management, the Council afforded to the Government and to the population a striking example of the best features of European financial administration. Adjudication of the tithes (taxes)[5] took place on schedule; accounts were closed on time; coupons on the consolidated debt were met at maturity. Within its own ranks, the Administration never condoned dilatory methods; in its business with the Government the Council was continually pressing matters for solution. Salaries of native officials and of laborers employed in the P. D. A. were adequate, and were paid when due. On no occasion did the number of

---

[5] *Infra*, p. 11 *et seq.*

Europeans employed in the Administration exceed seven or eight percent of the total. The policy of regular payment of sufficient salaries practically wiped out, within the Administration's ranks, the abuses of *baksheesh* (bribery) and of retention of collected receipts by local revenue agents, two vices which had sorely troubled the Imperial Government in attempts to reform its financial administration. Indeed, to become an employee of the Administration was the ambition of many a Turk and Ottoman Christian.

Moreover, direct benefits to the native peasantry can be traced to the coöperation of the Council with foreign railway companies and banks. In the adjudication of tithes assigned as railway guarantees, or as security for government loans, the agents of the P. D. A. had an "effective voice" in all proceedings. These employees spurred on procrastinating Government officials who were charged with the auctioning of pledged tithes; the Council in Constantinople was an exacting master, and obligations to the Ottoman Bank and to the *Deutsche Bank* had to be rigidly discharged. Thus, under ordinary circumstances, the peasants were assured a fair price for their grain, and could depend on the auctions being held at favorable moments. The operation of the railways increased the productivity of the regions traversed by assuring the natives of means of transportation for all production beyond local requirements. In 1889 the value of the tithes in the provinces traversed by the Anatolian Railway was Ltqs. 145,378 (Turkish pounds); for the year 1898 this figure was Ltqs. 215,470, while in 1909 it reached Ltqs. 291,919.[6]

The Debt as an Example of Financial Control

That the Administration of the Ottoman Public Debt was not a typical example of foreign financial control is shown by several facts. Its organic statute was not an international treaty, nor even a diplomatic act. The salaries of the members of the Council were paid by the Ottoman Government; the expenses of the P. D. A. were met out of receipts from ceded taxes. Barely a third of Turkish revenues were under the control of the Council.

[6] Ltqs. is the abbreviation for *Livres Turques*, Turkish pounds. Normal exchange of the Turkish gold pound is Ltqs. 1.10 (110 piasters) to the pound sterling, or about $4.40.

Five different nationalities were here represented, yet these delegates were not appointed by their governments but were representatives of unofficial bondholders' syndicates.

Nevertheless, the vague sanctions of the Decree of Mouharrem gave to that instrument a quality of elasticity which allowed the powers of Europe to keep their hands free to act, in case of need, on motives of expediency, rather than on the basis of strictly defined obligations. The "unofficial" character of the Council's membership signified a minimum of mutual official responsibility between each representative and his government. At the same time this condition permitted each delegate to extend his interests and activities almost without limit. The relatively small proportion of Ottoman revenues administered by the Council created the illusion that in fact the Imperial Government remained the dominating factor in Ottoman finance. Nevertheless, the Council was sufficiently influential to guide Turkish financial policy in directions advantageous to the Council and its associated enterprises. The diversity of nationalities represented in the Council made that committee the representative of a class of European society, rather than the deputy of a single European state or group of states. The supposed inadequacy of the Decree of Mouharrem in reality was its most potential attribute.

In this chapter have been sketched in barest outlines the activities of the Administration of the Ottoman Public Debt; in the chapters that follow these outlines will be elaborated—this mere skeleton will be given flesh and blood and the breath of life.

Chapter II

THE BACKGROUND OF THE BORROWING

European financial control was instituted in the Ottoman Empire because of Turkish inability to administer finances in a manner satisfactory to Occidental tenets. Not unnaturally, Frenchmen and Englishmen who lent their money expected loans to be managed according to European fiscal principles. Aside from the fact that these principles demand a rigid adherence to the rule of punctual discharge of obligations (the importance of which was not apparent to Ottoman officialdom), internal conditions in the Empire precluded the possibility of honest and efficient handling of revenues. The twenty years preceding 1875, during which the pre-Decree foreign debt was contracted, were characterized by administrative disorganization throughout the Sultan's domains.

Turkey Handicapped by Internal Chaos

The real authority in the vast extent of the Empire was in the hands of the high officials, usually *pashas* (generals in the army), who were the governors of the *vilayets* (provinces). Except the Sultan himself and the ministers of the central departments in Constantinople, these provincial governors were the most influential persons in the Empire. The *valis,* as they were called, were indeed the keystone of Ottoman administration. They were appointed by the Sultan himself, and were removable by him only. At the other extremity of the bureaucratic ladder were the subordinate provincial officials who were responsible in each province to the *vali.*

The *vali* was charged with the execution of the laws within his province, the administration of justice, and the collection of the taxes. In these matters his responsibility was great, but the temptations to which he was subject were even greater. There was constant opportunity to discriminate between Moslems and non-Moslems in the enforcement of laws relating to the inheritance and transfer of property. Trade and commerce within a province were hampered according to the frequency and severity of arbitrary tax levies visited upon the non-Moslem elements, who controlled most of the trade. After 1856 the testimony of Christians was supposed to have been accepted in the courts of the Empire; yet within his province the *vali* was able, by properly exerted pressure, to bring this provision to naught.[1] The collection of the most important direct tax, the tithe, could easily be made his personal privilege, and here the chances for lining pockets were enormous. The energy and impartiality of a capable and conscientious administrator could be impressed upon the lower members of the bureaucracy. Just as easily could an unscrupulous and dishonest governor so influence the ranks of his subordinates as to preclude honesty and efficiency in local administration. In these key positions, therefore, good local government demanded the presence of skilled and scrupulous men.

Unfortunately, for the most part, the *valis*, even if skilled, were unscrupulous. In the selection of these officials influence and collusion at Constantinople were more powerful factors than personal integrity and administrative ability. Because of the opportunities for enriching one's self, these positions were eagerly sought by active, yet dishonest and scheming, members of the ruling class. Backstairs methods were the rule; traffic in these positions became a regular occupation of unofficial, yet powerful, retainers of the Sultan's court. When a *vali* was removed, the selection of his successor was, in the heyday of corruption, in effect a case of auctioning the office to the highest bidder. The necessity of procuring money to attain the position usually placed the successful person under obligations to a *saraf* (native banker). To his original desire to fill his pockets the governor had added the necessity of discharging financial obligations to his various official and unofficial backers. One of the two reasons for Turkey's existence, according to an English merchant in Constantinople, was "for the benefit of some fifty or sixty bankers or usurers, and some thirty or forty pashas, who make fortunes out of its spoils."[2]

The "Law of the Vilayets", of 1861, had intended to grant to the provinces a large measure of self-government, in which both

[1] Engelhardt, E., *La Turquie et le Tanzimat* (2 volumes, Paris, 1883-4), pp. 242-5.

[2] Cited in Senior, N. W., *A Journal kept in Turkey and Greece, 1857-58* (London, 1858), p. 84.

Moslems and Christians were to participate. In reality, however, the government of the Empire was centralized more than ever in the Sultan's hands. In effect this meant that opportunities were multiplied at Constantinople to exercise influence over the Sultan. The *valis* of the various provinces were in his undisputed power, while the *ex officio* official members of the local councils instituted by the Law secured a perpetual Moslem majority. "Under such a system, and the legal protection enjoyed through it by the Ottoman functionaries against evil consequences of their own misdeeds, corruption was rife throughout the Empire."[3]

Local government in the provinces was intimately related to administration of finances. The Sheriat, or Holy Law, prescribed the important taxes. Of these the tithe was the oldest and most firmly rooted in the life of the Empire. It could only be collected, however, in one of two ways. Either it could be apportioned among the various provinces and farmed to privileged persons for a fixed sum, or it could be collected directly by agents of the Treasury. In both systems there were almost insurmountable difficulties. The policy of farming the tithes had been followed for decades before the middle of the century, and it had been found that opportunities for corruption and dishonesty were many. The *vali* had often been the tithe farmer.[4] As he invariably possessed

---

[3] *Encyclopedia Britannica*, 11th Edition, Volume XXVII, p. 428.

[4] Theoretically, farming the tithes was abolished by the *Hatti-Humayoun* (Imperial Edict of February 18, 1856) which provided that "the law will enjoin any discrimination against individuals; the evidence of Christians is to be accepted in the courts of the Empire; the abuses in the collection of taxes will be corrected, and the tithes, instead of being farmed out as formerly, will be collected directly by agents of the Treasury. . . . The laws against corruption will be applied indiscriminately to all those who contravene them." Practically, this Edict had little effect in changing the earlier method of farming the tithe.

The *Hatti-Humayoun*, and the *Hatti-Sherif of Gulhané*, November 3, 1839, together with the laws and decrees promulgated to enforce them, are known collectively as the *Tanzimat*, or Series of Reforms. Together they formed the attempts made by Sultan Abdul Medjid (1839-61) and his ministers to improve the condition of the Christian elements of the Empire, and to reorganize generally the central and local administrations. A Western observer contributes this criticism of the *Hatti-Sherif*: "The motives that led to the framing of the *Gulhané* edict, and the project of thereby reforming the administrative system of the Ottoman Empire were doubtless praiseworthy. They were the creation of a benevolent and liberal mind, but not of a political economist conversant with the counter-prejudices and correlative position of the vast majority of his fellow-countrymen, or with the objects and restless ambition of the minority. Before changing the character of the connection between rulers and people

friends in high positions, he could procure the privilege of collecting the tithe for a price low in comparison with that realizable at a real public auction. In collusion with a banker of questionable methods the *vali* would purchase the privilege at a farcical auction; the two would then collect sums from the taxpayers far out of proportion to the tithe for which they were legally accountable. The difference between the price paid for the privilege and that actually received from the taxpayers would be divided among the *pasha*, his *saraf*, and subordinate officials coöperating with them. The taxpayer could not make a complaint heard in Constantinople, once the central government had received the amount paid by the farmer; and, in attempting to complain to his provincial governor, the peasant would find himself face to face with the person who had taken from him more than the law stipulated.[5]

---

individually, and, above all, before attempting to imitate foreign institutions, it was essential to have considered how far these changes and imitations were applicable to the subjects of the Sublime Porte." Charles White, *Three Years in Constantinople* (London, 1845), pp. 296-7. The texts of the two *Hatts* are to be found in Nouradounghian, G., *Receuil d'Actes Internationaux de l'Empire Ottoman* (4 volumes, Paris, 1878-1902), Volume II, p. 287, and III, p. 83.

[5] While traveling in Turkey Nassau Senior had the following conversation with an English resident in Constantinople: "It is absolutely impossible for a *pasha* to remain poor, unless he be absolutely indifferent to money. Reshid Pasha's palace and park on the Bosporus are worth at least 200,000 pounds sterling; the land is worth perhaps 300,000 pounds. At the death of the last owner, who died without male issue, this property escheated to the Sultan, and was sold at public auction. Reshid was Grand Vizier, and bought it for 25,000 pounds. According to custom, no one overbid the Grand Vizier." When Nassau Senior asked what would have been the consequence had someone overbid him, the answer was: "It is useless to ask what would have happened under impossible conditions. An idea as strange as overbidding a vizier, or even a *pasha*, never enters anyone's head. Reshid was very generous in valuing these grounds at 25,000 pounds. He could have had them knocked down for a thousand." Senior, *op. cit.*, p. 101. The unenviable position of the taxpayer, both Moslem and Christian, is described in Du Velay, A., *Histoire Financière de la Turquie* (Paris, 1903), pp. 59-98; see also Georgiades, D., *La Turquie actuelle* (Paris, 1892), pp. 31-3.

Du Velay's *Histoire Financière* is a classic on Turkish finance. Written by a former official of the Ottoman Bank, and utilizing documents obtained from that source, the entire history of financial mismanagement, the breakdown of the system of taxation, reform and finance, and the story of the Public Debt Administration until 1903, is told in detail and with authority. The author maintains quite successfully an unbiased point of view, but it is evident that he sees conditions through European glasses. Unfortunately, the work has not been brought up to date. The other indispensable secondary source for the student of this subject is Morawitz, Charles, *Les Finances de la Turquie* (Paris, 1902). This likewise has not been brought up to date, is not so comprehensive as Du Velay, but

If the method of farming was not employed, the only alternative was the system of collecting the tithe *en régie,* that is, in kind, by Treasury agents. This course involved expense with which the central administration could not be burdened. A large organization of agents was necessary, and, what was more important, it was essential that this body of collectors be honest and efficient. Moreover, inasmuch as the tithe was collected in kind, there remained the expense of providing warehouses where the produce could be stored until a favorable time for its sale. Although the necessity of transforming the tithe into money was a process demanding absolute honesty, the opportunity for fraud by which a corrupt local administration could profit was ever present.

Besides the tithe the two other direct taxes were the tax on land and the head tax on non-Moslems. Here, too, favoritism in the designation of tax collectors together with discrimination between Moslems and non-Moslems, and between taxpayers of wealth and those of modest means, resulted in an inequitable distribution of taxation.

Nature itself emphasized the difficulties encountered in local administration. The extensive coastlines encouraged smuggling and the introduction of contraband. Topographic features were inhospitable; different sections of the country were separated by mountain ranges; the central Anatolian plateau was visited by periodic droughts and inundations. Distances were enormous. From the Bosnian frontier to the Persian Gulf is farther by four hundred miles than from Kansas City to New York, and mountains and deserts intervened. The African provinces were separated from Constantinople by wide stretches of sea and desert. These extensive territories and the lack of a satisfactory system of communication encouraged revolutionary movements. Parts of the Empire, like Egypt and Tunis, became tributary provinces with their governors practically sovereign. The European provinces were inhabited for the most part by minority races who welcomed the European sentiment of nationalism, and turned the Balkan question into an apparently inextricable tangle. Most of

---

the descriptions of early financial conditions (prior to Mahmoud II, 1808-39) are extremely interesting and enlightening. Morawitz writes with wide knowledge of the Orient and introduces many interesting characteristics of the people, but his point of view is likewise European. He was for many years an official of the Anglo-Austrian Bank in Vienna.

the rivers were short and swift, and unsuited to navigation and commerce. The topography of the country made it difficult and expensive to construct roads and highways. The development of maritime steam transportation drew traffic from the caravan routes which formerly connected the Arabian provinces with the capital. Remote sections of the country were unconnected with the sea ports and cities by roads suitable for quick travel. Lacking means of transportation, the Government could not readily move troops for the suppression of revolt. The Empire possessed few railways. Short lines like the Smyrna-Aidin, and Mersina-Adana lines, were constructed in the 1860's; Baron Hirsch's Orient railway was not constructed until the 1870's, and it was not until 1888 that Constantinople was linked by rail with central and western Europe. The German project for a trunk line across Anatolia to the Persian Gulf was not begun until the early years of the twentieth century, and even now (1929) is not completed.

Obsolete Methods at Constantinople

The dishonest administration of the taxes in the provinces was matched by the lack of organization in the central ministry of finance. Prior to 1839 there had been no office of minister of finance. The highest fiscal official in the state was the grand treasurer (*defterdar*) who, as his title suggests, was more a general guardian of certain state funds than a person charged with the administration of revenue and expenditure. After the creation of the office of minister of finance, the duties for which its occupant was responsible were not comparable in any way with those of a modern finance minister. Although budgets were published after 1863, these were nothing more than vague estimates of what expenses and revenue might be. Indeed, it was impossible for them to be otherwise. The Civil List, or private income of the Sultan, was not the property of the state. It was under the control of a special minister, responsible to the Sultan only. If the monarch and his family desired to exceed it, they could do so with impunity. The minister of the Civil List realized that his tenure of office depended upon remaining in the good graces of his master; therefore, it behooved him to uncover sources of revenue to meet expenses not met by the Civil List. The extravagant tastes of Medjid and Aziz during the middle of the nineteenth century necessitated a series of incumbents of this position ingenious enough to realize sums to meet royal demands.[6]

No less demoralizing was the use of drafts (*havalés*) to pay state bills. These were mere orders to pay, signed by the finance minister, issued on the revenues of different provinces. They were delivered by ministers of state to creditors and contractors and were often negotiated at a considerable discount. Favoritism among ministers and between ministers and creditors created the gravest abuses in this system. Moreover, certain ministries possessed special revenues that were in no way accountable to the minister of finance. Thus it was impossible to integrate the total estimated expenses of the state, and the finance minister was unable to balance revenue against disbursement.[7]

To add to this confusion of organization the state itself made grievous financial errors in attempting to provide revenues to meet constantly increasing demands. The Government purposely de-

[6] A detailed account of the organization of the Treasury is given in Du Velay, *op. cit.*, pp. 38 *et seq.* The remnants of the old organization, and its duties, persisted into the twentieth century: "The ministry of finance (*malié*) is the modern counterpart of the old grand treasurer (*defterdar*). In the extent as well as in the nature of his attributes, the head of the ministry resembles this officer of the old régime, rather than a European minister of finance. Since 1881 relieved by the Public Debt Administration of almost all the responsibility for the service on the consolidated debt; since 1900 subordinated to the financial commission of Top-Hané [an offshoot of the Council of State established by Abdul Hamid II] for the solution of all important financial questions, and deprived of all effective control as a result; disturbed, moreover, in its internal functioning by a financial system which does not allow the finance minister to centralize receipts in his tills nor to control the expenditures of ministers by coördinating revenue and disbursements in a budget, the *malié* has become a correspondence and accounting bureau, concerning itself only with the means of meeting the daily expenses which fall upon it. . . ." Young, George (ed.), *Corps de Droit Ottoman—Receuil des codes, lois, règlements, ordonnances, et actes les plus importants du droit intérieur, et d'études sur le droit coutumier de l'Empire Ottoman* (7 volumes, Oxford, 1905-6), Volume V, pp. 14-17. The functioning of this extraordinary organization was rendered all the more difficult by an attitude described thus: "Respect for a fixed time of payment is a notion absolutely foreign to the Ottoman intelligence, which has an instinct as well as a taste for petty expedients, subterfuges, and deferments until the morrow or the following week. But one must not exaggerate the importance and gravity of the incidents which arise. On the whole, with more or less good will, after more or less delay, under more or less energetic pressure, Turkey pays what she owes." Morawitz, Charles, "The Public Debt of Turkey," in *The North American Review*, Volume CLXXV (August, 1902), p. 287.

[7] Young, *op. cit.*, Volume V, pp. 14-17; Morawitz, *op. cit.*, p. 67; Du Velay, *op. cit.*, p. 117; Charmes, J., *L'Avenir de la Turquie* (Paris, 1882) pp. 287-94.

based the value of the specie in circulation, issued large amounts of paper money with no reserve, and embarked on a policy of meeting annually recurring budget deficits by floating loans in the money markets of Europe, the interest and sinking funds of which increased from year to year and finally proved too heavy for the revenues of the Empire to carry.[8]

Such grievous errors might have been avoided and the obstacles inherent in the financial administration might have been overcome had there existed an intelligent, honest, and public-spirited group of civil servants. Here, too, all the conditions were against the forces of regeneration. The average of official intelligence was low. The professions of civil service and religious teacher appealed to those of the population who did not become soldiers or farmers. The Ottoman bureaucracy was permeated with inertia and shortsightedness. Capable subordinates when acting under rigid supervision, Turks proved to be good public servants; but it was essential that they be regularly and adequately paid, and that opportunities for dishonesty and intrigue be reduced to a minimum. But, as has been indicated, the faults and inherent qualities of the financial system encouraged dishonesty and deceit. The incentive of advancement hardly existed, as favoritism and influence determined the appointments to the higher positions, and only infrequently did ability and merit receive their reward. The salaries of the army and of civil servants were usually in arrears, and the only means of livelihood was to live off the country by *baksheesh* and dishonesty. Writing in the *Edinburgh Review* in 1854, a western critic observed that "the present state of things is a scramble for private advantages of the lowest kind, and the idea of public duty to the collective interests of the Empire has scarcely a representative in the service of the Grand Seigneur."[9]

With the Turkish population lived a group of communities composed of subject races, who had been granted special privileges under the direction of their religious officials. By factors of language, race, religion, and social custom, these groups were set apart from the Moslem population. Maladministration and the lack of an efficient and impartial judicial system encouraged the temptation to discriminate against them. Although it was for the

[8] Du Velay, *op. cit.*, pp. 55-8, 123-6; see also *infra*, Chapter III.

[9] Volume XCIX (January, 1854), pp. 282-314.

benefit of these populations that Europe had insisted on reforms, the absence of responsibility and initiative in high places continued much of the abuse existing before the attempts at reform.[10]

Two other factors reduced public spirit and sanctioned a policy of self interest. The Ulema, or body of religious teachers, expounders and interpreters of the Holy Law, set their faces against any reform in favor of non-Moslems. In their opinion it was contrary to the spirit of the Koran. The division between the faithful and the *giaur* (non-Moslem) was established by the Koran itself. Not only was the *giaur's* lot after death unhappy, but his condition on earth was likewise unfortunate because, by the prescriptions of the Koran, he was liable for the payment of higher taxes than his Moslem neighbor. To the Ulema, therefore, it was inadmissible that existing conditions could be changed, although impartial judgment would undoubtedly have established the existence of illegal excessive taxation on non-Moslem elements. An attempt to prove this in a court of law, however, would have been quixotic. True, the Christian elements were exempt from military service at this time, but invaluable as was this exemption to the non-Moslems, it was attributable to the belief that participation in the exploits of Turkish armies should be open only to disciples of the Prophet. Moreover, the Ulema was composed of persons of a circumscribed conservative outlook, trained in the fanatical mosque schools, and bound instinctively to combat liberal tendencies. This was likewise an attitude compatible with self interest, inasmuch as any liberal movement would tend to deprive the Ulema of its privileged position in the make-up of Ottoman society.[11]

---

[10] The civil service was dominated by a characteristic which Morawitz, *op. cit.*, p. 28, describes as follows: "Complete forgetfulness of everything, the absorption of the soul by the body, the total absence of desire! It is blessedness in idleness, resignation to decay, lack of any movement whatsoever! What matters it that everywhere else science and progress are changing conditions of human life? Why look for change, since everything here is for the best in this best of worlds?" In another place the same author suggests that this form of logic existed: "Why go out of our way to pay to the state the taxes we have collected, when the state will but distribute them later in the form of salaries? Is it not much simpler for us to be paid directly by the taxpayers?" p. 28.

[11] It was, however, a public demonstration by the *Softas* (theological students) before the palace of Abdul Aziz in May, 1876, which brought home to this Sultan the tenor of public opinion, and led to his subsequent deposition.

Another factor which tended to vitiate reform was the character of the sultans. From the viewpoint of personal character, the Ottoman rulers of the nineteenth century compare not unfavorably with the members of the House of Othman who directed the fortunes of the Empire during the years following its heyday under Suleiman. But their most virtuous quality was in having good intentions, rather than in possessing strength of character sufficient to execute them. Mahmoud II (1808-39) has been accused of being insincere in his desire for reform. He did achieve, however, the destruction of the Janissaries and some reorganization in the army. His son, Abdul Medjid (1839-61), recognized the need of reform and was sincere in his promulgation of the Hatti Sherif; he was "good and merciful, but weak and unable to resist suggestions made by his entourage." His instincts were good, but he did not realize the promise of his youth.[12] He lacked physical force and moral energy, was extravagant in his tastes, and, during the latter part of his reign, became intensely fanatical. Even the extravagances of his reign, however, were surpassed by those of his successor, Abdul Aziz (1861-76). This ruler had a mania for building palaces, mosques, barracks, and public buildings. He pretended an interest in the reforms instituted during the reigns of his predecessors. Like Medjid, he was unable to recognize the signs of financial danger. He continued the issue of paper money until his Grand Vizier, Fuad, negotiated a loan to make possible its withdrawal. Some order was restored in finance by the energy of Kiami Pasha, an Egyptian functionary. This was quickly nullified by the continued indulgence of Aziz, who refused to believe in the gravity of the financial situation.[13]

One more factor, this of an economic character, contributed

---

[12] But "it must be recognized that Mahmoud was not supported by Europe in his attempts at reform. . . . The organization of a powerful army inspired distrust amongst neighboring states which were interested in seeing the Empire remain weak." Ganem, Halil, *Les Sultans Ottomans dans études d'histoire orientale* (Paris, 1902), p. 212.

[13] *Ibid.*, pp. 209, 247. Commenting on Aziz's palace building, the *London Times*, on September 30, 1863, said: "This is indeed a tendency to be regretted, and one that might well be the subject of a gentle remonstrance from the friendly advisers whom France and England have at court. . . . Unless an end be put to the habits of life which these elaborate buildings are the expression of there can never be any hope for Turkey under its present rule."

to retard the reform of the country. Europe, probably subconsciously, was interested that the economic status of the Ottoman Empire remain as it was. A Turkey largely agricultural and with few native manufactures would always be a consuming country. European industry and commerce were expanding at an enormous rate during the nineteenth century, and a consuming Turkey would offer a large market for surplus European manufactures. On the other hand, a Turkey with liberal movements, with education, and with the practical sciences developing natural resources and production, would mean that many needs of the population would be provided by products of home manufacture, and would diminish Europe's market accordingly.[14]

Expansion of the European Economic Orbit

As a factor in the determination of foreign policy, the significance of funds invested in backward countries was not at this time fully appreciated. "Surplus" capital in western Europe, however, was a very important element affecting the Ottoman Empire of the nineteenth century. Perhaps it is the irony of history that created a large amount of European capital available for investment abroad at the very moment in Ottoman history that witnessed not only the failures to reform the degenerated internal administration of Turkey, but also the reign of vacillating and spendthrift rulers. In any event, the coincidence of these two phenomena, coupled with the interests of Europe, led to a condition which, until the birth of the Turkish Republic in 1923, consolidated European ascendancy in the economy and politics of the Ottoman Empire.

The industrial revolution was born in England during the end of the eighteenth and the beginning of the nineteenth century. It was during this period that the important inventions of spinning machines, power looms, steam engines, and new metallurgical

[14] "If administrative reform had been accomplished in Turkey, it would have given a great impetus towards progress, and the Ottomans would have become a producing people instead of remaining essentially consumers and a tributary to Europe for manufactured goods. This is the motive which has inspired European policy for a century. It is neither noble nor enlightened, but it adapts itself to the economic needs of the peoples of the Occident and is in accord with their modern aims. It is an unworthy policy with no outlet towards an ideal, but eminently practical." Ganem, *op. cit.*, p. 212. The same point, applicable to the period after the institution of the Public Debt Administration in 1882, has been emphasized in a memorandum prepared for the author by J. E. Gillespie, of the American Embassy in Constantinople.

processes were made. The perfection of technique accompanying these inventions was carried forth in England at an astounding rate. Their development in England, Great Britain's natural wealth in coal and iron, and her superior merchant marine, gave to her industrialists a practical monopoly of the production and distribution of machine-made goods in Europe during the first three-quarters of the nineteenth century. The increase in the volume of manufactured products and the solution of difficult technical problems caused a large increase of capital for which its owners sought profitable employment. Early surpluses found their way back into home industry. The new free trade economy of the mid-nineteenth century, although it allowed greater expansion of home industry due to the ever-widening orbit of possible markets, was not sufficient, however, to allow of the profitable absorption of all the surplus capital produced. Hence large amounts became available for investment in new and undeveloped countries, or for the purchase of securities of foreign governments which sought the privilege of floating loans in Europe.

In preference to ploughing surpluses back into home industry at relatively low interest rates, British investors found in foreign issues more remunerative employment for these funds, both private and corporate. A writer in the *Edinburgh Review* notes this fact in the followng language:

> The main object of the new system of investments is to lend money abroad at a higher rate of interest than can be secured at home. . . . Thousands of men, who, under the old system [foreign investments reserved to a few, large, private firms] would rather have invested their money at three percent at home than risk it abroad at fifty, are now ready to place it abroad at fifteen, rather than keep it at home for five. Thus it is that a class of merchants which had hitherto been comparatively small has now been increased by an indefinite number of investors, who are not only willing but eager to add to their approved and traditionary investments a few shares of a more modern, less certain, but more remunerative character.[15]

Another factor which stimulated export of British capital was the development of the joint stock form of investment; this is the

---

15 "Seven Percent," *Edinburgh Review*, Volume CXXI (January, 1865), pp. 223-51.

"new" system (it was, of course, not entirely new) referred to in the first sentence of the quotation just given.

> . . . This growing availability and diffusion are the consequences of the new organization provided by the comparatively sudden and vast expansion of the joint stock system, and of the birth of so many financial companies capable of undertaking the largest operations. . . . Joint stock enterprise has been less anxious [than in the 1820's] to invent fancy branches of commerce, or to find mysterious and recondite sources of wealth, than to get the highest rates for their capital by lending it to foreigners. To satisfy the foreign demand for capital in all its forms seems to be the leading idea. To assist landowners by mortgage banks; merchants by discount establishments; governments and cities by loans, and generally to introduce capital into countries where the rate of interest habitually stood at twelve percent and often reached eighteen: such are the professed objects of the most prominent among the new companies.[16]

Modern industrial development in France dates from the third decade of the nineteenth century. In industry, at that time, France was still working with her hands when England was, by means of the new tools of the industrial revolution, turning out machine-made goods more rapidly and at a lower cost than could be done elsewhere. Not until the third quarter of the century did France experience a notable expansion in industry which made her a competitor of England in the world market. The period marked by the most rapid rate of development was that of the Second Empire, during which a free trade policy was followed after 1860. However, two-thirds of the population of France till the soil, and it is this group that for a century has been the source of the seemingly inexhaustible capital for which France is famous. Each peasant has been a capitalist, usually owning the farm on which he lives and, by virtue of his traditional thriftiness, able to accumulate enough cash to fill the bottom of a stocking. These modest savings, multiplied by the millions who compose the French agricultural element, have constituted the reservoir to which the nations of the world have come for capital. In 1860 the income of the agricultural class was estimated at an amount equal to nearly a billion dollars; this represented sixty-seven percent of the total

[16] *Ibid.*

wages of the nation, and was four times greater than industrial wages.[17]

The significant fact is that England and western Europe were experiencing a remarkable expansion in finance, industry, commerce, and agriculture. The financial activity of the period is an index of the contemporary development in other fields. Commenting on the number of new government bond issues then in process of negotiation, the *Journal des Débats,* on March 24, 1862, observed that "At London and Paris there is sufficient credit for all the governments of the universe." In France, the decade following 1852 witnessed an increase in the length of railroads in operation from 3,800 to 11,000 kilometers, nearly 300 percent. During the same period, horse power in French industry mounted from 75,500 to 205,600. From 1850 to 1870 world marine tonnage propelled by steam advanced from 217,000 tons to 1,100,000 tons; total world tonnage, steam and sailing vessels, doubled during this period, increasing from seven million to fourteen million tons. The total length of railroads in operation in the world rose from 38,592 in 1850 to 206,651 kilometers in 1870. Average salaries of workers in ten French building trades increased from 43.00 francs weekly in 1853 to 68.10 in 1881. In England, the index number of salaries in the building industries was 57 from 1840 to 1849; between 1865 and 1870 it was 77 (100 for 1900). Savings establishments in France numbered eleven in 1829; ten years later they had increased to 264; within the following fifty years the number became 547 with 987 branches. On January 1, 1889, there were 5,364,000 subscribers to these institutions, with deposits totalling 2493 millions of francs, an average per depositor of 464 francs. Western Europe was being rebuilt, and as tools and methods she was employing the new discoveries of the industrial revolution and the principles of the science of finance. Europeans were working, saving, investing, and speculating.[18]

---

17 Marshall, F., *Population and Trade in France, 1861-2* (London, 1862), p. 50. "No peasantry in the world pursue the acquisition of a piece of land with such restless perseverance as the French; the satisfaction of this desire is the great object of their existence. This thirst after property is universal in France; it shows itself in every class, but in none to so marked a degree as among the agricultural population who scrape up the means of satisfying it by years of willingly borne privation." *Ibid.*, pp. 52-3.

18 Cauderlier, Em., *L'évolution économique du XIXme siècle* (Brussels, 1903), pp. 78 *et seq.* and sources there cited; Page, W., (ed.), *Commerce and Industry—An historical review of the economic conditions of the*

But the material evidences of this outburst of human energy are less important for the present purpose than the consequences which it produced outside the borders of western Europe, and it was in this connection that the Ottoman Empire was particularly affected. It was during the twenty years from 1854 to 1875 that Turkey borrowed over a billion dollars from Europe. In other geographical areas important sums also found their way into government bonds. Even before the middle of the century, Portugal and Spain had borrowed money in the London market. Likewise Argentine, Peru, and Honduras had come to Paris to partake of the rich bounty of surplus capital. The governments of these countries defaulted on their bonds, bankruptcy having resulted from the attempt to carry interest and sinking fund charges. Was the nineteenth century to witness the ascendancy of the idea of the sovereign national state, and was this victory to be tarnished by a series of state bankruptcies? Were the rulers of these new states too inept in their management of national revenues, and too naïve to realize the danger of defaulting on their bonds, when European money was at stake? In the African provinces of the Ottoman Sultan, the nominally dependent but actually sovereign rulers found it easy to borrow money, and difficult to acquit themselves of the contingent responsibilities. In the 1860's the Bey of Tunis followed this policy, and twenty years later was compelled to sign a treaty accepting French protection. During the same period English and French money was invested in Egypt, whose Khedive proved him-

---

British Empire from the Peace of Paris in 1815 to the declaration of war in 1914, based on Parliamentary Debates (2 volumes, London, 1919), Volume II, Tables 1, 23, 56, 57, 66, 72, 121, 122; de Foville, A., "L'épargne en France," extract from the *Annales du Conservatoire des Arts et Métiers* (Paris, 1889), *passim*. "In the years between 1852-54 . . . France was in a most feverish state of industrial and speculative activity. Joint stock enterprises of every kind came before the public with subscriptions of shares; half the population devoted itself to Bourse speculations, and the national characteristic seemed to suddenly change, abandoning the habits of hoarding and solid investments for the sake of profits which suddenly tempted it in a new direction . . . Building went on in France with astonishing rapidity. In Paris, Lyons, Marseilles, and many other great towns, whole districts were covered with new houses. . . . " Marshall, *op. cit.*, pp. 137-8. "The Turkish minister of finance has left no stone unturned to obtain for the Treasury the best possible conditions, and his task has been facilitated by the plethora of money in the European markets, and by the readiness of capitalists to seize every opportunity for advantageously placing their funds. . . . " *Levant Herald* (Constantinople) quoted in the London *Times*, August 14, 1869; see also *infra*, Chapter IV, note 24.

self an even more extravagant spender than the Bey. In 1882 British troops were introduced into the country. Was the foreign loan becoming an instrument in the determination of foreign policy?

Early Restriction of Turkish Sovereignty

Many years before the establishment of foreign financial control in 1882, the powers of Europe had obtained the right to interfere in other important spheres of Ottoman administration.

In point of time, Europe's position was established in 1535 by the treaty which Suleiman the Magnificent signed with Francis I of France, renewed and developed by Mahmoud I in 1740, and confirmed by other later treaties with France, as, for instance, those of 1802, 1808, and 1861. Their most important stipulations were three in number: the right of subjects of foreign governments who resided within the Empire to be judged according to their own laws and in the established consular courts; second, freedom from Ottoman taxation; lastly, limitation on the customs duties to be levied on goods of foreign origin. The first two of these provisions placed foreigners outside the law of the Empire; the third gave a privileged position to imports and eventually placed the bulk of trade in the hands of foreigners.[19]

France and Russia first claimed the right to protect Christian minorities, France originally by the treaty of 1535, which recognized her right to protect the Catholics in the Empire. Russia's claim was more doubtful, but, in any event, she claimed the right by virtue of the Treaty of Kuchuk-Kainardji (1774). These two powers fought the Crimean War for this privilege. Concerning the rights of the European Concert as a whole, "the gradation is evident. At first, foreign intervention is limited to the holy places, to their caretakers, and to foreign visitors. It is next extended to

---

[19] Eversley, G., *The Turkish Empire* (London, 1917), p. 287. The weak character of Sultan Medjid and of Sultan Aziz, and their pliability seem to Eversley to explain why Europe assumed the tutelage. This undoubtedly gave European diplomats in Constantinople an opportunity to assume leadership in the institution of reforms, etc. No time was lost, however, in placing Europe's privileged position under the sanction of treaties, which are of infinitely more durable character than the influence of diplomatic representatives. See also Engelhardt, E., *Le droit d'intervention et la Turquie* (Paris, 1880), and Brown, P. M., *Foreigners in Turkey—Their Juridical Status* (Princeton, 1914).

include the Catholic and Greek Orthodox faiths; and finally the protection of Ottoman Christians devolves on the Powers. . . . "[20] This last point was gained in 1856 by the Treaty of Paris, which guaranteed the integrity of the Empire itself. But an interpretation of Article 9, "which seemed to guarantee the independence of the Sultan with his subjects, on the contrary has been used by the cabinets of Europe to claim the right to restrain this independence insofar as its exercise might bring harm to the Christians of the Empire."[21]

In the negotiations which culminated in the Treaty of Paris Europe first obtained the right to interfere in Ottoman domestic administration. The Hatti-Sherif (Edict of November 3, 1839), which was the first attempt to define the rights of the Christian subjects, had been very vague. An article of the Protocol of Vienna, February 1, 1855, therefore, envisaged "the immunities of the Christian populations of the Empire." Lord Stratford de Redcliffe, British Ambassador at Constantinople, in January, 1856, dispatched a note to the Sultan's Government "making clear the necessity 'of including in the same chart' the religious privileges of the Christians *and the administrative reforms* which must reconstruct their social and political condition."[22] A month later, while the Paris Congress was in session, the Hatti-Humayoun (February 18, 1856) appeared, and by Article 9 of the Treaty of Paris the Sultan communicated this chart of reform to the powers. The chart contained a statement of "the religious privileges of the Christians and the administrative reforms" necessary to guarantee their security. European diplomacy, originally interested in protecting the minorities in the exercise of their religions, added the right to oversee the necessary administrative reforms. In effect this granted a right which could be exercised at any time, inasmuch as the minorities were widely scattered, and new methods of administration necessitated recasting much of the machinery of local government throughout the Empire.

In the field of finance the progress is no less patent. To begin with, a government which is prohibited by treaty from raising

[20] Engelhardt, *op. cit.*, p. 30.

[21] *Ibid.*, p. 40; for a detailed argument sustaining this position, see Du Velay, *op. cit.*, p. 113, where is cited the contention of d'Avril, Adolphe, taken from his *Négociations relatifs au Traité de Berlin.*

[22] Cited in Engelhardt, *op. cit.*, pp. 34-5. The italics are the author's.

its customs duties certainly has its fiscal powers qualified. In 1856 the Ottoman Bank was established, and a year later England claimed a substantial control over the operations of this institution.[23] Also in 1856, the Austrian Government, at the request of the Porte, dispatched a financial adviser, M. Lackenbacher, to assist in the proposed administrative and fiscal reform. Two years later, British and French delegates joined with the Austrian expert to form the consultative High Council of the Treasury. In June, 1860, this Council was transformed into a *Conseil Supérieur des Finances* to supervise the new financial administration. In three different loan contracts Turkey admitted the principle of having representatives of the holders of the bonds on the commissions to administer the revenues ear-marked for their service.[24]

The period from 1875 to 1882 is too full of influences exerted on Ottoman ministers in regard to finance to allow of treatment here. To strengthen this brief statement of the attitude of Europe, it may be added that it was at the instigation of the Russian Ambassador, General Ignatieff, that Mahmoud Nedim Pasha, the Grand Vizier, suspended the service on the foreign debt in 1875. The Congress of Berlin exercised sufficient pressure on the Porte for the Administration of the Public Debt to be set up in 1882. During the last two decades of the nineteenth century a series of loans were floated with the aid of the Public Debt for the purpose primarily of railroad construction. In almost every case the administration of these loans was confided to the Council or to the Ottoman Bank. In 1896 the Russian Ambassador dispatched a note to the Sublime Porte calling to its attention the sanctions of the Decree of Mouharrem.

In truth Europe's attitude was that of a tutor: "Turkey is in tutelage," wrote the Duc Décazes, French Foreign Minister, on January 10, 1876. Three years later Lord Derby uttered the same opinion, "The daily surveillance of which Turkey is the object in her domestic affairs has reduced her sovereign authority to practically zero." [25]

---

[23] Its functions were very limited, however, as compared with those following the reorganization in 1863, and the extension of its privileges in 1875. See *infra*, Chapter IV.

[24] *Infra*, pp. 28-29, 40, 50-1.

[25] Cited in Engelhardt, *op. cit.*, p. 61.

Chapter III

INCREASING OTTOMAN INDEBTEDNESS

In spite of frequent wars, of inefficiency in the system of taxation, and of the corruption for which it was famous, the Ottoman Government did not resort to foreign loans to supplement state revenues until the middle of the nineteenth century. At this time, however,

> the poverty of the Treasury was extreme and the Government was reproached for collecting the taxes through bankers who absorbed the greater part. No one went back to the real causes of the crisis. They can be put under three heads: a weakened monetary system, absence of budgetary control, and a wasteful administrative organization.[1]

Legitimate Loans Inaugurate the Process

The earliest of Turkey's foreign loans were contracted with her allies, England and France, and were destined to meet extraordinary war expenditures necessitated by the struggle with Russia during 1853-56. Expedients which had been previously employed by the Government in moments of financial embarrassment were insufficient in this emergency. The sums needed for purchase of war material and for payment of troops were larger than the bankers in Constantinople, accustomed to granting short term advances to the Government, were willing to lend. A long term loan was the alternative. On August 4, 1854, Sultan Abdul Medjid issued a *firman* (edict) authorizing a loan of three mil-

[1] Engelhardt, E., *op. cit.*, Volume I, p. 99. The economic result of this condition was constant depreciation of Turkish as compared with foreign money, and consequent public impoverishment. According to Engelhardt, "It is the influence of this disastrous decrease in public wealth to which the real decadence of the state must be attributed. Effectively bound by the Capitulations, and possessing no native industries, Turkey was compelled to import all manufactured goods; in exchange she traded her agricultural products, represented by an inferior currency which was continually losing its normal value, and the total resources of the country were reduced, therefore, in the same proportion." *Ibid.*, pp. 99-100. Interesting material concerning financial difficulties in Turkey is available in Belin, M., *Essais sur l'histoire économique de la Turquie* (Paris, 1865), pp. 262-6 and 309-11. Original sources are consulted by M. Belin in this work.

lion pounds sterling. The contract was awarded to Dent, Palmer, and Company, of London, and their Paris agents, Goldsmidt and Company. The interest rate was six percent, with one percent annual amortization, and the issue price was eighty.[2]

Underwriters' commissions and the low issue price decreased the receipts from this loan to half of the nominal amount. The sum realized by the Ottoman Treasury was inadequate to meet the demands of war. Less than a year later, therefore, another loan was necessary. On June 27, 1855, a contract was signed by the Turkish Government and the British and French Governments for the guarantee by the latter of the interest on a loan of five millions sterling, "the proceeds of which will be devoted to the pursuit of the war."[3] This guarantee of interest brought the most conservative bankers into the field, and the bid price reflected this competition. Rothschild of London floated the issue at a premium of two and five-eighths; interest was at the rate of four percent, with amortization one percent annually.

This transaction contained the seed of the idea of foreign control. In consenting to guarantee the loan, the British and French Governments demanded, as a sanction that the loan would be devoted to war expenditure, the right to designate two commissioners to exercise a control over the employment of the funds realized under the loan, and to verify the Treasury accounts. Lord Hobart was named as the British delegate, and the Marquis de Ploeuc as the French representative. They made a report to their respective governments, but Du Velay characterizes their activities in Turkey as "platonic" and observes that "to the same extent that the [Ottoman] Government showed a spirit of willingness to accede to the demands of the allied powers, it employed ruses and evasions to turn aside the two commissioners in their work of verification."[4]

---

2 Details concerning this loan and the others referred to in this chapter have been taken from the following sources: *54th Annual Report of the Corporation of Foreign Bondholders* (London, 1928); Jenks, L. H., *The Migration of British Capital to 1875* (New York, 1927); Roumani, A., *Essai historique et technique sur la Dette Publique Ottomane* (Paris, 1927); Du Velay, *op. cit.*; and various publications of the Public Debt Administration itself, the most important of which are listed in note 1, Chapter VI.

3 See the extracts from the House of Commons debate caused by the introduction of a Government bill to guarantee this loan, *infra*, Chapter IV, p. 62.

4 *Op. cit.*, p. 143.

The successful conclusion of the Crimean War in 1856 relieved Turkey of further war expenses, and enabled her to devote herself to internal fiscal reform. Violently fluctuating prices were a source of unrest throughout the Empire. Not only was dissatisfaction produced among the peasants, but the Government itself was handicapped in estimating revenue and expenditure. Debased metallic currency together with large issues of paper money (*caimé*)[5] were the roots of the wide variation in prices. Partial improvement in the former was effected in 1842 by an issue of coins of good metal, an operation which followed the restriction of the use of the paper money to Constantinople and suburbs. Attempts made in 1851 to withdraw the *caimé* from circulation had been interrupted by the Crimean War. Indeed, during the course of this struggle the Government had been compelled to issue further amounts.

The withdrawal of the paper money was the object of the 1858 loan. Of the nominal total of five million sterling contracted for by the Government with the London firm, Dent, Palmer, and Company, the issuing house bought outright three million at eighty-five percent; the remainder was placed at sixty-two and one-half in 1859.[6] Annual interest and amortization rates were again six and one percent respectively. In the contract for this loan also was a provision for a modified foreign control. The octroi and customs duties of Constantinople were pledged as security for the service of the loan. According to the contract, these revenues were to be collected under the direction of delegates chosen by the bondholders. This provision was little more than a gesture, however, for lack of organization among the bondholders themselves caused it to remain unfulfilled.

The 1858 loan relieved the financial situation only temporarily.

---

[5] This medium of exchange was first issued in 1839, bore interest at the rate of eight per cent, which was reduced in 1842 to six. Interest was payable in *caimé* itself. The disorders caused by the periodic issue and withdrawal of this paper money embarrassed the Government through the period of the Russo-Turkish War, 1877-78.

[6] The London firm of Dent, Palmer, and Company figures extensively in this period of Ottoman financial history. Private sources in Constantinople are responsible for the assertion made to the author that Mr. Palmer was sufficiently powerful to cause the downfall of one grand vizier who refused to succumb to Mr. Palmer's contention that the Imperial Treasury was in need of another loan. The succeeding prime minister was more amenable to the suggestion, and Mr. Palmer floated his loan.

Funds realized from this issue were sufficient to retire only a part of the paper money. The annual charges on the foreign debt were beginning to mount, already having reached nearly a million pounds sterling. In spite of an imperial edict promulgated by Abdul Medjid on August 26, 1858, in which rigid economies were prescribed, palace debts continued to assume large proportions, the commotion among imperial retainers caused by this decree proving only momentary, for it was violated with impunity by a favorite member of the Sultan's slave household who purchased jewels of unprecedented value immediately after the edict's promulgation.[7]

Abdul Medjid himself could not pose as an example for his palace followers. At this time he was in the midst of indulging his pet fancy of constructing palaces. The jewel of his collection was the superb building of Dolma Bagtché. The Sultan manifested sufficient interest in its cost to inquire concerning it of his minister of the Civil List. The figure supplied by this official, thirty-five hundred piasters (thirty-two pounds sterling), shocked the intelligence of the Sultan, until he was further informed that this sum represented the expense entailed by the Treasury in having issued promissory notes to the amount of the real cost of construction, 2,800,000 pounds sterling.[8] This extravagance prompted the following caustic comment from a Constantinople banker: "It is monstrous that the finances of a great empire should be ruined by the fantastic desires of a fool who, already having fifty palaces, wants to construct fifty more." [9]

Nevertheless, the following year a more or less emphatic gesture was made to rehabilitate imperial finances. Since 1857 a member of the Austrian Ministry of Finance, M. Lackenbacher had been delegated, at the request of the Sublime Porte, to consult with the High Council of Reform in its labors of administrative and fiscal improvement. In October, 1859, the Sultan ordered an investigation of financial conditions, and requested the British and French Governments each to name a representative. M. Falconnet, director of the Ottoman Bank, was delegated by the British; the Marquis de Ploeuc was the French commissioner.

---

[7] Morawitz, *op. cit.*, p. 28.

[8] Du Velay, *op. cit.*, p. 124.

[9] Senior, *op. cit.*, p. 108, quoted by Girardin, St. M., "La moralité des finances turques," in *Revue des Deux Mondes*, January 15, 1861, p. 471.

Together with M. Lackenbacher and four Ottoman officials, the British and French representatives were attached to the Ministry of Finance in a consultative capacity.

In this relation, however, the commission was unable to effect much improvement. The foreign commissioners were capable, no doubt, and were willing to be consulted concerning possible remedies for the situation. But the Ottoman Government showed little disposition of utilizing their services. On October 5, the patience of the foreign delegates having become severely tried, a communication was dispatched to their respective governments. This note expressed "regret to see that Turkey is not helping herself; that she is not proceeding to a gradual and forceful application of the reforms, and that sufficient initiative is not manifest to obtain the object of the Decree of 1856." [10]

As a result of this action the Imperial Government designated one of the foreign members to summarize the financial situation. When submitted to the Porte, this résumé formed the basis of a note to the interested powers, in which were presented details of the proposed financial reforms and a definition of the powers of the commission. This action failed to satisfy the British, French, and Austrian members, who desired their functions defined for them by the Imperial Government itself. The Government, however, past master in dilatory methods, always devised some excuse why this should not be done.[11] At a later date this commission was given greatly extended powers.[12]

Bold Schemes for Foreign Financial Control

The unwillingness of the Government to use the consultative commission to better the financial situation prompted several proposals for the surveillance of Turkish finance. In 1859, the British Ambassador at Constantinople, Sir Henry Bulwer, proposed that modifications should be effected in the laws regulating the holding by foreigners of real property in the Empire, that

---

[10] Cited in Du Velay, *op. cit.*, p. 115.

[11] Girardin, *loc. cit.*, pp. 477-8. Commenting on the strategy of sending a note based on the foreign commissioner's report to the powers, he says: "The Porte never thought for an instant of doing what the European note asked, that is, of creating a real authority which would proceed seriously and sincerely to the reform of Turkish finances." p. 479.

[12] *Infra*, p. 34.

certain of the lands belonging to the state should then be leased to a syndicate of foreigners, and, on the security afforded by these properties, bonds should be issued to raise sufficient capital to effect the desired administrative and fiscal reforms. The French Ambassador, Count de Lavalette, suggested an even bolder plan. He proposed the collective guarantee of a loan to the Sublime Porte by the signatories of the Treaty of Paris, and forwarded this plan to the representatives at Constantinople of the interested governments. Moreover, during the course of an interview with the Prince Regent of Prussia in 1860, the Austrian Emperor Franz Joseph suggested the idea of a collective guarantee of a loan by the federated German states.[13]

The French Ambassador's plan was the object of extended criticism in a dispatch from the Prussian Government to its representative in Constantinople, Count Goltz, under date of August 3, 1860. After reviewing general conditions in Turkey, the Prussian Foreign Minister continued:

> Under these circumstances the idea of the French Ambassador at Constantinople relative to a loan guaranteed by the Great Powers has raised serious objections with us. Evidently any sum of money, no matter of what proportions, will accomplish no good, if it is delivered to an administration which has neither adopted nor put into execution the fundamental principles of political economy and continues its original system. It can be stated with certainty that such an administration would not only be unable usefully to employ the product of the loan, but also it would not be long before the necessary means would be lacking to meet interest and sinking fund charges. This act would place the governments of Europe in the difficult alternative of themselves meeting the obligations of the Ottoman Empire, or of taking coercive measures which would place the Empire in the greatest danger, and which would form a singular contrast to their good intentions.

The Prussian Foreign Minister was unable to recommend the project for legislative action, and, after remarking that it was probably in foreseeing the eventuality of default that the Marquis had made "as a condition of the guarantee that the Porte not only submit the administration of its finances to the control of agents

[13] Morawitz, *op. cit.*, p. 28.

of the Powers, but should even place them entirely in their hands", added: "It is difficult for me to believe that the Sublime Porte could consent to such a condition." [14]

All of these various plans were abortive, partly because of their impractical nature, but more because at this time there was little if any widespread feeling of the need of placing Turkish finances under foreign control.[15] The acceptance by the Imperial Government of any of these proposals would have implied tacit admission of its inability to manage its own fiscal matters. Moreover, revenues were coming in after a fashion; coupons of the early loans were being paid; and, if there was an indefinite, but persistent, undertone of skepticism concerning ultimate improvement, there was also the assertion that Turkey's "magnificent resources" would always be sufficient to pay interest on the foreign debt.[16] Also at this moment a diplomatic battle was being waged between the British and French Ambassadors at Constantinople to determine who should fall heir to the prestige and influence formerly possessed by the "Great Elchi", Lord Stratford, who had resigned his post as British Ambassador at Constantinople in 1858. The proposals of Sir Henry Bulwer and Count de Lavalette were part of this struggle. In any event, neither plan was pressed by the government whose representative had called it forth.

In the meantime, however, the financial situation had again become acute. The floating debt of four million pounds sterling, with interest at twelve percent compounded annually, doubled itself every six years. To eliminate or reduce this snowball-like obligation was necessary. The Government sought a reputable firm in London to float an issue to accomplish this object. But bankers in both London and Paris fought shy of the proposal. Finally, on October 29, 1860, a Parisian financial wizard of the day, M. Mirés, contracted to deliver to the Porte the proceeds of

---

[14] *Ibid.*, p. 29.

[15] But cf. Senior, *op. cit.*, pp. 109-10, where he cites the following statement of a Constantinople banker: "As much as I detest the idea of foreign interference in the domestic affairs of a country, just so much am I convinced that here is a point upon which the diplomatic corps should confer. The ambassadors should show the Sultan the necessity of fulfilling his promises, of establishing a civil list, and of keeping his expenditures within its limits. This is the most important clause of the *Hatti-Humayoun.*"

[16] As, for example, are referred to *infra*, Chapter IV, pp. 63-4.

an issue of sixteen millions sterling, at an issue price of fifty-three and three-quarters. Supported by several of the more conservative Paris newspapers, such as the *Journal des Débats,* the public subscription achieved an initial success.[17] Rumors of irregularity in the employment of funds of his other companies, however, shook confidence in M. Mirés; the subscription was forsaken by speculating elements of the Bourse; and M. Mirés's arrest by the French Government pricked the bubble of confidence in the regularity of the transaction. Weakness appeared in other Turkish securities. Mistrust soon spread to the foreign exchanges, and Galata banks and business houses sought to realize on matured notes of the Ottoman Treasury. Turkish exchange on London and Paris broke under the pressure of heavy selling of discounted bills. In late December, exchange on Constantinople stood at 190 piasters to the pound sterling (par 110). To check the process the Ottoman Government sent a call of distress to London; the British Government responded by dispatching two members of the Board of Trade, Lord Hobart and Mr. Foster, to Constantinople to perform the inquest. A French writer in the *Revue des Deux Mondes* felt called upon to "state how widespread is the idea that Turkey needs to be placed 'en tutelle' by Europe." [18]

At this moment there were, however, some bright spots in the situation. In June, 1860, the advisory financial commission had been transformed into a *Conseil Supérieur des Finances* with powers which enabled it to coöperate with Lord Hobart and Mr. Foster in liquidating the evil results of the Mirés loan. True, " . . . the revenue was pledged for six months or a year in advance; but as those who got it in from the people lent it out again to the Government, things in a certain way at least went on." [19] A new Sultan, Abdul Aziz, who professed principles of retrenchment and economy, had succeeded Abdul Medjid on his death, June 25, 1861. The Government was utilizing the *Conseil Supérieur* to make a thorough-going examination of receipts and

17 M. Mirés's letter containing the prospectus for this loan appeared in the December 8, 1860, issue of the *Journal des Débats,* and ran to three and a half columns of type.

18 Girardin, *loc. cit.*, p. 473.

19 Extract from a letter from Sir Henry Bulwer to Admiral Martin of the Mediterranean fleet, dated September 22, 1860, printed in Drummond Wolff, Sir Henry, *Rambling Recollections* (2 volumes, London, 1908), Volume II, pp. 1-6.

expenditures. On December 7, 1861, the two representatives of the British Board of Trade submitted a report to their government, a report which was distinctly favorable to the possibility of ultimate improvement. There was, according to this report, nothing fundamentally bad in Turkish financial management. Revenues were capable of expansion; increase them, and many former evils would be removed. The misfortunes of preceding years had been many, to be sure, but they had been caused by ignorance of sound principles, and not by bad faith. Outside advice could remedy this defect.[20] There was no proposal to institute foreign control. Moreover, faith in the future of Ottoman finance was stimulated by rumors that the Government was on the eve of granting a wide extension of privileges to the Ottoman Bank. Finally, the Finance Ministry, with the aid of foreign assistance, had completed its survey of the situation, and had drawn up a budget. Fuad Pasha, the Grand Vizier, embodied this statement in a famous report to the Sultan early in 1862.

Thus the stage was set for a favorable reception to the proposal of the Imperial Government for another loan. Paper money still circulated in the capital of the Empire; the amount had even been increased by heavy issues which in December, 1861, brought the *caimé* to a low point of a quarter of its nominal value. But the Government was willing, if a loan could be devoted to withdrawing the paper money, for a foreign expert to direct this process. The Hobart-Foster report received favorable comment in the House of Commons; Lord Palmerston delivered a eulogy on the virtues of Abdul Aziz. Under the unofficial sanction of the British Government, the loan, which had been underwritten by the Ottoman Bank and Devaux and Company, of London, achieved a phenomenal success in the money markets of Europe. An issue rate of sixty-eight, however, brought to the Government's coffers little more than half of the nominal amount of ten millions sterling. Nevertheless, under Lord Hobart's direction, the paper money was withdrawn from circulation.[21]

---

[20] *Parliamentary Papers*, Turkey (1862) Volume 64, pp. 475 *et seq.*

[21] See the statement made in the House of Commons by Mr. Layard, Undersecretary for Foreign Affairs, *infra*, Chapter IV, pp. 49-50; Lord Palmerston's panegyric, *ibid.*, p. 50.

Growing Frequency of the Loans

The expedient which had been adopted to meet the demands of war, and which also had been employed as a means of retiring the paper money, was now viewed as a method of meeting budget deficits.

> The Turk, finding he could borrow money easily, spent it more lavishly. But with the financial system derived from Europe, they had no knowledge of managing, as Europeans manage, their finances either in checking expenditures or collecting taxes. Thus borrow! borrow! borrow! was their only resource as immediate payments became necessary; and this on those terms by which the money wanted could most quickly be procured.[22]

In 1863, reorganization of the Ottoman Bank, with greater prerogatives than heretofore, had taken place as rumored; in exchange for the new concession, the Bank granted another loan. The floating debt again showed signs of increasing; with the proceeds of the 1863 loan of a nominal total of eight millions, issued by the Ottoman Bank, the Government's debts to local bankers were again transferred to foreign creditors. Two years later no ready cash was available with which to meet the January, 1866, coupons; no alternative appeared but another loan. The annual charges on the foreign debt, already over two and a quarter million sterling, were by this loan increased another half-million. In May, 1866, when Fuad Pasha was searching for means to meet the matured coupons on early issues, the British and French Ambassadors at Constantinople expressed their uneasiness concerning the lot of the holders of bonds of these issues, fears which were calmed by Fuad, who gave assurances that the Government would respect its external obligations. In the same year the internal debt was funded by using the proceeds of a series of bonds secured on the general revenues of the Empire.

The quickened pace of the process was not regarded, however, as cause for undue alarm. Revenues were rising. According to the 1863 budget receipts were estimated at something over fifteen million pounds sterling; five years later the Government estimated its income at nearly twenty millions. Although Sultan Abdul

[22] Drummond Wolff, *op. cit.*, Volume II, p. 5.

Aziz manifested an uncontrollable desire to increase his navy, the European ambassadors in no way impeded him.[23] No syndicates were appointed for the collection of interest for the 1858 and 1862 loans, as the Ottoman Bank maintained that payments on these loans were being met regularly.[24]

Nevertheless, unlooked-for demands for money continued. Foreign monarchs paid return visits to Abdul Aziz, who had made a circular European tour in 1867. Diplomatic and regal amenities had to be lived up to, and the Sultan entertained his royal guests on an oriental scale of lavishness. Insurrection in Crete demanded increased outlay for war materials. In 1869, proceeds from a six percent loan of a nominal total of twenty-two million sterling, issued at sixty-one by the *Comptoir d'Escompte* of Paris, allowed the Government to discharge its immediate obligations on the foreign debt, and to meet the increased day-to-day expenses created by the Cretan rebellion.

Lottery bonds issued in 1870 by Baron Hirsch as a means of financing the construction of the network of railways for which the concession was obtained in April, 1869, were of a total nominal value of nearly thirty-two million sterling, but the Government received less than a third of this amount.[25] In June, 1871, Dent, Palmer, and Company floated another six percent issue of a nominal total of five million seven hundred thousand. This allowed the Government to meet charges on its external obligations for another short period.

A series of nine percent Treasury bonds was issued by Raphael, of London, in April, 1872, for a nominal total of eleven million. Barings, Rothschild, and the Ottoman Bank, combined in September of the following year to bring on the market an issue of eight million, at fifty-eight and a half. The culmination occurred in 1874 when the Ottoman Bank floated the issue of largest nominal total, forty million sterling, at the figure of forty-three and a half!

---

[23] Newton, *Lord Lyons, A Record of British Diplomacy* (2 volumes, London, 1913), Volume I, pp. 151-2.

[24] Du Velay, *op. cit.*, pp. 151 *et seq.*; Newton, *op. cit.*, Volume I, p. 152; Constantinople correspondence to the *London Times*, June 17, 1872.

[25] For the details of the management of this issue of bonds by Baron Hirsch, and the railroad constructed, to say nothing of the profits realized on the transaction, consult Du Velay, *op. cit.*, pp. 250 *et seq.* Cf. also the article by Bent, T., "Baron Hirsch's Railway," *Fortnightly Review* (London) Volume XL, New Series (August 1, 1888), pp. 229 *et seq.*

This proved to be the end. Revenues had increased, but not in the same proportion as the charges on the foreign debt. Estimates by the Government of receipts from state revenues touched twenty-two million sterling in 1874. But after the Ottoman Bank flotation of that year interest and sinking fund charges amounted to twelve million sterling! The limit had finally been reached. The foreign debt theoretically absorbed fifty-five percent of the total resources of the Imperial Government.

This procedure was like a snowball: the more money Europe lent, the more ways Turkey spent. The Imperial Government sought the loans. It was simpler to pledge next year's tithes as guarantee for a new loan than to effect economies in the local administration and to retain control of the tithes in order to meet current expenses. Or it was easier to fund a constantly reappearing floating debt by a foreign loan than to abolish wasteful methods in the central administration. Continuous and increasing palace debts were met by internal loans. When the limit of saturation appeared, internal obligations were converted into a foreign loan. Transfer the floating debt from Galata bankers to French *rentiers!* Substitute Englishmen from the Midlands for the bearers of internal bonds! Money comes easily; life is good; borrow, borrow, borrow!

On the other hand, western bankers urged the Sublime Porte to borrow. Available diplomatic documents do not reveal the complete rôle played by embassies; but an obscure newspaper item narrates that one loan, at least, is supposed to have been forced upon the Porte by the French Embassy.[26] Private financial archives are closed to the public gaze; nevertheless, the representative of one London firm is reported to have been sufficiently powerful to cause the downfall of an obdurate grand vizier, who refused to accept a proffered loan.[27] Moreover, European advice was well-intentioned, but wide of the mark. Never mind reducing expenses; increase the revenues. Natural resources can be exploited when agriculture fails. Competition for loans was keen; the Government needed money; our company would lose out, un-

---

[26] *Levant Herald* (Constantinople) quoted by the London *Times*, October 30, 1868.

[27] *Supra*, note 6. A hypothetical case of the negotiations prior to the opening of the public subscription is described in Drummond Wolff, *op. cit.*, Volume II, pp. 63-6.

less influence were exerted. Closet yourself with the Grand Vizier! A pliable finance minister! It's not our money that is used! Quick profits! Opportunity of a lifetime! Lend, lend!

Initial profit realized by underwriting firms and interest drawn by investors are two outstanding points to be noted. The average issue rate was approximately fifty-eight percent; this must be reduced further by six or seven percent to represent underwriters' commissions. In many of the contracts an option clause was introduced, according to which the issuing house, having bought outright a part of the issue, reserved the right to float the remainder at its convenience. The proceeds from the portion at option were realized by the bank at any rate which the market would bear; the Government, however, received proceeds therefrom on the basis of the quotation in the optional clause. It involved a risk for the underwriter, but the hardship worked on the Government was invariably greater. "It is worthy of note that every time the option was altered, there was also a change in the original conditions of the contract, a change always in favor of the issuing persons and to the detriment of the interests of the Treasury." [28]

Bankers in Galata (the section of Constantinople containing the financial district) who had engaged in lending to the Government retired to Paris and constructed mansions in the Parc Monceau.[29] A host of credit establishments sprang up in Constantinople during the decade 1865-75; their avowed purpose was to lend money to the Government, because, when the opportunity for profits was removed by the default in 1875, the majority immediately went out of business. One of these firms, the *Crédit Général Ottoman,* placed twenty thousand of its shares on the Constantinople market on August 18, 1869. Orders for 957,000 were received.[30] Successful purchasers realized handsomely on their investment. In its report of April 7, 1873, the board of directors of this company announced the distribution of a dividend of 2.94 Turkish pounds, that is, 26.74 percent on the paid-up per share capital of eleven Turkish pounds.[31] The normal annual dividend paid by the

[28] Du Velay, *op. cit.*, pp. 340-1.

[29] Morawitz, *op. cit.*, p. 25.

[30] *London Times*, August 18, 1869.

[31] Du Velay, *op. cit.*, p. 305, who doubted at first whether this profit might be attributed entirely to the business of loaning to the Government, but concludes that "this marvellous dividend . . is nothing more than

Ottoman Bank to its British and French shareholders from 1863 to 1873 was between twelve and thirteen percent.[32] The low issue price of the loans indicated not only profit for the banks; but also it signified the realization by the ultimate purchaser of ten percent, for instance, on a bond paying nominally six percent. Varied were the persons and institutions who purchased Ottoman bonds. The shock of the crash in 1875 was even felt within the Vatican, which had invested in Turkish securities! [33]

Profit and the Political Status Quo

In these twentieth century days, when capital is recognized as a powerful instrument for the extension of economic and political influence over "backward" areas, the critical student must ask whether this huge investment of the savings of Europe was effected for political ends.

The answer must be sought in the obvious political aims of England and France in the Ottoman Empire, and in the dominant economic doctrine of the time. The loans made during the Crimean War were frankly political in purpose. The political alliance of February 25, 1854, was not sufficiently potent to bolster up the weak structure of the Ottoman Government. The aims of the alliance had to be backed by money, the sinews of war. Thus Turkey received from her allies approximately eight million pounds sterling. Moreover, the treaty of alliance was offensive and defensive in character, guaranteeing the independence of the Empire and the integrity of its territory. Thus the political aims of France and England were indicated.

Whatever may have been the skepticism with which some financial circles in France and England regarded Turkey, the loans during the Crimean War were deemed necessary. In its financial columns, the *Journal des Débats* of August 25, 1854, observed that "The Turkish loan has attracted the best capital in Paris." A leading London financial magazine, during the flotation of the 1855 loan, spoke of its object in these terms: "That the means adopted to recruit the resources of Turkey for maintaining her

---

the profit realized on advances or loans contracted by the Ottoman Government, to the exclusion of all industrial transactions."

32 This fact is exposed to public view on a marble slab in the main corridor of the Ottoman Bank in Constantinople.

33 Morawitz, *op. cit.*, p. 28.

position against the aggression of Russia will prove successful, is the devout desire of every one favorable to the cause of civilization." [34]

Five years later, after the successful conclusion of the Crimean War, another English periodical favored the principle of guarantee, which was the official policy of the British Government: "The preservation of the Ottoman Empire from ruin and dismemberment is, at least for the present, an object of the highest importance to the interests of England, as well as to the general tranquillity and prosperity of Europe." [35] In 1861, the *London Times,* although it wondered if a change in British policy were imminent, admitted that "a few years ago . . . everybody recognized the importance of keeping the Bosporus in the hands of a power too weak to be aggressive, and of the advantage of having a semi-civilized but progressive state as a sort of outpost of Europe against Asia." [36]

On May 29, 1863, Gladstone, then Chancellor of the Exchequer, said in the House of Commons:

> Let us firmly adhere to the ancient policy of this country, that whether the existence of the Ottoman Empire in Europe be in itself desirable or not, it is a matter of profound European concern that the destruction of that Empire be not made the means of introducing more serious evils and dangers more menacing than any which may attend its continuance.[37]

By 1867, however, the *Times* recognized that Britain's attitude was expedient, as is shown by the following extract from a leading article: "Of all her [Turkey's] neighbors, only England and Austria are really favorable, and their good will arises more from the notion that the downfall of the Turkish Empire would exalt their own rivals than from any real friendship for the threatened power." In the same article France was called a "lukewarm" friend and Russia and Greece "unrelenting enemies." [38]

In 1864 a policy of expediency was likewise advised for France.

[34] *Banker's Monthly,* Volume XV (September, 1855), p. 559.
[35] *Fraser's Magazine,* Volume LXII (October, 1860), pp. 483 *et seq.*
[36] June 19, 1861.
[37] *Parliamentary Debates, House of Commons,* third series, Volume 171, (1863), p. 147.
[38] September 13, 1867.

> The best policy is, in short, that which the signs of the times indicate, one that takes account of the new needs and legitimate hopes of peoples. The rôle of the Powers, and that of France in particular, seems to us clearly defined. M. Guizot thus clarified it so judiciously in a passage from his Memoirs: "Keep the Ottoman Empire together in order to maintain Europe in equilibrium, and, when some dismemberment takes place or some province detaches itself from that decadent Empire by the force of circumstance or the natural course of events, be in favor of changing it into a new and independent state which will take its place in the family of nations and one day will form part of a new European equilibrium. This is the policy which suits France, and to which she has been naturally led, and the one which she will do well, in my opinion, to follow." (Guizot, Memoirs, T. V.)[39]

This author adds that such a policy was also advocated by another French writer, M. St. Marc Girardin, in an article written shortly before.[40]

Maintenance of the political and economic status quo in Turkey was compatible, moreover, with self interest in Britain and France. Free trade connotes the unrestricted exchange of goods and services between individuals and communities. Upon this doctrine British commercial policy had been based since 1846, and French policy since 1860. Restrictions imposed on British industry earlier in the century had been removed. An economic policy based on the doctrine of official non-interference with trade and industry refused to take cognizance of the uses to which capital was placed. Capital was composed of earnings and savings; these were fruits of the factory system. As a part of this system, capital enjoyed the same unlimited freedom of action that belonged to trade and industry. Earnings might be ploughed back into home industry, or exported to other countries: to the government either of these policies was acceptable.

When capital could be profitably disposed outside of national boundaries, it should be allowed to migrate. As the country in which industrialization had progressed further than any other, England was the first to experience a supposedly "saturated" capital market. More lucrative fields than those available in the "saturated" area, therefore, should be sought abroad.

---

39 Ubicini, M., *Revue des Deux Mondes*, May 15, 1864.
40 *Ibid.*, March 15, 1862.

For the most part official attention was unconcerned about areas in which investments were made. Governmental defence of foreign investments could be invoked only in case of a flagrant breach of international law, amounting to a denial of justice. At this moment assistance to disappointed bondholders was not conceived as being consonant with broader national interest.[41] Not yet had the voice of economic nationalism sounded its call to make the nation economically self sufficient by restricting imports and by employing national capital to develop native and infant industries. Nor indeed had zealous defence of economic interests abroad been evolved as a primary factor in the determination of foreign policy. Thus British and French gold went into Turkish bonds with little political significance save that of seconding in a weak manner official desire to keep the status quo intact.

Here is a reason explaining why there existed so little desire to institute foreign control over Turkish finances. Irregularity in the administration of the service on foreign loans was considered the concern of the issuing houses and of the bondholders. Diplomatic representatives who were personally interested might, of course, display interest in rectifying gross errors. Official opinion, however, envisaged foreign investments as good or bad; in the former case the individual bondholder reaped the benefit to the exclusion of the broader interests of the government and the country. In the latter case, the bondholder should bear the loss; he should not expect the government to assume expense or to risk involving the country by attempts to pick chestnuts from the fire.

Of course, at this time bondholders were hopelessly disorganized. Even if organization had existed, experience later showed that little could be expected from the underwriting houses in effecting the execution of provisions for syndicates to collect earmarked revenues. "The contractors of the [1858 and 1862] loans,

---

[41] Speaking of British policy, Jenks, *op. cit.*, p. 123, says: ". . . It need not be supposed for a moment that disregard of bondholders arose from any fine sensitiveness about using the resources of the nation to forward the interest of a few subjects. It simply had not been conceived as a national interest to help bondholders." The gradual transition in the attitude of the British Foreign Office during the nineteenth century is thus described by this author: "What had been an embarrassment to Castlereagh, a subject to be virtually shunned for Canning, was appearing to Palmerston as an opportunity and as a right to be employed with discretion, and was forshadowed as a possible national duty." *Ibid.*, p. 125.

to whom belongs the right of nominating the syndicates, have not asked the execution of this clause."[42] The Ottoman Bank, indeed, requested the Turkish Government to refrain from recognizing agents of the bondholders.

Although in 1870 the Grand Vizier, Aali Pasha, upon the representations of the British Foreign Office, had appointed members of the syndicate for the 1862 loan, this commission was never set to work. At this time such a course was about the extent to which a foreign government would venture. Even in those days establishment of foreign control over the finances of a debtor country presupposed on the part of the creditor definite diplomatic aims and a favorable opportunity to effect them. But only one first-rate power, Russia, was avowedly hostile to the Empire, and Russia elected more drastic measures than the institution of financial control. Moreover, no Ottoman bonds were held in Russia. Diplomatic influence exercised at Constantinople by representatives of the other European powers had to be both subtle and graceful in its course, and exercised with due consideration for possible effects on relations in other areas. Prussia's opposition to the French Ambassador's scheme[43] in 1860 seems to have been sufficient to sterilize it. When a single government is sub-

[42] "In 1870, Aali Pasha, the Grand Vizier, upon the representations of the British Foreign Office, appointed the members of the syndicate of the 1862 loan, whose function it was to receive, according to the contract, the revenues especially hypothecated. The syndicate, although appointed, was, however, never set to work, and on the introduction of the six per cent. loan of 1871 by Dent, Palmer, and Company, opposition was threatened on the ground that Turkey had not fulfilled some of the special conditions of the 1862 loan. Similar views were taken by a holder of the bonds of the 1858 loan, who pressed them upon a committee of the Stock Exchange. It was then understood that the Turkish Government gave a distinct promise that the syndicates of the 1858 and 1862 loans would be put in force, and on that promise the quotation of the 1871 loan was granted. Still, from that time to the present no action has been taken by the Turkish Government with respect to the syndicates, and in the absence of such action it is insisted that no new Turkish loan can be introduced upon the London market." Private correspondence to the London *Times*, June 12, 1872. "The contractors of these loans (1858 and 1862), to whom belongs the right of nominating the syndicates, have not asked the execution of this clause. Last year the Imperial Ottoman Bank suggested to the Turkish Government to not recognize agents of the bondholders, as it (the Ottoman Bank) was paying the service on these loans as regularly today as formerly." Constantinople correspondence to the London *Times*, June 17, 1872. Cf. also *Parliamentary Papers*, No. C. 1077 (1874) pp. 1-27, for official correspondence concerning the 1858 and 1862 loans.

[43] *Supra*, Chapter III, p. 32.

jected to diplomatic influences springing from a number of sources, these impulses can usually be made to counteract each other, leaving practically a free hand to the supposedly "weak" government. A comparable situation existed at Constantinople during this period. And what the Turks consented to give with their right hand, was frequently taken away with the left.

Nevertheless, even at this time political rivalry on the basis of economic interests was envisaged as a possible outcome of the situation. A French correspondent in Constantinople submitted to the Government at Paris an open report in which he called attention to the recrimination which Lord Stratford had undergone as a result of the numerous public utility concessions which had just been awarded to British promoters. "To speak frankly, France has taken no part in the great enterprises which are destined to change completely the face of Turkey, and from which she [sic] may obtain immense advantages. But who is in fault? Is it not to the apathy of her children that she owes it rather than to the intrigues of Lord Stratford?"

An English reply to this appeared on February 20, 1857:

> The whole matter is simple enough. The people of this country want no accession of territory at the expense of Turkey, nor do they wish to influence the counsels of the Porte, except that they may insure its stability and independence and promote the prosperity of the people. But our capitalists and men of enterprise have gone to Turkey because they see in it a country of great capability, where money and industry judiciously [sic] invested may bring large returns. . . . The Turks have a fine territory and no money, energy, or skill; we have all three, and they pour into Turkey as naturally as water finds its level. However, we are far from saying that this extension of individual enterprise will not have political results. It is one of the benefits of freedom, and of the energy and self-dependence which it gives to the individual, that any private man may influence the destinies of this country. Our capitalists, our schemers, our travellers are not directed according to any plan of British policy, but, on the contrary, the Government merely follows the routes they indicate and supports the enterprises they have initiated. . . . The British Government has no plan for the establishment of its influence; it merely leaves things alone; and yet, though the [Turkish] Empire will always, we trust, maintain its political independence, there can be no doubt that the relations with England must in the course of

> a few years become more intimate and the effect of English enterprise most remarkable.

From the development of trade, the construction of telegraphs and railways, and the necessity of maintaining communication with the Indian and Australian dominions, "we cannot, therefore, but expect . . . such an extension of our influence as will enable us to effectually uphold the integrity of the Empire."[44] The elements of imperialism were already at hand, and the events of the late nineteenth and early twentieth centuries were already anticipated in the 1850's.

[44] *London Times*, February 20, 1857.

Chapter IV

EUROPEAN POINTS OF VIEW

The investment of English and French money in Turkish Government bonds before 1875 was made without imperialist motives. The possible consequences of such investment in a territory like the Ottoman Empire were not realized. As a step in the process of acquiring "backward" areas the worth of economic interests had not yet been fully developed.[1] The real reason for this migration of capital was the desire for pecuniary profits.

> The period had been one of extraordinary financial invention and enterprise, partly legitimate, partly otherwise. . . . The public were eager for speculation and easily found purveyors of financial sensation. The principal feature of the period was the procuring of enormous profits and great results by the shifting rather than by the subscription of capital.[2]

This quotation furnishes the key to the situation. The negotiators of early Turkish loans were seeking profits, while providing the Empire with cash to meet war expenditures. Contractors of later issues were interested primarily in realizing easy money at the expense of the Ottoman Treasury. Investors in Turkish bonds were attracted by the expectation of liberal returns on their money. Speculators strove to cause fluctuation in Turkish securities that their holdings might be disposed of, leaving them the richer. Those who participated in the activities of the credit establishments which sprang up in Constantinople during this period looked for nine or ten percent from their shares, while public utility and industrial shares in England were yielding four

[1] But cf. the following excerpt from the *Times* of February 12, 1856: "The removal of all obstacles to the purchase of land by foreigners, [and] the establishment of a sound financial system and of the guarantees for the security of the capital invested in roads or harbors, must be the diplomatic labors most immediately productive of large results. A rich and unworked land is before us, and the industry of the West may go in and possess it! We may be content, therefore, to allow time to aid us in our labors."

[2] Drummond Wolff, *op. cit.*, Volume II, p. 54.

or five. Concessionaires for public utilities in Turkey thought first of lining their pockets and later of providing decent public service, or of developing the resources of the country for the benefit of the native population.

Perhaps part of the odium surrounding the action of the Sublime Porte in 1875 was removed by the fact that some at least of these greedy individuals were caught in the resulting crash. Unfortunately, it was the small investor who suffered real privations, but even to him must be attributed an undue amount of credulity. It is true that he was encouraged by actions of his government and of the Sublime Porte which, however worthy in their object, were none the less productive of a false sense of security. Statements of private individuals and organizations interested in maintaining Turkish credit were far from presenting a true state of affairs. It will be enlightening to inquire into official and private actions which supported high hopes for Ottoman creditors in Europe. Moreover, there were two opposite points of view concerning the ability and willingness of the Empire faithfully to discharge its financial obligations. Finally, the victory of avarice and speculation over sober thought and unbiased judgment will be manifest if some sources are uncovered which tell of the reception of Turkish bonds by the European public.

Official Advocacy of the Loans

The "man in the street" was first lured into investing in Turkish bonds by the support which the British Government was pleased to accord the loan negotiated in 1854. In the prospectus for this loan the following statement appeared:

> The undersigned [banking house] has the satisfaction to acquaint the public that they are authorized by the Earl of Clarendon, H. M. principal Secretary of State for Foreign Affairs, to state that this loan is negotiated with the knowledge of the English Government; that H. M. Government is satisfied that the loan and the appropriation of the . . . 282,000 pounds sterling per annum of the Egyptian tribute are duly authorized by H. M. the Sultan; and, further, that the representatives of the Sublime Porte at Paris and London are empowered in virtue of imperial firmans to ratify the contract of the loan in the name of His Majesty the Sultan; and Lord Clarendon relies with confidence upon the Turkish

> Government fulfilling with good faith the engagements they have entered into.[3]

In 1875 this was cited by an English writer as evidence that, in his opinion, the Government stood

> morally responsible. This does not, of course, amount to a guarantee by this country in any legal sense, but it is morally something of the kind; and people with some show of justice might turn around to our government and say: "It was by your counsel that we lent our money to this loan. . . . You ought to indemnify us." [4]

Criticism of this kind was easy after default had occurred; it is offered here as a point of view which had some currency. Certainly the 1855 loan, the interest on which was guaranteed by the French and British Governments, caused no such loss to its holders as other issues. Yet this guarantee, coupled with the above statement concerning the 1854 loan, provides adequate basis for the contention that these loans were issued under the sanction of European governments.

Mention has already been made of the unfortunate outcome of the 1860 loan, and of the dispatch by the British Government of two representatives of the Board of Trade to assist in liquidating the losses suffered by English commercial houses. While Lord Hobart and Mr. Foster were in Turkey they utilized their opportunity to make a survey of the economic condition of the country. Their report, which was submitted to Lord John Russell under date of December 7, 1861, regarded the financial situation "as susceptible of the greatest improvement." [5] They considered that the tax on the tobacco industry, for instance, was capable of being multiplied five times. The statement concerning this report made by Mr. Layard, Undersecretary of State for Foreign Affairs, in the House of Commons on March 14, 1862, was very hopeful:

> Perhaps the most gratifying feature of the report was that it showed there was nothing fundamentally rotten or bad in the state of Turkish finance, that the difficulties into which it had fallen arose entirely from mismanagement and want

---

[3] Quoted by Wilson, A. J., "The Turkish Default," *MacMillan's Magazine*, Volume XXXIII (November, 1875), pp. 88 *et seq.*

[4] *Ibid.*, p. 89.

[5] *Parliamentary Papers*, No. 2972 (1862), Volume 64, pp. 475 *et seq.*

> of experience, and that with a very little sound management and good will, those difficulties could be got over, and a balance restored between revenue and expenditure.[6]

When questioned on May 29, 1863, concerning the extent to which Turkish credit depended upon the good will of the British Government, Mr. Layard said:

> It must be remembered to the great honor of Turkey that she has never failed to pay her debts with the greatest punctuality, and that the credit she may command in the market, and the power she has of raising money, is not to be attributed to . . . the undue assistance of the English or any other Government, but to the simple fact of people being willing to lend money to a state which has hitherto faithfully discharged its obligations.[7]

During the debate on Turkey on March 31, 1862, the Prime Minister, Lord Palmerston, spoke in glowing terms of Abdul Aziz, the Sultan who had mounted the throne but a year previously:

> Fortunately Turkey has a sovereign who possesses in an eminent degree, qualities calculated to enable him to regenerate that Empire. He is a man of great vigour of mind, of determined patriotism, of the most frugal and even parsimonious personal habits, indefatigable in industry; from the habits of life formerly imposed upon him, not, perhaps, so well versed in the details of government as others, but most anxious to learn, most desirous of always arriving at the truth, and firm in setting his face against corruption and jobbing, favoritism and all those abuses which of late years tended so much to the decay of the Turkish Empire.[8]

This debate in the House was precipitated by the announcement by the Government of its appointment of Lord Hobart as special commissioner to oversee the use of the proceeds of the 1862 loan. On this occasion Lord Palmerston outlined the Government's reasons for acceding to the request. He considered that Lord John

---

[6] *Parliamentary Debates, House of Commons,* third series, Volume 165 (1862), pp. 1519-26.

[7] *Ibid.,* Volume 171 (1863), pp. 6-147. But cf. this statement with the opinion of a contemporary French writer, Girardin, St. M., that "the incurable malady of Turkish finance is not the lack of administration but the absence of good faith." *loc. cit.*

[8] *Parliamentary Debates, House of Commons,* third series, Volume 166 (1862), p. 297, March 31, 1862.

Russell, Secretary for Foreign Affairs, (whose action in regard to the loan had been interpreted as similar to an official guarantee), had merely "acted upon the commonest dictates of prudence and statesmanship in a matter which deeply concerned the interests of a friendly power, and a power, moreover, the maintenance of which is a point of very great importance to England. . . ."

The Turks had applied to England for funds to retire the paper money, and had "represented" that the possibilities for their obtaining, on tolerable terms, the amount which they required would be increased if H. M. Government would consent "not to assume any responsibility, or enter into any engagement as to the payment of the interest" but to commission a competent person to go to Constantinople to see that the money raised was applied to the purpose intended. A refusal to comply with this request could have been interpreted as "indifference" by the British Government towards the prosperity of Turkey. "I will simply state," said Lord Palmerston, "that the British Government take upon themselves no responsibility whatever for the payment of the interest of the loan, and all that Lord Hobart's functions will extend to is simply to see that the money raised is applied solely to the purpose for which it is raised."[9]

The French Government likewise lent its support in floating the loans destined for Turkey. In conjunction with the British Government, it had guaranteed the 1855 loan, and was also represented by an official delegate on the advisory commission on finance. French official influence at Constantinople was evidently considerable, if we can believe the following news item taken from a Constantinople paper: "The transaction [conclusion of a contract for a five million sterling loan with the *Société Générale* of Paris] has challenged a good deal of local criticism, all the more that it is said to have been in a measure forced upon the Treasury by the French Embassy."[10]

The participation of the British and French Governments in the appointment of delegates to the advisory commission on finance in 1859 was shared by the Austrian Government. In this respect three of the most powerful European states lent their official support to the policy of the Ottoman Government for financial reform.

---

[9] *Ibid.*, p. 295.

[10] Foreign correspondence of the *Times*, October 30, 1868.

A few voices in official circles were raised against the official backing under which Turkish borrowing proceeded. When the Government's proposal to ratify the convention of June 27, 1855, for the guarantee of the 1855 loan, was placed before the House of Commons on July 30, it encountered an opposition as formidable as its constituents were distinguished. Ricardo, Disraeli, and Gladstone all disagreed with Lord Palmerston's estimate of Turkish resources and ability to pay her debts. Ricardo opposed the form of common guarantee and preferred a distinct and separate guarantee, or better, he asked, why didn't Turkey come into the market and float a loan without the support of her allies, if her resources were as Lord Palmerston had maintained? Cobden, who affiliated himself with the opponents of the measure, was most outspoken in declaring: "Do not delude yourselves that you are lending money when you are giving it. . . . If you are going to advance money at all, take the simple course of making her [Turkey] a present of it. . . . Do not complicate yourselves with any joint or separate guarantee." The measure was adopted by a vote of only 135 to 132.[11]

Again, in 1862, when the Government was questioned concerning Lord Hobart's appointment, Mr. Hubbard, member for Buckingham, criticized Earl Russell's action in favoring the loan issued by the Ottoman Bank and Devaux and Company. Inasmuch as the loan was five times oversubscribed, he considered that this "furnished a clear proof of the action of governmental interference in the matter, but he entertained very serious misgivings as to the policy of that interference." If the loan had been a success mainly on account of the part the Government had taken with respect to it, Mr. Hubbard desired to know what the consequences would be in case of any disappointment in the future. "In the event of any obstacle to the future completion of the contract between British capitalists and Turkey, would not the subscribers to it say to H. M. Government: We contributed to this loan owing to the encouragement you gave us; we ask you now to interfere to obtain for us the fulfillment of our expectations . . ." [12] The Government disagreed that any unseemly or impolitic action had been taken, and Lord Palmerston stated his conception of the responsibility

[11] *Parliamentary Debates, House of Commons,* third series, Volume 139 (1855), pp. 1211-70.
[12] *Ibid.,* Volume 166 (1862), p. 290, March 31, 1862.

of the Government.[13] But the Government's favor of the issue undoubtedly increased its desirability, even though Lord Hobart's report had not been issued when the loan was floated. This course, in the opinion of the *London Times,* indicated that the Government "had either been slow or awkward in its friendship, or the Porte had been imprudently precipitate" in its desire for funds, since the rate of issue had been very low (68).[14]

Cobden maintained his original position, and, when Turkish good faith and resources were again discussed in the Commons, on May 29, 1863, he "maintained that she has never paid any interest at all, because she has borrowed all the money to pay the interest."[15] Lord Stanley, Foreign Secretary in 1868, was pessimistic concerning the state of Turkish finance, and in a speech uttered a warning "of the inevitable peril of the Ottoman Empire from financial collapse and rebellion."[16]

The French Ambassador at Constantinople, the Marquis de Lavalette, in 1861, some time before French influence was predominant at the Sublime Porte, recommended to his nationals "to engage their resources only in those enterprises which are clearly based on foundations of the most perfect integrity."[17]

But the voices of opposition were of little avail, for the Ottoman Government itself, although on occasion acting in a manner to throw doubt into the minds of its creditors, in the main presented a policy which was interpreted by sanguine observers as directed towards an eventual reorganization of finances on a solid and lasting basis. Into the treaty of alliance with France and England, Turkey had consented to introduce an article which made important concessions to the Christians of the Empire, concessions of such a nature that "there could be none better to dispose favorably the public opinion of England."[18] The *Hatti-Humayoun* of 1856 was considered by many as an indication that financial reform would follow in the footsteps of administrative reform. In 1858 the Sultan prescribed stringent economies. The Government in 1859 created the advisory finance commission, transformed it in

---

[13] *Supra,* p. 51.

[14] April 1, 1862.

[15] *Parliamentary Debates, House of Commons,* third series, Volume 171 (1863), p. 136.

[16] Reported in the *Times,* November 13, 1868.

[17] Cited in Du Velay, *op. cit.,* p. 119.

[18] *Ibid.,* p. 139.

1860 into a *Conseil Supérieur des Finances,* and, at the same time, notified the French, British, and Austrian representatives at Constantinople of the functions which the Government had delegated to it. Both Aali Pasha and Fuad Pasha had expressed their desire for the creation of a state bank with the best English and French capital supporting it, a desire that resulted in 1863 in the creation of the Imperial Ottoman Bank. The first budget of the Empire was struck the same year; two years later the internal debt was consolidated and inscribed in the *Grand Livre de la Dette Publique.* Aali Pasha paid tribute to the useful function of foreign capital in Turkey in these words: "The capital engaged in our enterprises will attract the attention of the countries which have furnished it, and, as a result, the policy of economy which was forecast in 1856 . . . will become more certain and more effective." [19] In 1870 the Imperial Government showed itself willing to appoint representatives of the holding syndicates for the administration of ear-marked revenues. Finally, each new contract for a loan, and the prospectus describing it to the public, contained the provision that certain revenues of the country were designated specially for its service, revenues the amount of which on paper were always sufficient to meet the demands of maturing coupons and sinking fund. From the point of view of published intentions British and French investors had little reason to think that the favor of their governments was less than they considered it, or that the actions of the Ottoman Government might be questioned.

Warnings in the British Press

Representative organs of British and French journalism added the weight of their opinion to the official activities of their governments. Although the *London Times* had expressed an unfavorable opinion concerning certain operations in connection with the 1854 loan,[20] when the project for ratifying the convention for the

[19] *Ibid.*, p. 248.

[20] Discussing a fall of two points in the 1854 loan, due to the signatures having been stamped, instead of written, on the bonds, the *Times* said: ". . . it contains a lesson which may be turned to good account by all individuals or states who may ever entertain the prospect of becoming borrowers. It is the penalty which Turkish credit is forced to pay for the way in which, under Russian influence, the reactionary party contrived, by repudiating the acts of their agents in the contract for the former loan,

1855 loan was discussed in Parliament, all the influence of this journal supported the Government. The *Times* adopted this policy in spite of objections to dealing with a country like Turkey which possessed a "barbarous state of finance."[21] But, when the war was ended, and Turkey had been momentarily freed from Russian aggression, this organ adopted a decidedly cautious note in its advices concerning Turkey and Turkish finance. In its issue of December 27, 1856, is the statement:

> We are told that the Council of State contains a section who are especially entrusted with the audit of government accounts and the duty of punishing peculation, and that this very body contains men who are notorious themselves for peculation. Who shall guard these guards? Who shall oversee these overseers?

Commenting on the measures of economy which had been decreed by the Sultan in 1858, a leading article maintains that

> . . . it would be folly not to recognize the connection between this sudden conversion to economy and the demand for the new loan. Without presuming that the Porte is desirous of enticing foreigners into lending money by a false pretense of reformation, . . . we must take the Sultan's present determination for what it is worth. . . .[22]

As a matter of fact, the *Times* was almost vehement in its opinion that Turkey was finding it too easy to float loans in the European markets. While the 1858 loan was in the process of subscription, it warned English investors:

> In our opinion the present loan which Turkey is contracting. . .should be the last at least for a long time to come . . .The time has come when Turkey should help itself. Both England and France have done enough and spent enough for the present. . . .We cannot but feel that the Turks have suddenly acquired a strange relish for this borrowing

to throw an element of uncertainty into all the future transactions of the Government, which nothing but years of regular conduct will now efface. Although nothing has since occurred to damage the financial honor of the country in its intercourse with foreigners . . . the public have now become possessed of a vague and unreasoning feeling that leads them at once to magnify even the mere rumor of an informality into a serious difficulty." November 9, 1854.

[21] *Ibid.*, July 23, 24, 31, 1855.

[22] *Ibid.*, September 13, 1858.

> . . . There is too much reason to believe that Turkish *pashas* are a little captivated by this easy means of bringing sovereigns and napoleons to the Bosporus. . . Such a state of society [as that of Turkey] is one which will naturally tend to the contracting of loans, and the wasting of funds which the borrowers need not trouble themselves to repay. It is not necessary to stuff them in feeding them well. The vices of Musulmans are sloth and pride, and in furnishing funds which others must pay, we are only encouraging these vices. Let our capitalists be wise and prudent. They have lent Turkey sufficient to put her on her feet. . . and not enough to turn her head nor to render her accustomed to it. We have felt it our duty to say this . . . lest the principle of trusting vast sums to this anomolous and untried state be too easily accepted by the public.[23]

Ten days later the easy terms which characterized the market at that time caused these words to appear:

> There is at present something like a plethora of capital, and it may well be that our suffering countrymen will seek relief by endeavoring to fill the exhausted veins of Turkey. . . The crying sin of Turkish governments for many generations has been financial profligacy. To get money by any means has been the great art of statesmanship,—to spend it with profusion the great art of ambition. . . . To live within its means, to borrow only on great occasions, and then with a certainty of inflicting no wrong on the lenders, are the first duties of an honorable community. Till Turkey has shown a firm resolve to carry out these principles she ought not to expect further assistance as a state; and our capitalists, if they turn their attention to the east, would do well to confine themselves to definite enterprises, of which they can hold the management in their own hands, rather than to constitute themselves creditors for large amounts to the Imperial Government.[24]

But even in the matter of such enterprises as are alluded to, the *Times* drew a gloomy picture of what Englishmen might expect in Turkey:

> The great wealth of England and the desire for more profitable investments than are offered within the limits of a country of redundant capital, have caused, and will cause,

[23] *Ibid.*, September 15, 1858.
[24] *Ibid.*, September 25, 1858.

> the East to be explored by the enterprising and speculating . . . But one thing ought never to be lost sight of—the Turkish state is different from any other with which we are familiar.

Having recognized the fact that behind the façade of Ottoman functionaries were to be found Armenian and Greek bankers in whose debt most of the Turkish officials usually found themselves, this journal continued:

> If this gaudy frontispiece of Imperial sway does not truly represent the financial power of the country, if the Sultan and his ministers cannot really control the commercial concerns of the Empire, we may find too late that guarantees and concessions are but a delusion, and that vast sums of money and a great opportunity have been lost. . . We would advise our countrymen not to trust too sanguinely to [Turkish] political support. The Turkish functionaries are in commercial matters both ignorant and corrupt. . . . The Porte is, we believe, totally untrustworthy in its dealings with foreign enterprise. . . . While capitalists are bidding for concessions, the Porte has demanded as its price, first a loan of five million pounds, then of eight millions, rising in its exactions as the competition grows hot. . . . Such a state of things should make our countrymen more cautious in their dealings in this new field of enterprise.[25]

Some years later the financial editor of this paper offered this observation:

> . . . Until a different state of affairs is witnessed it will be well for our people not to give an eager reception to any new appeals to our money market, however cleverly their introduction may be manipulated by the large financial operators, the safety of whose personal speculations may depend upon its success.[26]

The agitation current at this period over the safety of Turkish bonds prompted the following severe indictment of the actual state of affairs:

> No argument can be necessary to show the great danger of such loans so long as the daily quotations are published.

---

[25] *Ibid.*, November 1, 1856.
[26] *Ibid.*, November 8, 1869.

> When a government stock is quoted at terms to pay from nine to twelve percent interest to the investor, those terms are a danger signal sufficient for any person capable of understanding signals or advice of any kind. . . . It must be admitted that the interests of investors are cared for to a much less extent than would be practicable if the keenness of financial competition were regulated by decent scruples. . . . There are scarcely a dozen houses in London by whom any large loan could be properly conducted and if these, instead of constantly opposing each other, could be brought to recognize, in deference to the public interests as well as to their own, some principles of mutuality, they might make in the aggregate much larger profits without anxiety, and at the same time keep foreign governments straight by showing them that a reckless or dishonest course would at once close every avenue of assistance. This is precisely what is now wanted in the case of Turkey . . . but the idea of such a consummation would be quixotic, and it may be expected that, as in the past, so in the future, each rival establishment will strain every nerve to find the point at which, by the most dexterous manipulation, it may venture to outbid others in supplying her demands.[27]

When London was informed in 1871 that the new Finance Minister, Sadik Pasha, desired to settle outstanding accounts with foreign railways, that economies were to be introduced, and that the civil list was to be cut by 250,000 pounds, the *Times* thought that "these statements must, however, be received with caution. The step which would tend more than any other to revive confidence in Turkish securities would be a strict compliance with the letter of the bonds of the various loans."[28]

The above quotations from this leading London journal may create the impression that its attitude during this period was constantly hostile to Turkish borrowing. The following extracts, however, show that on occasion it uttered opinions which might be compelling enough to induce further investment. Its attitude concerning the 1855 loan has already been mentioned.[29] The appearance of the first budget in 1862 was received somewhat skeptically, but finally the opinion was presented that another opportunity for regeneration might be allowed:

---

27 *Ibid.*, November 23, 1869.
28 October 31, 1871.
29 *Supra*, pp. 54-5.

> We are too well accustomed to the splendid protestations of nations on the eve of contracting loans to allow ourselves to be dazzled altogether even by this array of well-balanced figures and sound economic principles. . . . The sinking fund may show that alacrity of sinking into an annual deficit which has so frequently characterized the sinking funds of other nations from whom more was to be hoped. The expenditure may not be kept within reasonable bounds. *Caimé* may not be called in; palaces may continue to be built. . . . We know all this, and yet it is so pleasant to find that a thing is going to be done at last that we will try yet once more to believe positively for the last time in the regeneration of the Turkish Empire.[30]

The continued ability of Turkey to find money evidently strengthened belief in her vitality:

> Our countrymen have placed enough money abroad on very doubtful security, and have the recollection of enough foreign insolvency, to make them anxious when they hear of the decay of the Musulmans, the threatening aspect of the Christians, the designs of the Russians, and the other facts and tendencies that go to make up the eastern question. Happily for the state of mind of those who are pecuniarily interested in the east, creditors are a sanguine and confiding race, and when, in the view of mankind generally, black clouds are gathering, they can only see that the heavens are a little grey. If the Turks be encamped in Europe, so are the British in India, so are the French in Algeria, and yet in neither of these cases do people allow the prospective termination [sic] of the rule to have any practical effect on their dealings. So with respect to Turkey: the Ottoman Porte has borrowed, is borrowing, will borrow. . . . Yet the Turks keep on their way after a stolid, obstinate fashion of their own, and they find means to levy taxes, to maintain order, to get new money from various quarters, and to pay the interest on old. . . . To those who make inquiries concerning the "sick man" the bulletin must therefore be "the patient is no worse."[31]

Even the contribution of a most unfavorable criticism of Turkey from an English resident in Smyrna was envisaged with calmness by the financial editor. To the arguments of a false budget, the prodigality of the government, its policy of borrowing to pay

[30] The *Times*, March 24, 1862.
[31] *Ibid.*, January 14, 1868.

interest, and the alleged hollowness of the phrase "Turkey's extraordinary resources," the following answer was given:

> The moment Turkey allows her credit to collapse she must fall to pieces; such a territory will then not be allowed by the European powers to pass into anarchy, and whatever may be the government or governments to be established, it or they can take no solid stand without an honorable assumption, sooner or later, of all recognized public obligations.[32]

But in 1871 anxiety finally manifested itself, when a rumor reached London that a project of repudiation had been discussed in a ministerial council. It happened that the only ground for this rumor was "a suggestion thrown out by one of the ministers unconnected with the department of finance that the rate of interest of the general debt might with advantage be reduced from five to three percent, a suggestion which, as might be expected, died a natural death."[33] The *Times* observed that "notwithstanding this satisfactory correction, it would be more pleasant if in the Imperial Council there were no repudiating elements, even though limited to a minority of one."[34]

Various items in other English journals contributed to the belief that money lent to the Turkish Government was exposed to no more than ordinary risks. The *Daily News* of September 2, 1858, emphasized the particularly liquid revenues which were designated to meet the charges on the 1858 loan. It also considered as most gratifying the stipulation for the erection of a special commission to collect the revenues, a commission on which two Englishmen would sit. This was termed "a considerable innovation from the political point of view as well as from the point of view of finance." In the *Daily Herald* of September 3, 1858, appeared this observation:

> Everything which has been said in regard to the instability of the Ottoman Government, of the irregular employment of the customs revenues, and of the absence of authority for contracting the loan . . . has only been circulated to obstruct the course of the loan, or for accomplishing a quotation

32 *Ibid.*, financial section, October 29, 1869.
33 *The Levant Herald* (Constantinople) quoted in the *Times*.
34 October 27, 1871.

of a discount, and it is affirmed that it is devoid of any foundation.[35]

But in the *Morning Advertiser* the opinion was expressed that "any sort of plan which will draw a large amount of capital from this country, and which will produce only a small annual return must be regarded with disapproval and even with a certain amount of uneasiness by those who are interested in watching the march of events, and, in particular, certain happenings which later might be accompanied by unfavorable results."[36]

The *Banker's Magazine* (London) was skeptical of the smooth course which the guaranteed loan of 1855 might be expected to run. After recognizing the apparent security of the loan, this journal was of the opinion that:

> Such disasters have attended the previous financial transactions entered into on behalf of the Sultan, that it would be imprudent to predict a perfectly satisfactory fulfillment of the engagement. . . . The stock itself . . . presents, all contingencies avoided, a most stable and satisfactory security, but in all such operations . . . a proportional amount of risk is incurred, which the chances of the market or other circumstances may naturally influence. . . . The arrangement of a money transaction such as the one now contemplated will induce considerations which may affect the pecuniary interests of the capitalists who take the lead in negotiations.[37]

In 1860 another publication expressed the opinion that "wanton extravagance and general corruption are the two concurrent causes which have produced the ruined condition of Turkish finance." [38] The same article registered violent disagreement with the state of Turkish finance as presented to the European public in the *Al-*

---

[35] "The *Morning Herald*, expressing views said to be those of the British Government, predicted a brilliant future for the Ottoman Empire. This journal does not consider the present disorganized condition as incurable. It is thought to have been halted, at least for the present, by the singular energy which the Sultan has just manifested . . . Everyone knows that England's debt is larger proportionally than the Turkish debt; there is hope for Turkey then, and the best proof of this is the rush in England to cover this last loan." *Journal des Débats*, September 12, 1858. Cf. also the *Banker's Magazine* (London) Volume XIII, (April, 1853), pp. 252 *et seq.*

[36] September 6, 1858.

[37] Volume XV (September, 1855), pp. 558-63.

[38] "The Financial Condition of Turkey," *Fraser's Magazine*, Volume LXII (October, 1860), pp. 483 *et seq.*

manach de Gotha. In the latter the private purse of the Sultan was entered at 250,000 pounds sterling. But to this figure, according to this article, should be added at least twice as much again, and it adds that any passing whim of the Sultan or of any member of his family may result in a large unpredicted demand on the Treasury.

On the introduction of another loan in 1873, the *Banker's Magazine* uttered further words of precaution:

> Severe fluctuations in the prices of Turkey's stocks have corresponded to the vaccilation in public opinion between the belief as to her ability to meet her liabilities, and the fear that her late heavy borrowings had exceeded at last her capacity to pay interest, and had exhausted the patience of her European creditors. The presentment of so large a loan as that just introduced and the reception it met with go far, it must be confessed, to warrant apprehension as to the future. Turkish loans have hitherto met with great favor, and, in spite of several alarms as to the payment of the dividends, each new financial overture from that quarter has been fairly successful. With this last demand, however, there appears to be some considerable difficulty. In inducing the public to take it, there have been the usual assertions as to the purely formal nature of the requisition, its intended appropriation to the consolidation of the debt, and the excellence of the hypothecations in its favor. But only eight million pounds of the twenty-eight million has been subscribed for; and this poor response is naturally regarded as tantamount to proof that, for the present at all events, Europe has had enough of Turkish indebtedness.[39]

On October 9, 1873, the *Times* again thought fit to call to the attention of the investing public the risks incurred in sending any more money into Turkey:

> The only service which can now be rendered to Turkey is to refuse her a single additional shilling of money on any

[39] Volume XXXIII (October, 1873), pp. 999 *et seq.* Among qualifying reasons as to the too ready assertion of this opinion, the article mentioned the prices of the various loans on the market, paying about nine per cent., which he did not consider excessive; the "process of issuing foreign loans under the auspices of a syndicate has only recently come to the knowledge of the public, and it is now no secret how the system is worked and that many of these bodies have yet on their hands large amounts of the various foreign loans of modern issue." p. 1000. For this reason, in the opinion of this magazine, the unsubscribed remainder of the last Turkish loan should not cause surprise.

> pretext whatever until she shall have placed her system of revenue and expenditure under solemn guarantees in the hands of statesmen conversant with true principles, and protected by checks and restrictions so established as to be beyond even imperial interference.

A final note of warning was uttered by the financial editor on November 7, 1874:

> Subscribers to every new loan must be aware that they are but feeding a flame which in the end will consume everything if the whole system is not radically altered.

Divided Opinion Elsewhere

These opinions culled from representative English newspapers and reviews must be recognized as possessing a distinctly cautious tone. Supporting this general viewpoint are expressions of individual opinion which should be compared with those appearing in the public press. Here again were two different points of view, one favorable to the reports of Turkish resources, of Turkish ability to pay, and of general financial rehabilitation, the other defending the opposite contention.

On October 12, 1861, a meeting was held of bearers of Turkish bonds of the 1858 issue, presided over by Mr. W. A. Mackinnon, M. P. During the course of remarks on the general situation, he said:

> In considering the question of a debt from a foreign government, these points should be especially looked to: the amount, the moral character of the debtor, and the means for meeting the interest.

In applying these tests to the Turkish situation, Mr. Mackinnon said:

> The principle of the Turkish debt is only two and one-half times the total income of the country, while in England it is nearly twelve times. Second, the Turkish nation bears a reputation for honesty equal to any other people, and the present Sultan is believed to be especially anxious to reduce the public expenditure and keep out of debt. Third, Turkey possesses some of the finest portions of Europe, Asia, and Africa, with unequalled means of production, which are capable of great improvement.[40]

[40] Reported in the *Times*, October 12, 1861.

In the report of this meeting in the press it was also observed that Sir Henry Bulwer, then British Ambassador at the Sublime Porte, estimated that the public revenue of Turkey might be raised one third to 15,250,000 pounds sterling and the expenditure reduced one third to 7,800,000 pounds, leaving a surplus of nearly seven and a half million pounds. Earl Russell had also expressed a favorable opinion concerning the resources and prospects of the Turkish Empire.

Again, in 1868 the *Times* carried a letter from a person signing himself "Anglo-Turk" who disagreed entirely with Lord Stanley's unfavorable remarks concerning Turkish finance. After a long analysis of the situation, this correspondent finally arrived at two conclusions: first, the increasing wealth of Turkey, and second, its increasing capacity to pay. He admitted, however, that "There are, no doubt, waste and extravagance at Constantinople; but the tendency is toward correction. . . . For myself, I may speak from a personal knowledge of Turkey (something which Lord Stanley cannot) in describing it as a progressive and not a retrogressive state." [41]

In a report to his government on the Turkish budget of 1872-3, Mr. Horace Rumbold, British Consul in Anatolia, made the following significant declaration:

> It would not be fair to argue that the expansion of productive power is only apparent, or that increased revenue is solely the result of unsparing taxation. On the contrary, so rich in natural resources is this Empire that it is probable that, in spite of defective administration or ill-considered financial measures, its inherent wealth creates wealth again, and defies, as it were, the process of exhaustion.[42]

The *Times,* which devoted a leading article to this subject on August 3, 1872, "concurs entirely with this view."[43]

---

[41] December 10, 1868; on July 19, 1867, the *Times* printed the following extract from the *Turquie* (Constantinople): In reference to a three year loan concluded with the Paris *Société Générale* for two million pounds sterling, ". . . we may remark that it is creditable to the Grand Vizier and the Minister of Finance to note the readiness with which foreign capital is offered to Turkey of late, showing that, notwithstanding interested detraction, the credit of the Empire has never been firmer."

[42] Cited in the *Times,* August 3, 1872.

[43] But cf. the editorial of October 9, 1873, *supra,* pp. 62-3, stating an opinion concerning the administration of this "inherent wealth."

The publicity given to these views drew forth just as zealous a defence of the opposite point of view. An English resident of Smyrna considered the favorable reports which were appearing in the English and French press as misrepresenting the situation:

> It is easy to conceive that all those interested in Turkish financial schemes should endeavor to influence the general public to uphold the [Turkish] Government's credit. . . . But that any leading papers in London or Paris should endorse the monstrous fiction of real progress or stability in Turkey is sadly reprehensible, as by such misrepresentations the general public become the unconscious victims of those highly respectable and eminent capitalists who lend their name and influence to bring the loan upon the market, and by clever combinations run up the value and then sell out as quickly as they can with handsome profits in premiums, commissions, etc., well knowing that at any moment the whole artificial fabric of Turkish credit may crumble to the dust, and bring ruin upon all those who have been induced by influential names and plausible arguments, together with the allurement of high interest, to invest their hard-earned savings in these mis-named securities.[44]

These conflicting ideas concerning Turkish resources, administrative efficiency and integrity, and concerning the desirability of her securities have been taken exclusively from English sources. Was there a comparable amount of comment stimulated in France, where there was quite as much interest in placing surplus funds favorably? If we may judge from one representative organ, the *Journal des Débats,* it would seem that editorial comment was much scantier and far less frequent than in the English press. During the fifteen years prior to 1870 hardly a single leading article was devoted to a discussion of the arguments for and against the wisdom of purchasing Turkish bonds. In the financial columns observation and comment appeared more frequently, but in nothing like the volume which the above quotations indicate was the case in England.

An editorial in the issue of August 18, 1855, was favorable to the contention that Turkey's assets were sufficient to pay her debts. In 1858, on the occasion of the dismissal of four of his ministers by the Sultan, this journal interpreted this action in this manner:

---

[44] Correspondence in the *Times,* October 29, 1869; compare the retort of the financial editor, *supra,* p. 60.

> Everything contributes to the belief that this measure is related to the resolution taken by the Sultan to terminate the financial disorders [in the imperial palaces and harems] which have recently been commented upon in the *Times* and other quarters.

Some days later the *Journal* offered a more extended comment on the situation:

> Can one hope for the establishment of more order in the finances and for the wiser and more trustworthy employment of the revenues of the Empire? The English seem to count a great deal on the direct functioning, in the collection of the revenues, of the commissioners provided for in the last loan contract. If this foreign interference might have as a result the introduction of European ideas of book-keeping into the finances of the Empire, never would a loan have been more useful to the borrower, and the increase of Turkey's debts would this time have sensibly slowed up her ruin.[45]

The appeal made to the individual investor was commented on in an issue some years later:

> Now we are witnessing the search for capital in every quarter. We find nothing to criticize in this, because it demands publicity and this calls forth examination and criticism of the motives on which is based the transaction seeking subscribers. Thus, on the eve of the subscription to the Turkish loan, M. Mirés set forth the situation in Turkey. . . . Are we not correct in remarking that times have changed, and that the Bourse is no longer the place where all the large issues are floated? . . . This helps to sustain interest in the transactions submitted to the public.

The *Journal des Débats* was one of the Paris papers which had supported the 1860 loan contracted by M. Mirés. It was unfortunate that the financial editor chose this particular operation on which to comment, inasmuch as the extremely favorable resumé of conditions in Turkey made by M. Mirés and published in the *Journal*, and other papers, failed to harmonize with the conception held by the public. The ideas of M. Mirés were discounted heavily, a factor which contributed to the ultimate failure of the transaction.[46]

---

[45] September 12, 1858.

[46] December 10, 1860; the prospectus appeared on December 8. A severe criticism of its contents is found in "La moralité des finances

Naturally enough, although little editorial space was given to Turkish fiscal problems, comments are to be found from time to time in the financial columns. The temporary weakness in Turkish stocks in 1863 caused this comment:

> The recently issued Turkish six percent is a security which stood in great need of the prestige of a large credit establishment in order that it might enjoy the confidence which is not inspired in issues based entirely upon the pleasure of the Ottoman Treasury.[47]

The demands from various quarters made on the Paris market during 1865 caused this ironical comment:

> The last foreign loan of the year 1865 is the Turkish loan. It follows those to Mexico, Tunis, Austria. In truth it seems that the doors of Paradise have opened:
>
> *On voit arriver, en chantant,*
> *Un Turc, un juif, un protestant,*
>
> Thus goes the song, and the refrain adds: *Rendez-moi mes clefs, disait St. Pierre!* This is the real refrain sung by ministers of finance.

As security the Turkish Government had pledged the product of the Arghana copper mines and the tax on Anatolian sheep. The ironic strain continues:

> The sheep of Anatolia formerly laughed at the sheep of Roumelia [the taxes on which had already been pledged], but now they have no desire to laugh in a country where the eating of pork is heresy, wine is forbidden, and the flocks of cattle a delusion, but where the sheep, to his misfortune, is worth his weight in gold. This does not apply, however, to the sheep of Anatolia, on which an annual revenue of fourteen million francs can certainly not be raised. As regards the mines of Tokat, they are part of the private wealth of the Sultan, and a king has never been forbidden to place his crown in pawn. . . . Turkey is making an admirable effort in attempting to open and to close a "Grand Livre": in opening it in order to consolidate all her debt therein, and in closing

turques," by Girardin, St. M., *loc. cit.*, pp. 474-5, particularly in regard to the activities of the advisory finance commission. Cf. also leading article in the *Times*, July 13, 1861. The loan itself is briefly described *supra*, Chapter III, pp. 33-4.

[47] *Journal des Débats*, July 15, 1863. The "large credit establishment" was the *Banque de Paris et des Pays-Bas*.

it to allow the capitalists of London and Paris an opportunity to get their breath.[48]

In Paris, as in London, rumors were current in 1869 that the political aspect of the situation might soon be evident:

> The negotiators of the Turkish loan deny that the shadow of a small black cloud is beginning to appear in the region of the Pyramids, but anti-Turkish bankers perceive a menacing and overhanging problem, the whole Eastern question.[49]

Criticism of the Imperial Ottoman Bank

It is hardly surprising that sharp divisions of opinion existed among representative newspapers and in other quarters in England and France concerning the wisdom of investing in Turkish bonds. One establishment, however, occupied a strategic status in Turkey, one in which there was adequate opportunity to obtain substantial and accurate information concerning Turkish finance.

Of all financial institutions operating in Turkey, the Imperial Ottoman Bank was in the strongest position to make its presence felt on the side of reform and retrenchment.[50] It is an open question, however, whether the ultimate effect of this establishment on the fiscal situation before 1875 was for good or evil. In 1863 a reorganization of the English-chartered Ottoman Bank took place, and the new lease on life enjoyed by Turkish credit in London and Paris financial circles after that date must be attributed to great degree to the confidence inspired by this measure. Again, after Turkish credit weakened in the early 1870's, the Government in 1875 granted further privileges to this institution, which again bolstered up Turkish credit in Europe. An unidentified correspondent to the *London Times* wrote:

> The prevailing notion appears to be that, on its new basis, the Bank will stand to the Porte very much in the relation of the Treasury and the Bank of England to our own government; or, in other words, that it will practically control the entire financial administration of the Empire. It is not too

[48] *Journal des Débats*, December 18, 1865.

[49] *Ibid.*, November 29, 1869.

[50] For a description of the personnel, objects, and nature of the privileges of this important institution, see Young, G., *op. cit.*, Volume V, Chapter 83; Du Velay, *op. cit.*, pp. 189-96 and *passim;* Biliotti, A., *La Banque Impériale Ottomane* (Paris, 1909); also, for a statement of the economic activities of the Bank in recent years, see *infra*, Chapter IX.

much to say that this misconception was very favorably discounted during a recent subscription to the first instalment of the loan, when the credit of the Bank rather than of the Porte led to so brilliant a success for the operation.[51]

These measures, although of a highly profitable character to the Bank, can only be described as a compromise, in that the Ottoman Government never went far enough to concede complete control of its fiscal system, but only delegated a sufficient number of privileges to impress European investors with the probable eventual rejuvenation of the finances of the Empire.[52]

The Bank, on the other hand, was criticized for its failure to halt the accelerated process of borrowing by the Ottoman Government. "If the Imperial Ottoman Bank is sincerely interested for the bondholders, their first act should be to stop further borrowing, whereas the contrary is the fact." [53] After having criticized the British Government for its support of Turkish financial transactions, an English critic says:

> The Imperial Ottoman Bank has been the chief offender, as it has been the most unsatisfactory "friend" that the Sultan ever had. Knowing the corrupt character of the Turkish Government as its Constantinople officials must have done, it is strange to see how greed of gain, and, no doubt, also some remains of the old enthusiasm about Turkey's great resources, have blinded them to the true state of affairs. In

[51] Correspondence in the *Times*, November 4, 1874. J. C. M., the correspondent, continues: "But the facts are not at all as thus popularly supposed. Shortly stated, the new reform is limited to this: first, that the Porte once again promises to issue regular budgets, framed by a commission on which the Bank shall have one delegate out of ten or twelve named by the grand vizier for the time being. Second, that the departmental outlay shall, as a rule, be kept within the limits as thus fixed. Third, that the Bank instead of the Malié (Treasury) shall receive the revenue and pay it against the ministerial checks, or in other words, that it shall do for the Porte what other banks do for their private clients, and that is all. There is no stipulation whatever that the annuities of the foreign debt shall be a first charge on the revenues, nor any provision which gives the Bank, as such, the least effective control over departmental extravagance or, least of all, over the Civil List."

[52] News items of the following nature appeared from time to time in the leading London and Paris journals: "According to each official monthly statement of the Imperial Ottoman Bank the revenue collections continue to increase in large proportions." Constantinople report in the *Times*, June 26, 1867.

[53] The *Times*, November 17, 1874. "The consolidation of the floating debt is a mere pretext for transferring debt from local to foreign creditors, and is, moreover, an encouragement for Turkish bankers to tempt the Government into every kind of extravagance."

> the light of what has happened, many of the announcements issued under the sanction of the Bank read as if they could hardly have been made in good faith. . . . The true status of loan contractors and the extent of their responsibility are things that need defining above almost every other business question, and this would be a good case to try it on, for the Ottoman Bank indubitably led the public to put faith in its character of regenerator of Turkey more than in the Turk himself.[54]

The protests of statesmen who opposed this wholesale emigration of capital, and the warnings and ironical criticism of leading Paris and London papers, were unavailing. This period was one of the wildest speculation. The early material guarantee of the French and British Governments, the subsequent favor of the latter, the skill of the Porte's ministers in playing off rival financiers against one another, its published series of proposed reforms, and the false sense of security created by institutions like the Ottoman Bank, were sufficient to send good money after bad. The tales of Turkey's wealth, of her inexhaustible resources, and of the ease with which reform would produce handsome dividends on corporate investments, were met with equally sincere contentions that undeveloped wealth would never pay dividends, that the people of the country were already overtaxed, and that reform, if successful at all, would come only after a long period of time. Western Europe's capacity to produce and save was comparable only to Turkish ability to squander and spend. But Turkish profligacy was encouraged by avaricious bankers, who, in turn, were able to raise money by plausible arguments addressed to the public of Europe. At the bottom of the situation may be noted the lack of a sufficiently strong public opinion, based on elementary economic principles, to stop the process before it was too late. Such opinion as there was was fragmentary and uncrystallized, and varied according to the interests of different groups. Not until 1875, when the crash came and Turkey acknowledged bankruptcy, was there a generally accepted idea among creditors about the Turkish financial situation. Then, of course, it was agreed that the circumstances were desperate. Few were those who could point to their early statements and say that what they had pre-

[54] Wilson, A. J., "The Turkish Default," *loc. cit.*, pp. 90-92.

dicted had come to pass. The majority agreed that it was Turkey's fault, and Turkey, therefore, should take the blame. Nine and twelve percent were indeed handsome dividends, and when they were cut in two, or stopped altogether for a time, the outcry was great.[55] For the investing public there seems to be no medium ground between timidity and recklessness.[56]

What was, in fact, the reception which Europe accorded Turkish calls for financial help? The 1854 issue attracted the best capital in Paris; the rate of the public offering of the 1855 loan was nearly three percent above par. The subscription list for the 1858 loan comprised the names of seven hundred notable persons in London. So great was the rush to purchase the 1862 offering that English Consols were disposed of in order that the Turkish six percents might be purchased. The nominal total of this loan was eight million sterling, but applications were received for a total of thirty-four million. "Hundreds of the wisest, the shrewdest, and the richest of Englishmen have been rushing to declare in language which cannot be doubted their conviction that the 'sick man' is convalescent." [57]

The 1863 flotation glided to success on the wave of popularity which characterized the loan of the year previous. The 1870 and 1872 Lottery Bonds were "trés recherchés" in Vienna. In 1874, only a year before default occurred, "the subscriptions for the Turkish loan were . . . stated to be of extraordinary magnitude, the total in London alone being considerably in excess of the whole amount." [58]

In all fairness it should be added that the 1860 loan was a failure; that the subscription to the 1865 issue "dragged along

---

[55] *Edinburgh Review,* Volume CXLIV (October, 1876), pp. 545-6.

[56] There was, in reality, no dearth of warnings in the public press. See, for example, the following group of letters, Constantinople advices, protests against new quotations on the Bourse, experiences of difficulty with Turkish securities, etc., in the *Times,* November 9, 1854, February 9, 1856, March 27, 1862, August 17, 24, 1867, November 23, 1868, March 5, 9, 10, 20, 26, 27, 30, November 20, 1869, May 18, 1872, February 12, 1874, June 12, 16, 1874.

[57] The premium on the 1855 loan is hardly to be wondered at, in view of the official British and French guarantee. *Journal des Débats,* August 25, 1854; *Daily Herald,* September 3, 1858; *Journal des Débats,* March 31, 1862; London *Times,* April 1, 1862.

[58] *Économiste Autrichien,* quoted in Du Velay, *op. cit.,* p. 256; London *Times,* September 18, 1874.

haltingly"; that in 1871 opposition was encountered in obtaining the quotation on the London exchange for the loan of that year; and that "some considerable difficulty" was experienced by London bankers in disposing of the 1873 issue. Nevertheless, the catastrophe in 1860 can be attributed mainly to M. Mirés's loss of personal prestige. The slowness of the public in consuming the bonds of the 1865 issue was attributed by the *Journal des Débats,* on January 8, 1866, to a bear attack on all foreign issues, while the system of underwriting an issue by a syndicate which often carried untaken bonds in its portfolio for some time, seems to the *Banker's Magazine* (London) to explain the "considerable difficulty" in connection with the 1873 loan.[59]

The economic doctrine of the third quarter of the nineteenth century, that is, governmental non-interference with capital movements, together with the prevailing western European political opinion concerning the Ottoman Empire—maintenance of its integrity—precluded the placing of capital in Turkey for any ulterior political motives. At that moment, financiers, promoters, and business men did not, of course, rationalize and at the request of their governments create economic interests in any given locality. Initiative and energy always strive to widen the circle of material activity. The expansion of the European capitalistic system during the nineteenth century was bound to push Europe's interests and influence in an ever-widening orbit. The Ottoman Empire fell within this area, and for peculiar reasons was the object which attracted large amounts of capital set free by the expansion of industry and credit. To lend money to Turkey had little political object other than the strengthening of the Empire, an object the success of which may be doubted in the light of subsequent events. To allow Turkey to borrow money, on the other hand, offered an opportunity to the speculator and financier to realize quick and easy profits, and to the small investor a chance to obtain high interest. These were the real motives at the bottom of this transfer of European gold to the gateway to the East. But the course of history transformed a series of profitable transactions (with a secondary political motive) into an opportunity to establish European financial administrators in the capital of the Empire. With

[59] Volume XXXIII (October, 1873), p. 1000.

the quickened economic pulse of the Near East in later years, this establishment of European representatives, albeit unofficial, was to aid in the acceleration of the "civilizing mission" which Europe assumed in the Near East. To the events resulting in the institution of the Ottoman Public Debt Administration, and to its rôle in Turkey during the following forty-five years, the following chapters will be devoted.

Chapter V

THE FOUNDING OF EUROPE'S OUTPOST

That profit was the obvious as well as the underlying reason why Europe was willing for so much "surplus" capital to find its way into Turkish hands has been shown. Also a less well-defined, but clearly present, political motive has been detected, namely, the desire of England and, to a less degree, that of France, to use financial means to maintain Ottoman independence and political integrity.

Turkey's need of money was ever-present. This fact, coupled with the administrative weakness of the Empire and its lack of public-spirited servants, shortly produced the fatal result of practically ruining its credit abroad. Before detailing the steps which brought this about, time must be taken to sketch hurriedly the political and economic background. Insurrection in Herzegovina, war with Serbia and Montenegro, and uprisings in Bulgaria, all occurring between the spring of 1875 and the fall of 1876, were merely the prelude to a far greater calamity, the Russo-Turkish War of 1877-78, an event far-reaching in its effects which was to push the Empire still farther into debt. The situation was so complicated that European administrative assistance proved the only way out of the morass. European recklessness and Turkish profligacy resulted in bankruptcy; bankruptcy caused the further attenuation of the sovereignty of the Sultan, by alienating important revenues and by causing the institution of a foreign-directed administration within Turkish borders.

It is surprising that the Ottoman Empire, possessing considerable latent resources should, in the short space of twenty years, have undertaken a foreign indebtedness amounting to two hundred million pounds sterling without a commensurate development of these resources. In a way, those who contended that Turkey could pay the charges on a foreign debt of this size, were correct. There is no doubt that its resources were immense and, with proper development, could have produced sufficient revenue to discharge interest and sinking fund.

It was a vicious circle, however, in which Turkey attempted to function. Potential resources existed within her borders, but Turkey lacked the technical skill and capital for their development. The limited amounts of native capital were in the hands of the subject races, Greeks, Armenians, Jews. It is doubtful whether sufficiently large sums could have been realized from this source to develop Turkish natural resources effectively. In any event, capital which Ottoman subjects did advance to the Government was used for more pressing needs, such as the payment of the fighting forces and of the administrative departments. Foreign capital was a necessity, therefore, if the natural resources of the Empire were to be put into condition to bear a just portion of the charges on the foreign debt.

Foreign capital, however, had already made its appearance in Turkey, in response to demands for meeting war expenses, and for improving the weakened monetary system. Charges on these early loans were, of course, prior charges on any future foreign capital which might enter the country. The later loans were largely mortgaged even before they were in the Government's coffers. Imperial requirements of the Sultan, administrative demands of the army and of the civil service, charges for the consolidation of the internal and floating debts, service on foreign loans already contracted: these were the burdens under which well-intentioned grand viziers and finance ministers labored. They were, moreover, the reasons which caused the indefinite postponement of the execution of a program involving the development of the resources of the Empire.

Under these circumstances, therefore, it is perhaps surprising that Turkey discharged her obligations to creditors abroad as long as she did. There were numerous occasions upon which responsible ministers might have stooped to the suggestion which was constantly being presented, that a decrease in the rate of interest, or postponement in paying the coupons, should be effected. Tribute must be paid to the Viziers, Aali Pasha and Fuad Pasha, who realized the demoralization which would accompany such a policy, and who refused to accept this suggestion.

But the period of relative tranquillity which the Ottoman Empire enjoyed during the fifteen years following the Treaty of Paris (1856) could hardly be extended indefinitely, with her traditional enemy, Russia, ready to denounce the restrictions of this treaty at the first opportunity. This came in 1870 in the midst of the Franco-Prussian War, and from that date on a new Russo-Turkish war was only a matter of time. The insurrection in Crete in 1869, and the uneasiness noticeable in the European provinces were danger signs regarded with apprehension by those who feared Turkey's ability to maintain order within her boundaries. For the holders of Turkish bonds these signs of domestic discontent and of Russian territorial aims caused the future to be envisaged with fear. If, in the midst of domestic strife and under the fear of foreign aggression, Turkey were to experience the misfortune of having an unscrupulous grand vizier, Turkish bonds might indeed become the speculation they had so often been called.

The Dark Outlook in 1875

The situation in 1875 inspired the gloomiest forebodings. In spite of the success of the 1874 loan domestic conditions in the Ottoman Empire were far from satisfactory. The harvest of that year had been poor in several provinces; the Government had been compelled to distribute provisions to some sections of the populations in order to prevent famine; floods were more severe than for years; disease broke out in several localities. The result was that the collection of the tithes and of other taxes was undertaken only under the greatest difficulties. The Government was unable to realize the estimates of its revenues. Insurrection in Bosnia and Herzegovina which broke out in the early summer soon spread to the rest of the European provinces and called for the use of force by the Government.

To the desperate economic situation was added the burden of meeting the charges on the external and internal debts, larger at that moment than at any earlier time. The foreign debt amounted to two hundred millions sterling; the annual charges reached the sum of nearly twelve million pounds. The revenue with which to meet this charge had to be found in the general revenues of the Empire, which, according to the 1874-5 budget, amounted to approximately twenty-two million pounds. Although this figure represented an increase of some sixty-five percent over the budget estimates of 1863-4, the meeting of the foreign debt charges from the general revenue would have left a remainder of only ten million pounds with which to carry on the departments of state for the year, an obviously impossible proceeding. There was also a floating debt of some sixteen million pounds.[1]

The disordered economic life of the Empire and the huge charges on the foreign debt coincided with an increased uneasiness in Europe concerning the ability of Turkey to proceed under these burdens. Although the coupons of the various loans had usually been met at maturity, the payment of those of the general debt due July, 1866, had been postponed for three months. Again, in 1871 the provisions concerning the charges of several of the foreign loans had not been kept, and part of the coupons remained unpaid. Europe was troubled not only in the matter of meeting the charges on government bonds, but various of the railroad companies which had constructed lines as the result of concessions also had outstanding accounts with the Government dating back, in some cases, several years. This inability of the Government to fulfill its engagements began to manifest itself in the late 1860's. Holders of defaulted securities and shareholders and officers of the public utility companies protested at this time to the committee of the Stock Exchange in London on the occasion of new issues of Ottoman loans. Their protests, however just, had little influence in slowing up the process of Turkish borrowing.[2] But they are indicative of a growing feeling of unrest among the holders of the early issues and those commercially interested in the Empire. Moreover, the English financial houses which had interested themselves in early loans, began to be more exacting in their demands regarding the hypothecation of revenues. The Paris houses which, with the exception of the 1871 loan, had been more successful in concluding the later loan contracts, were not so exacting, but with the Franco-Prussian War, their position was perceptibly weakened by the demands made on French capital to meet the war indemnity.[3]

---

[1] Du Velay, *op. cit.*, pp. 318, 324.

[2] *Supra*, Chapter IV, note 56.

[3] " . . . The question of a guarantee is one to which English capitalists will look with far more rigid scrutiny than the French establishments with whom Turkey has dealt of late years have been accustomed to, and more stringent conditions than have heretofore been required will now probably be demanded for placing the hypothecated revenues under the immediate control of the syndicate of the loan." *Levant Herald*, quoted in the London

Thus, the increased demands of the London money market, the growing skepticism in Europe concerning Turkish good faith, the requirements of a large foreign debt, and the troubled economic condition of the country, combined to require the services of an honest, capable, and energetic statesman as grand vizier, if Turkey was to have a fair chance to emerge from the entanglements into which she had fallen. But the hopes inspired in Europe by the appointment in 1872 of Midhat Pasha were tempered by the realization that intrigue was too strong to allow him to retain the position. There followed a succession of incumbents, none of whom was sufficiently strong to hold the office in the face of palace wire-pulling and of administrative problems demanding immediate attention. The inability of Hussein Avni Pasha and Essad Pasha to settle impending difficulties brought Mahmoud Nedim Pasha to the office in August, 1875. As Europe had no confidence in his integrity, the situation looked dark indeed.[4]

It was he who accomplished the destruction of Turkish credit, as it was under his viziership that the decrees were promulgated which announced Turkey's inability longer to carry the charges on her debt. The predominant foreign political influence at this time was the Russian Ambassador, General Ignatieff, who was thoroughly in sympathy with the aims of his government concerning the debasement of the Ottoman Empire and the establishment of Russia in Constantinople. He carried this policy to extremes. Appointed to Constantinople in 1864, he lost no time in ingratiating himself with the Sultan and his viziers.[5] Mahmoud

---

Times, March 21, 1871. But cf. this opinion: "In fact, since 1868, the fear of bankruptcy and its effects on the financial and commercial world have resulted in more loans than the confidence of bankers in the solvency and good faith of the Sublime Porte." Brunswick, B., *La Banqueroute Turque* (Paris, 1875).

[4] For an insight into the details of this period of Turkish history the following works are suggested: Midhat, Ali Haidar, *Life of Midhat Pasha* (London, 1903); "Leouzon le Duc, L.," *Midhat Pacha* (Paris, 1877); Y. A., *Midhat Pacha: la Constitution ottomane et l'Europe* (Paris, 1903); Midhat Pasha, *La Turquie, son passé et son avenir* (Paris, 1901); Izzet Riza, *La Turquie réformatrice et Midhat Pacha* (Lille, 1913); Djemaleddin Bey, *Sultan Murad V* (London, 1895); de Regla, Paul, *Au pays de l'espionage* (Paris, 1902); Ali Vahbi, *Avant le débâcle de la Turquie, Pensées et souvenirs de l'ex-Sultan Abdul Hamid II* (Neuchâtel, 1916).

[5] Nicholas Pavlovitch Ignatieff was born in 1832. He first distinguished himself in China during the restless years between 1856 and 1864, and succeeded in obtaining from China many concessions for Russia. Appointed to Constantinople in 1864, he remained there until the break-up

Nedim Pasha had been grand vizier in 1871 and had been followed by Midhat Pasha, who, in fixing the blame for the disappearance of certain public funds, traced their peculation to his predecessor. This information, although not strong enough to impede Mahmoud's appointment again in 1875, furnishes an idea of his character, as he lacked the slightest conception of public and private honor.[6]

Unfortunately for the historian, influence is exercised more often orally and through personal contact than by written dispatches, and the part which Ignatieff played in the suspension of the service on the Turkish debt can be arrived at only by inference. It is obvious that such a step would react unfavorably on Turkish prestige in Europe.[7] No less apparent is the fact that a measure of this nature would contribute greatly to the reopening of the whole Eastern question, and, in such an event, Russia would again have an opportunity to realize her century-old ambition to install herself on the Bosporus. However, it is difficult, if not impossible, to establish a direct connection between Mahmoud's

---

of the Conference in 1876. By his thorough knowledge of Orientals, combined with remarkable ability and unscrupulousness, he gained great influence at the Porte, though known by the public as the "Father of Lies," and greatly disliked by the Liberal elements, both Turkish and Greek. In 1881 he succeeded Louis Melikoff as Minister of the Interior, but, failing dismally in that capacity, he was dismissed by the Czar, and died in obscurity. Elliott, Sir Henry G., *Some Revolutions and other Diplomatic Experiences* (London, 1922), note p. 186.

[6] Mahmoud was so completely under the domination of the Russian Ambassador that he was popularly known as "Mahmoudoff." "The Grand Vizier, Mahmoud Pasha . . . was entirely in the power of the celebrated Russian Ambassador. It is from him that he drew all his inspirations." Poulgy, G., *Les emprunts de l'état Ottoman* (Paris, 1918), p. 66.

[7] "Ignatieff, who pursued the idea of the destruction of the Turkish Empire by every means, saw in the situation an admirable opportunity to attain his object. Any suspension of debt service constitutes bankruptcy for the state resorting to it. For Turkey the consequences of such a measure could not fail to be even more serious." *Ibid.*, p. 67.

"If we are not misinformed, General Ignatieff, whose influence over the late Sultan was paramount and who had a large share in the most improvident and oppressive acts of his reign, had brought matters to a point very nearly resembling the alliance of Unkiar-Skelessi (July 8, 1833). . . . Russia was again to protect him, a corps of troops was ready to sail for the Bosporus, and the demand for their intervention was either signed or on the point of being signed by the Sultan, when the manifestation of the Softas, speedily followed by the deposition of Abdul Aziz, cut short the intrigue. . . . The fall of that unhappy and misguided sovereign was the death-blow to a whole system of policy, based upon his subserviency to the Russian Empire, and nothing remained but for General Ignatieff to quit for a time the scene of his discomfiture." *Edinburgh Review*, Volume CXLIV (October, 1876), p. 563.

action and the Russian Ambassador. Nevertheless, in the opinion of a contemporary writer, "It is generally believed . . . that he [Ignatieff] instigated the late Grand Vizier to the financial measures which destroyed Turkish credit in Europe. . . . It is at any rate a remarkable circumstance that the very worst period of Turkish misrule was that during which authority of General Ignatieff was undoubtedly paramount."[8]

Suspension of the Debt Service

On October 6, 1875, the Ottoman Government inserted in the Constantinople newspapers the information that "in the presence of a budget deficit of five million pounds Turkish, it has decided to pay only half of the coupons [on the foreign debt] in cash." The other half of the obligations represented by the coupons would be discharged during the next five years by the issue and delivery to the bondholders of bonds bearing five percent (Ramazans). This decision was elaborated and explained in an official decree of October 9. On the 14th, Savfet Pasha, Minister for Foreign Affairs, communicated to Ottoman representatives abroad the decision of the Government (which had been included in the earlier decrees), that the Ottoman Bank, in conjunction with its committees in Paris and London, was to collaborate with the contractors of the various loans in naming representatives to collect the revenues assigned for meeting the service on the debt.[9]

The régime set up by these decrees was observed for three months only. In March, 1876, the coupon for the 1858 loan was passed, and the payment of the coupons for the 1869 and 1873 loans was deferred. The insurrection in Montenegro occurred simultaneously, and in June the Turkish frontiers were crossed by Serbian forces. In reality these occurrences and the deposition

[8] *Ibid.*, Volume CXLV (January, 1877), p. 277; cf. Morawitz, *op. cit.*, p. 51. The opinions of contemporary French and English writers concerning Russian activities at Constantinople would conceivably reflect the suspicious attitude of the French and British Governments concerning Russian aims at that place. The biographical note 5 and the assertions in notes 6, 7, and 8 are corroborated, however, by an American writer, Latimer, E. W., *Russia and Turkey in the Nineteenth Century* (6th Edition, Chicago, 1903), pp. 209, 300, 331, 335.

[9] Brunswick, *op. cit.*, and *La crise financière de la Turquie* (Paris, 1874); Court, Georges, *Deux mots sur les fonds turcs* (Nice, 1876); Czunt, D., *Encore deux mots pour la défense des intérêts des détenteurs de fonds Ottomans en Turquie* (Constantinople, 1878).

of Abdul Aziz in May, 1876, were the first of a chain of events which culminated in the accession of Abdul Hamid II, in the Constantinople Conference of December, 1876, and in the establishment of the Constitution. But the temporary settlement of these outstanding political problems was soon followed by the outbreak of the Russo-Turkish War.

The period from October 6, 1875, to December 20, 1881, has been called the "period between the two decrees," that is, the decree reducing the payment of interest by half, and the Decree of Mouharrem, which finally settled the financial problem, the solution of which had been postponed by domestic strife and by foreign war. To this crowded period of Turkish history space will be given only to relate the efforts of bondholders' committees to secure the settlement of their claims, and the outstanding financial developments prior to the Decree of Mouharrem.

Inasmuch as the majority of the bondholders were located in France and England, it was in these two countries that the greatest outcry was heard against the action of Mahmoud Pasha.[10] The percentage of bonds held in other countries was small, and the formation of syndicates relatively simple, the agents of the issuing London and Paris banks effecting the organization in Berlin, Rome, and Vienna. In Paris and London the bondholders found themselves drawn together into several well-defined groups, depending upon the security of their respective loans. Thus the holders of the 1855 guaranteed loan were secure in their position, as this loan had not been included by the Ottoman Government in its decree of October 6. The loans secured on the Egyptian tribute (1854, 1858, 1871) were naturally thrown together; the bearers of the 1862 loan felt that their claims to preferential treatment were well founded, due to the support of the British Government in its issue; the holders of the general debt, secured on the general revenues of the Empire, realized the weakness of their claims to priority, but hoped that any definite settlement would include their holdings. This division into groups was nearly as

[10] Among the host of voices raised in protest over the activities of the Turkish Government "there are those who are inflamed by the resentment of disappointed avarice, who lent their money by millions to support a bad government when it paid them seven percent, but who discover all its iniquities when the rate of interest is reduced to three." *Edinburgh Review*, Volume CXLV (January, 1877), p. 265. See also *ibid.*, Volume CXLIV (October, 1876), pp. 545-6.

marked in France as in England and produced the greatest confusion in the claims presented to the French and British Governments. It was due to this fact more than to any other that an earlier agreement was not concluded.

With the exception of the 1854 and 1855 loans, in whose favor joint official representations were made by the British and French Governments, the attitude of the British Government was to give unofficial support only. This policy, which had been followed by his predecessors, was clearly outlined by Lord Derby on November 5, 1875, in an interview with Mr. Palmer and certain others representing the Egyptian tribute loans. As Foreign Secretary, Lord Derby expressed the opinion that Turkey would be able to do nothing for her creditors for some time to come, and reminded the deputation that the Foreign Office had received similar representations from holders of securities of Spain, Greece, and several South American countries which had either reduced the interests on their debts or had repudiated them. In all these transactions

> our invariable rule has been to give moral and unofficial support where we thought it was merited or where we thought it would be useful, but to avoid committing ourselves to any official demand. . . . I think the principle is a sound one, because, if it were understood in this country that persons lending money to foreign states would be supported by the official assistance of their own government, the obvious effect of that would be to enable the poorest states, and those with the least credit, to get money on much better terms than they otherwise would. The question which arises here is whether any peculiar or exceptional circumstances exist in regard to these Turkish loans. Now, no doubt we have guaranteed Turkey, but that does not constitute an exceptional circumstance, for we have done the some thing for Greece; we have fought for Turkey, but that can not be looked to as forming an exceptional claim, for we have done the same thing for Spain. The question which really does create some difficulty is the language which has been held by some of our public men in Parliament in connection with these loans, but I do not think it goes so far as a guarantee in any case.

Lord Derby had examined carefully what Palmerston, Clarendon, and Russell had said; while of the opinion that they went further in extending real moral support to the Turkish Government than was expedient, Lord Derby did not think they spoke in a way

> which would reasonably justify the expectation that the Government would interfere forcibly to compel the payment of any debt in case of default. . . . I think the part which the British Government took does not go farther than to pledge those who now represent that Government to use such moral influence as they can bring to bear to secure its creditors.[11]

An indication of a similar policy on the part of the other powers is contained in a dispatch of November 30, 1875, from Sir A. Paget, the English Ambassador at Rome, to Lord Derby. The Italian Minister for Foreign Affairs, Signor Venosta, had been interpolated in the Chamber the preceding day concerning the policy of the Italian Government in defending the interests of Italian bearers of Turkish bonds. After informing the Chamber of the action which had been taken by the Italian Minister at Constantinople, the Foreign Minister stated that an exchange of views had been effected with the other powers "which shows that the other powers intend to act with great reserve." [12]

The frequent meetings of bondholders and the numerous representations to the French and British foreign offices prior to the outbreak of the Russo-Turkish War in May, 1877, failed to settle the question of the future of Turkish bonds. Sufficient interest and energy were certainly not lacking on the part of those concerned. It seems that the authorities of the Imperial Government on several occasions were disposed to accept the proposals brought forward for its consideration.[13] In every case, however, some new phase of the domestic situation would intervene, presenting more important problems for solution. With the outbreak of the Russian war, a settlement was definitely postponed. As a Russian victory became probable, interested bondholders began to write their

[11] *Parliamentary Papers*, Turkey No. C.1424 (1876) Dispatch 47. Mr. Hyde Clarke, of the Corporation of Foreign Bondholders, had been advised similarly four years earlier. *Ibid.*, No. C.1077 (1874) Dispatch 61. Prior to 1879, instructions of the British Foreign Office to its representatives in Constantinople, and replies to inquiries and protests from British subjects, were in all cases to the effect that unofficial support only would be given. *Ibid.*, No. C.1424 (1876) Dispatches 64, 65, 68, 69, 73, 90, 91, 97, 123.

[12] *Ibid.*, Dispatch 71.

[13] *Ibid.*, No. C.1744 (1877) and No. C.2136 (1878) *passim*. For the text and explanation of the Hammond project, see *ibid.*, No. C.1424 (1876) Dispatch 79, and Du Velay, *op. cit.*, pp. 346-54.

foreign offices, not about pressing claims on the Sublime Porte, but that the treaty of peace between Russia and Turkey should not deprive the bondholders of their security, or, in case of detachment of territory, that a proportional amount of the public debt should be borne by those peoples to whom territory might be ceded by Turkey.

Such was the substance of two letters forwarded to Lord Salisbury under dates of April 3 and 16, 1878, the first from Mr. H. Guedalla, chairman of the English committee of bearers of the five percent loans of 1865-1873, the other from Messrs. C. F. Hammond and James Landon, chairman and deputy chairman of the committee of English bearers of the six percent loans. Lord Salisbury was likewise urged to instruct the British delegates to any general congress of the powers to support officially the claims of the holders of Turkish bonds.[14]

Waddington, French Prime Minister, was interpolated in the Senate on this point on April 2, 1878, when he answered that "if we find ourselves in agreement with other powers as interested in this question as we are, it is not impossible that this question would be among those that could be submitted to the congress." When pressed by a communication from the Marseilles Chamber of Commerce, in which were set forth the claims of nine hundred and eighty holders of Turkish securities, he referred to his statement in the Senate, and added that "if a congress should assemble, the French Government would be glad to have the concurrence of other powers in bringing these claims before it."[15]

Salvaging the Wreck

It was in fact during the Berlin Congress that the claims of the bondholders first received the official attention of the powers. Hitherto attempts had been made to persuade individual governments to recognize the policy of officially presenting demands at the Sublime Porte. The failure of these representations has been noted. Here at Berlin, however, a joint Anglo-French committee, consisting of Messrs. Guedalla, Hammond, and Landon, of the British bondholders, and Count Keratry, of the French bearers,

[14] *Parliamentary Papers,* Turkey No. C.2136 (1878) Dispatches 31 and 42.

[15] *Ibid.*, quoted in Dispatch 45, Lord Lyons to Lord Salisbury.

persuaded Count Corti, the principal Italian delegate, to raise the whole question of Turkish finance.[16]

On July 11, 1878, Count Corti, in concert with his French and British colleagues, presented the following declaration:

> The powers represented at the Congress desire to recommend to the Sublime Porte the establishment at Constantinople of a financial commission composed of specialists named by their respective governments, which commission shall be charged to examine into the complaints of the bondholders of the Ottoman debt, and to propose the most efficacious means for satisfying them as far as is compatible with the financial situation of the Porte.

This statement was opposed by the principal Turkish delegate, Caratheodory Pasha, who said that "his Government will give all its attention to the question of finance, as it is a duty, and one in its own interest, for the Porte to do everything in its power to better the situation." But, when Bismarck asked if the representatives of the other powers present agreed to the declaration of the Italian delegate, the Austrian and Russian delegates assented. The declaration was accordingly entered in the official proceedings as Protocol XVIII of July 11, 1878.[17]

In the Treaty of Berlin itself were embodied the following principles: the payment by Bulgaria of tribute to the Sultan; assignment of a portion of the revenue of Eastern Roumelia to payment of the public debt; assumption by Bulgaria, Serbia, and Montenegro, of proportional parts of the public debt; and integral maintenance of the rights and duties of Turkey concerning the railroads of Eastern Roumelia. Provision was made, moreover, for the payment by the Ottoman Government of a war indemnity to Russia of Ltqs. 35,000,000, although it had been agreed in Protocol XI of the Congress of Berlin that the payment of this indemnity should not prejudice the prior creditors of the Porte.[18]

---

[16] "It was at the instigation of myself, Mr. Hammond, and the late Mr. Landon, the three delegates of the London Committee of Turkish Bondholders, and Count Keratry, the delegate of the French committee, that Count Corti brought before the plenipotentiaries at the Berlin Congress in 1878 the question of Turkish finance." *Ibid.*, Turkey No. C.2709 (1880) Dispatch 110, Mr. Guedalla to Earl Granville, July 15, 1880.

[17] *Ibid.*, Turkey No. 39 (1878) pp. 257-71.

[18] Hertslet, *Map of Europe by Treaty* (4 volumes, London, 1891), Volume IV, pp. 2771-2; p. 2865; pp. 2771-2, 2790, 2785. But see *infra,*

No sooner had the Treaty been signed than the representatives of the bondholders began to press the Porte with fresh proposals for the settlement of the financial question.[19] The unanimity which had characterized the actions of the English and French representatives at Berlin was dissipated, however, by the return of the rivalries between the holders of the different issues. To this fact must be attributed a further delay in the settlement of the problem. If unanimity of purpose was lacking among the creditors of the Porte, the Turkish Government, which had opposed the Protocol of July 11, 1878, was sufficiently shrewd to recognize the strength of its position. Such was the situation, and the example set by the other signatories of the Treaty of Berlin in executing various articles of that settlement could be cited by the Porte as evidence that there was little reason why it

---

Chapter VI, pp. 115-16 for a statement of the difficulties encountered in executing these Articles.

[19] The project presented to the Porte by Count de Tocqueville, acting for an Anglo-French Committee, was actually signed by the Porte in January, 1879. Its provisions comprised a consolidation of the foreign debt, the hypothecation of certain revenues for its service, these revenues to be administered by a commission composed of two Ottoman members, two British, and two French, all appointed by their respective governments, but to receive the delegation of their powers and their salaries from the Ottoman Government. Finally, a group of Paris banks was to loan 200 million francs to the Porte, the administration of the service on which was to be entrusted to the above-named commission.

Both the British and French Governments hesitated to support the scheme. There was opposition from bearers of the 1858 and 1862 issues; it appeared that the revenues concerned were already ear-marked, and there was no indication of their early release; effective control over the customs (one of the assigned revenues) was lacking. The French Government was unwilling to appoint the two French commissioners as long as M. Waddington had no evidence of the fulfillment of the loan feature of the concession. The concession lapsed on March 19, and the Porte denounced it. At this juncture the British Government was ready to name members to any commission if it was of a nature of which it could approve, a viewpoint with which the French concurred. The Italian Government opposed the de Tocqueville scheme, holding that "as long as the commission proposed by the 18th Protocol of the Berlin Congress is not convened, . . . it could not, in the interest of Italian bondholders, admit either a reduction in the value of the bonds, nor any alienation of the revenues which formed their security." The attitude of the Ottoman Government is contained in an answer from Caratheodory Pasha to Count Corti, in which it was maintained that "inasmuch as the proposed international commission had as its object to seek out the best means of satisfying the bearers, and since the de Tocqueville scheme was in process of execution, the application of the 18th Protocol was not to be considered. *Parliamentary Papers,* No. C.2709 (1880) Dispatches 21, 25, 46, 49, 51, 52, 53, and *passim.* Finally the Russian Government opposed the scheme on the ground that any new loan to the Porte was prejudicial to its interests. Du Velay, *op. cit.,* p. 385.

should be criticized in its opposition to the institution at Constantinople of an international financial commission, as long as equally important articles of the Treaty remained unexecuted.

The dilatory policy of the Imperial Government, and the failure of the other powers to compose their differences and proceed to the execution of the terms of the Treaty of Berlin, could hardly be expected, however, to continue indefinitely. In fact, the real force which impelled the Porte to a solution was the need of money in the Treasury. During the war with Russia the immediate financial needs of the Porte had been supplied by the local banks at Constantinople, loans which had been secured on the most liquid revenues of the country. The most important was negotiated in 1877, the Defence Loan, the contract for which had been concluded between the Government, the Ottoman Bank, and a London house, Glyn Mills, Currie and Company. The reception accorded the loan in England was unfavorable in the extreme; the subscription broke down so lamentably that the Ottoman Bank alone in 1878 came to the assistance of the Government. The advances from local bankers plus the Defence Loan amounted to some nine million pounds sterling. Most of these were short term credits, and a definitive solution of this particular problem was more pressing than the larger question of the foreign debt. The Ottoman Bank and the local bankers had functioned for the benefit of the Treasury at a time when the markets of Europe were entirely closed to the Porte. Not unnaturally the Imperial Government was anxious for a solution which would reopen to it doors of the local financial institutions, and one which might pave the way for a permanent settlement of the whole problem.

This is precisely what occurred. A naval demonstration by England in October, 1879, resulted in the appointment of Said Pasha as Grand Vizier, and Ibraham Effendi as Minister of Finance. These officials realized the seriousness of the situation, being endowed with more imagination than their predecessors. The benefits which would accrue from a settlement of the advances from the local bankers were evident. Thus, when the Ottoman Bank and the other local creditors brought forward a project in November, 1879, to accomplish this object, the Porte signified its willingness to sign. This was the first step in the solution of the difficulties so long outstanding between the Turkish Government and its creditors.

The outstanding features of the agreement of November 10, 1879, were as follows: the Government leased to the bankers, at an annual rent equal to the net revenue thereon from March 1, 1879, to March 1, 1880, plus ten percent, the four indirect revenues of the stamp tax, spirits tax, fishing tax in certain areas, and the silk tithe in certain districts, as well as the salt and tobacco monopolies. The administration of these revenues was confided to the financial group in whose interest the contract was drawn; the proceeds were to be applied to the liquidation of the advances from this group; the duration was for ten years. The Government reserved the right to make an agreement more advantageous to the holders of the external and internal debt, in which case the present agreement was to be denounced.[20] In consenting to this arrangement, the Government was actuated by the desire to initiate a program which would begin to satisfy its foreign creditors, while safeguarding the rights of local bankers, and avoiding official European intervention in the state finances.

This step was recognized locally as of value, but its effect on the Porte's creditors in Europe was less favorable. The bearers of the various foreign loans renewed their protests to their foreign offices,[21] protests which in this case resulted in official representations.[22] Moreover, Europe looked askance at the proposal to set up an administration composed largely of Turkish subjects. Had not all the difficulty in the past arisen from a similar situation? Disgruntled Government officials were likewise ready to criticize the least misstep which the new administration might take; this could be pointed to as evidence that an organization containing Europeans was unsatisfactory for Turkey.

The results of the first half-year, however, demonstrated that an administration of Turkish subjects, presided over by a small group of Europeans, was not only honest but efficient. Although

[20] Text in *Parliamentary Papers*, No. C.2709 (1880) Dispatch 89, enclosure 3 (French); Dispatch 96, enclosure 6 (English). Also Young, *op. cit.*, Volume V. pp. 61-2.

[21] *Parliamentary Papers*, No. C.2709 (1880) Dispatches 90, 93, 96, 105, 109.

[22] *Ibid.*, Dispatches 81, 82, and 102, to Sir Henry Layard to "protest officially against the execution of the Convention and the Decree so far as they purport to apply to the liquidation of the debts . . . the revenues arising from duties on tobacco, salt, stamps, and patents, which were pledged by the Ottoman Government to the bondholders of the Loan of 1862."

the internal situation was most unfavorable for the collection of revenue, proceeds were more than ample to meet the charges on the consolidated advances. Mr. Hamilton Lang, director of the administration, in his first half-yearly report, predicted substantial increases in the revenue as soon as the administration became consolidated in the country, and the Government was in a better position to combat contraband.[23] These favorable results were regarded with some envy by western European bondholders, whose representatives were not party to the contract of November 10. Their own insistence upon an official body to administer the foreign debt had been unproductive of results. Nevertheless, the Porte was desirous of settling the grievances of its creditors, as it was only after such a settlement that further recourse to European money markets was possible. The success of the administration of the six indirect revenues prompted the notes of October 3 and 23, 1880, proposals which finally resulted in the Decree of Mouharrem.[24]

---

[23] Du Velay, *op. cit.*, pp. 405-12.

[24] The Turks feared the dangers inherent in a policy which would institute the commission forecast by the Berlin Congress. In reporting to Lord Granville, Mr. Goschen, British Ambassador, related the contents of an interview with the Ottoman Foreign Minister in which a hint that "they must expect that steps would be taken very soon in connection with that protocol [XVIII], inasmuch as they had raised the question themselves, was received with dismay. . . . It is clear that the Government fear the Commission as much as any demonstration, and great resistance must be apprehended." But the powers were reluctant to press the matter: "I have repeatedly sounded my colleagues very carefully on the question and found as I have expected a certain reluctance to embark on a fresh and a very difficult problem." Mr. Goschen, however, thought "that a favorable opportunity has been offered by the note of October 3 to take the initiative as to the convocation of the commission, though whether the point can be carried, unless the powers show very great determination, is open to most serious doubt." *Parliamentary Papers*, No. C.3197 (1882) Dispatch 15, November 1, 1880.

But the Russian Government considered that the ambassadors of the powers at Constantinople should remain aloof from the negotiations between the Porte and the bondholders' representatives. Although France and Great Britain had agreed that the question of the international financial commission should be raised as soon as the cession of Dulcigno had been effected, the French Government had subsequently changed its mind and had abandoned the idea altogether, preferring that the "bondholders should themselves select delegates to treat with the Porte directly and without any ostensible intervention on the part of the Government." The Austrian Government desired the execution of Protocol XVIII, but only for the purpose of an inquiry. The Italian Government, although desirous of the application of Protocol XVIII, instructed its Ambassador at Constantinople, Count Corti, to "associate himself with Her Majesty's Ambassador and his colleagues in such steps as they may take as to the question of the Turkish public debt." *Ibid.*, Dispatches 10, 14, 22, 32, 36.

THE DECREE OF MOUHARREM: ITS PROVISIONS

The financial project contained in the note of October 3 was part of a strong program submitted to the powers by the Porte for the settlement of the outstanding questions of the Treaty of Berlin: a definitive solution of the financial claims against the Porte (including the Russian indemnity); the settlement of the difficulties in Montenegro and Greece; and the question of the reforms to be instituted in the Armenian regions of the Empire. No less emphatic in its tone was the feeling of the Porte that its willingness to conclude these questions should coincide with the renunciation, by the other signatories of the Treaty, of recourse to naval demonstrations and measures of coërcion against the Porte.

As far as the financial section of this program is concerned, it received elaboration in the note of October 23, whereby the Ottoman Government, through its representatives abroad "invites the bondholders to choose a certain number of delegates among themselves, who, being endowed with complete powers, shall proceed to Constantinople to enter into direct negotiations with the Imperial Government" in order to arrive at an agreement for the resumption of service on the foreign debt.[25] Considerable delay was experienced in designating these representatives.[26] In January, 1881, the French bondholders chose M. Valfrey, former subdirector of the political section of the French Ministry for Foreign Affairs. The English creditors designated Robert Bourke, former Undersecretary at the Foreign Office. In the summer of that year, Baron Mayr was elected delegate of the Austro-Hungarian holders, and M. Mancardi of the Italian holders. These last three delegates proceeded to Constantinople in September, 1881, where they joined M. Valfrey and Mr. Bourke, who had already started negotiations with the Ottoman representatives. The German creditors were represented by Herr Primker.

Discussions began early in September and were concluded by the signature of an agreement which received the sanction of a royal *iradé* on December 20, 1881, and was promulgated the same day. This contract has become known as the Decree of Mou-

---

25 Du Velay, *op. cit.*, pp. 412-15.

26 Certain quarters protested against this policy of the Ottoman Government, and still insisted on the international commission. *Parliamentary Papers*, No. C.3197 (1882) Dispatches 21, 51, 64.

harrem (from the Turkish month in which it was signed), and is a document calling for careful analysis.[27] Its twenty-one articles may be divided into three general groups: those which refer to the reduction, conversion, and consolidation of the internal and external debt, but excluding the Russian indemnity;[28] those which deal with the service of the consolidated debt and the revenues ceded to the administering body;[29] and those which are concerned with the erection of an executive body known as "The Council of Administration," the organization to function under its direction, and the relations between the Government and the Council.[30]

It was recognized in all quarters that the existing state of the imperial revenues did not warrant the assumption by the Empire of the charges on the total nominal debt as defined by the contracts of the various loans. A reduction was necessary. The bondholders desired as small a reduction as could be obtained; the Government, conscious of the usurious rates at which it had been compelled to borrow, was equally anxious to effect as large a reduction as possible. A compromise resulted, and the reduced amount of the debt was composed of three sums: first, the outstanding balance of each loan (reduced, in each case, according to fixed rates); second, an amount representing the provisional certificates (Ramazans) delivered in exchange for the bonds drawn under the stipulations of the Decree of October 6, 1875; third, an amount representing the provisional certificates given as

[27] Text (in French and in English translation) in *ibid.*, No. Cd.5736 (1911) pp. 653 *et seq.*

[28] Articles I-VII inclusive. The Imperial Government had expressed its desire to include in this Decree the terms for the payment of the Russian indemnity. The delegates of the bondholders had, however, opposed this policy, a point of view to which the Government finally acceded on September 15. *Procès-Verbaux et Annexes de la commission pour delibérer sur un mode de règlement de la Dette Publique intérieure et extérieure de l'Empire Ottoman* (Constantinople, 1915) published by the Public Debt Council, pp. 15, 25, 36. (Hereafter this source will be cited as *Procès-Verbaux et Annexes de la Commission de 1881*). On May 14, 1882, the Russian and Ottoman Governments signed at Constantinople a convention respecting the payment of the war indemnity. Russia waived her claims to interest on the capital sum of Ltqs. 35,000,000, which was to be paid off in annual instalments of Ltqs. 350,000. The annuities were to be met out of receipts from the tithe and cattle tax from the provinces of Aleppo, Konia, Kastamouni, and Sivas. *Nouveau Recueil Général,* 2me Série, Volume VIII, p. 218.

[29] Articles VIII-XIV inclusive.

[30] Articles XV-XXI inclusive.

interest according to the terms of the same Decree. On this basis the nominal outstanding total of 191 million pounds sterling was reduced to 106 million. The bonds representing the outstanding capital of each loan were to be registered by their owners at different places in Europe, and the owners were to receive in exchange new bonds representing the reduced value of the registered bonds.[31]

For the service of the reduced debt, the Imperial Government ceded "absolutely and irrevocably . . . until the complete liquidation of the debt" certain of its revenues. Briefly, these were the salt and tobacco monopolies, together with the stamp tax, the spirits tax, the fish tax, and the silk tithe in certain districts. It will be noticed that these revenues were the object of the Decree of November 10, 1879, with the Galata bankers.[32] This agreement was now denounced, and the debts which it was intended to liquidate were now included in the Decree of Mouharrem. In addition to these revenues certain others of a hypothetical value were also ceded. Thus, the excess of customs revenues arising from an increase in duties as a result of the revision of existing commercial treaties was to be added to the salt and tobacco monopolies and the revenues of the other indirect taxes. Similarly, any surplus resulting from a general application of the tax on shops and stores as compared with the existing revenue from the income tax was ceded to the bondholders. If these revenues were of somewhat doubtful value at the time, the Bulgarian tribute, the surplus of Cyprus revenues, the revenue from Eastern Roumelia, and *tombeki*[33] duties up to Ltqs. 50,000 were of a more material

[31] In fixing the rates at which the outstanding totals of the various loans would be reduced, the Government desired to employ the issue rates as they appeared in the contracts; the representatives of the bondholders, on the other hand, wished the outstanding totals to be reduced according to the issue rates which figured in the prospectuses. The compromise finally agreed upon was on the basis of averages struck between these two sets of figures. On this basis the reduced outstanding capital (excluding interest) was 96,736,291 pounds sterling. To this figure was added ten percent to represent interest in arrears for the years 1876 to 1880, making the total of the consolidated foreign debt 106,409,920 pounds sterling, or 117,050,912 Turkish pounds, at the rate of 110 piasters to the pound sterling. *Procès-Verbaux et Annexes de la Commission de 1881*, pp. 82-3, 90-94.

[32] *Supra*, p. 88.

[33] *Tombeki* is a special form of tobacco for use in the *narghilé* (water pipe).

character; they likewise were ceded for the service of the bonds.[34] Any income from Serbia, Montenegro, Bulgaria, and Greece, delivered to the Ottoman Government under the provisions of the Treaty of Berlin and the Constantinople Convention to be applied to the public debt, was also the property of the bondholders.

The income from these sources was to be applied "in its entirety to the payment of interest and to the redemption" of the bonds. The first obligation was payment of the service amounting to Ltqs. 590,000, on the Priority Bonds, representing the funded debt (Ltqs. 8,170,000) of the Ottoman Government to the Galata bankers. When this charge was met, annual interest at the rate of from one to four percent (to be determined by the Council, and depending upon the expansion of the revenue receipts) was to be applied on the reduced capital of the debt. Interest was due semi-annually. If four-fifths of the net revenue (after payment of the charges on the Priority Bonds) would meet the annual interest charges, the remaining one-fifth would be applied to redemption purposes. But the annual rate of redemption could never exceed one percent of the reduced total of the debt.

At this point it may be well to mention the provisions under which the Ottoman Government could profit from the operation of the Decree. The maximum rate of interest was fixed at four percent; the maximum rate of redemption, one percent. If the revenues ceded to the service of the bonds produced an excess above these maximum charges, the surplus was to be turned over to the Turkish Treasury. This provision must surely have been included as a sop to the Government's pride, as it was only under the greatest compulsion that the Imperial commissioners consented to the cession of sufficient revenue to meet total annual minimum charges of one and one-quarter percent.[35] In later years the provisions of this article were most irksome to the Government: in 1903 the article was abrogated, and a Supplementary Decree defined new provisions under which the Government might profit.[36]

---

[34] Ltqs. is the abbreviation for *Livres Turques*, Turkish Pounds. Normal exchange of the Turkish gold pound is Ltqs. 1.10 (110 piasters) to the pound sterling, or about $4.40.

[35] *Procès-Verbaux et Annexes de la Commission de 1881*, pp. 97-120.

[36] *Infra*, p. 98.

Amortization of the bonds was to proceed according to a definite schedule. In grouping the various issues for this purpose the priority claims of the bondholders finally received a measure of satisfaction. Thus the first group comprised the 1858 and 1862 loans; under the second heading came the 1860, 1863, 1864, and 1872 issues; the 1865, 1869, and 1873 issues followed in group three; finally, the bonds of the general debt and the Lottery Bonds were brought together in group four. The basis on which these groupings were reached was the relative security on which the issues had been floated.[37] The first group was to be amortized first, followed by groups two, three, and four in order. Amortization was to occur twice yearly by purchase or by drawings, at the discretion of the Council. When the interest rate was one percent, the rate of amortization would be sixty-six and two-thirds per cent of the capital value.[38]

Article XV establishes the executive committee of the administration. "In order to represent the bondholders and to look after their interests a Council of Administration is established." The Council was to have its headquarters at Constantinople, and was to be composed of representatives of the bondholders. One member was to represent the English and Dutch bondholders; he was to be appointed by the Council of Foreign Bondholders in London; or, in default of that, by the governor of the Bank of England; or, in default of that, by a resolution adopted by the English and Dutch bearers assembled in public meeting in London. One member was to represent the French bondholders, he to be designated, according to the Decree, by the syndicate of French banks which had responded to the invitation of the Ottoman Government in the note of October 23, 1881.[39] The member to rep-

---

[37] It will be noticed that the 1854 and 1855 loans do not figure in this grouping. The 1854 loan was secured on the Egyptian Tribute to the Turkish Government, and a special agreement concluded in 1877 provided for receipts for meeting the service to be remitted directly to England from Egypt. The 1855 guaranteed loan was not included in the announcement of October 6, 1875.

[38] The amortization rate was seventy-five percent if the interest rate was more than one and less than three percent, and one hundred percent if the interest rate was three percent or higher.

[39] *Banque Impériale Ottomane, Banque de Paris et des Pays-Bas, Comptoir National d'Escompte de Paris, Crédit Lyonnais, Crédit Mobilier Francais, Société Générale pour favoriser le développement du commerce et de l'industrie en France, Société Générale de crédit industriel et commercial.*

resent the German and the member to represent the Austrian holders were to be designated respectively by the syndicate of German and of Austrian banks, which had acted similarly to the French syndicate.[40] The Italian representative was to be named by the Chamber of Commerce of Rome. There was to be a representative of the Ottoman bondholders, who was to be named by a general assembly of these latter convened by order of the Prefect of Constantinople. The Ottoman Bank was to name the member to represent the holders of the Priority Bonds. These bonds had been created after the denunciation of the Decree of November 10, 1879, by which the Government had funded its indebtedness to local bankers, and they were largely owned by the Ottoman Bank. The nomination of each member of the Council, excepting the Ottoman representative and the member for the Priority obligations, was to be communicated to the official representatives of the Ottoman Government in London, Paris, Berlin, Vienna, and Rome. The notification of the nomination of the other two members was to be communicated to the Ottoman Minister of Finance.

According to the Decree no member of the Council might hold a position in the service of the Ottoman Government, or a position as the military, consular, or diplomatic representative of a foreign government in Turkey. Members were to be elected for a period of five years and could be reëlected. In view of the number and importance of Ottoman bonds held in England and France, the president during the first five years was to alternate between the English and the French members. If, at the expiration of this period, the situation had materially changed, the Council should elect its president. Each member had one vote; action of the Council was by majority; in case of a tie, the president cast the deciding ballot. "The Council will cease to function only on the complete liquidation of the loans to which the present Decree is applicable."

The powers of the Council included "the administration, collection, and direct encashment, for the account of the bondholders and by means of its agents, of the revenues and other resources" ceded to it. The total of its income, after deducting administrative expenses, was to be applied under its direction to the interest and redemption of the debt. The Council had the right to farm

[40] House of S. Bleichröder, of Berlin, and the Credit Anstalt, of Vienna.

or lease to third parties any of the ceded revenues; it appointed and dismissed employees of the administration, said employees being considered as functionaries of the Government in the exercise of their duties. It also designated a director-general of the revenues who, under the direction of the Council, managed its business. For the exercise of its functions the Government was to give the Council such assistance as was "in keeping with existing public organization"; the Government also agreed to apply the penalties of the law in the suppression of contraband.

One article of the Decree is devoted to the control to be exercised by the Government. "The administration of the ceded revenues will be submitted to the control of the Imperial Government." At first this seems like a considerable grant of authority, but the Decree provided further that "this control will be exercised by a commissioner and comptrollers to be named by the Government." They were to be accredited to the Administration of the Public Debt; the Commissioner was to be invited to each meeting of the Council where "he will sit with consultative voice." This Commissioner and the comptrollers were given powers to take cognizance of the proceedings of the Council, to examine books and documents relating thereto, and to verify the accounts of the administration. But the important provision is that "under no conditions will they be able to interfere with the administration." [41]

An important provision is to the effect that "any difference which may arise between the Government and the Council, concerning the interpretation and execution of the present Decree, will be submitted to four arbitrators for decision," two to be named by the Government and two by the Council. "In case of necessity, these arbitrators will elect an umpire."

The two final articles are also of importance. "In case the Government suspends or causes the present agreement to cease functioning, the bondholders will regain entirely the fullness of their rights established by the original contracts, insofar as their bonds will not have been redeemed according to the provisions of the

[41] The wording of this sentence in the draft presented by the Imperial commissioners was "without interfering in the administration." The much stronger phraseology ultimately embodied in this sentence was drafted by a mixed sub-committee, and accepted by the Commission. *Procès-Verbaux et Annexes de la Commission de 1881*, pp. 43, 58.

present Decree." Also, "The Imperial Government will immediately communicate the present Decree to the powers. . . ."

Such are the most important provisions of the Decree of Mouharrem. The Council of Administration entered upon its duties on January 1, 1882, taking over practically intact the administrative organization which had been built up by Mr. Hamilton Lang by virtue of the powers delegated to the syndicate of Galata bankers by the Decree of November 10, 1879. This establishment of a foreign council within the confines of the Empire was hardly regarded with great hope by western European bondholders.

On other occasions the Ottoman Sultans had been willing for foreign administrators to be designated to control the proceeds of certain revenues. In all previous instances, however, either the agreements had been too uncertain in their wording to insure their success or the good will of the Government had been lacking. In the present case the situation had radically changed. Bankruptcy had finally overtaken the Empire; the European provinces of the Sultan had been all but detached from the Empire by the Congress of Berlin; English and Austrian pressure had finally accomplished some attenuation of the disastrous Treaty of San Stefano. Turkish prestige was at a low ebb, and something was needed to reëstablish it. No doubt the new Sultan, Abdul Hamid II, realized the gravity of the situation better than had his predecessors. If he were a contrast to them in his personal habits, no less a contrast was visible in the shrewdness by which he was able to mollify the anger of his European creditors. Skillfully appraising the situation, he gave enough in the Decree of Mouharrem to reëstablish good will toward Turkey yet not enough seriously to weaken his sovereign powers. It may have been a wound to Turkish *amour-propre* to see a foreign council administering a portion of the revenues of the Empire; but it was less an evil than would have been the establishment of an official political organization for the accomplishment of the same object.

From 1882 to 1903 this Decree remained the fundamental law of this interesting and curious organization, unchanged by wish of the bondholders, and untouched by the hands of the Government. In the latter year, however, the agitation which had been brewing for some time finally crystallized, and a Supplementary Decree replaced certain of the provisions of the Decree of 1881. The wish of the Imperial Government to participate in the distribution of the profits coincided with the desire of certain groups of the bondholders to enjoy a higher rate of interest.[42]

The *Décret-Annexe,* or Supplementary Decree of September 14, 1903,[43] accomplished two definite objects: the unification of the unredeemed bonds, replacing them by a new issue; and the abolition of those articles of the earlier Decree concerning the ability of the Government to participate in profits. Twenty-two percent of the bonds had been redeemed by the operation of the 1881 Decree; the unredeemed bonds were replaced, at certain rates of exchange, by a new issue of unified bonds, all standing on the same basis as regards interest and redemption. The nominal value of the new issue was something under 32 million pounds (Turkish). The rate of interest was four percent; the rate of redemption, 0.45 percent per annum; a definite sum was fixed which represented the charges on the new issue, a sum something over two million pounds (Turkish). Everything over this amount was to be divided between the Imperial Government and the Public Debt Council in the ratio of seventy-five percent and twenty-five

---

[42] The operation of the Decree of Mouharrem, particularly of the sections disposing of excess revenues, is described by Mr. Young: "Under the régime of the Decree of Mouharrem, the Administration enjoyed the character of a corporation for the exploitation of Ottoman revenues to the sole profit of the shareholders, that is, the holders of Turkish securities." *op. cit.,* Volume V, pp. 102-3.

"The surpluses of the ceded revenues which resulted from good administration profited the bondholders only, as the Treasury had no right to these amounts until after the payment of a maximum interest of four percent and amortization of one percent. This was equivalent to the absolute exclusion of the State to any participation. The ceded revenues and their excesses formed an indivisible whole; they were placed exclusively to the raising of the interest and to the redemption of the bonds until complete extinction of the administered loans. The Government, having no right either to a proportional part of the plus-values or to the part of the ceded revenues which would be freed by the extinction of the credits to which these revenues had been placed, possessed no incentive to favor the raising of the interest rate, or in the redemption of the bonds.

"On the contrary, both the increased interest rate and the gradual redemption of the bonds had the natural effect of enhancing the course of the bonds and retarding the amortization. The Government saw the day receding when it could again undertake the administration of the ceded revenues. This increase in the value of the bonds, in rendering more difficult the operation of conversion and unification, deprived the Government of the best means offered it of profiting from its enhanced credit." *Ibid.,* p. 99.

[43] Text (in French and in English translation) in *Parliamentary Papers,* No. Cd.5736 (1911) pp. 653 *et seq.*

percent respectively. All articles of the Decree of Mouharrem, except those definitely affected by these new provisions, were continued in force.

The Decree of Mouharrem: Its Character and Sanctions

In its nature the Decree of Mouharrem is unique. It possesses elements of Ottoman public law, yet it is more than that, for it is not a unilateral decree of the Ottoman Government. It is a bilateral agreement between the Imperial Government and its creditors, which was given the sanction of the Sultan's Government by the official *iradé* under which it was promulgated. At the same time, however, the Decree is surrounded by an international atmosphere, for by Article XXI the Ottoman Government was bound to "immediately communicate the present Decree to the powers." Moreover, notifications of the nominations of the Council members were, by Article XV, to be made to the official diplomatic representatives of the Ottoman Government abroad. Yet it did not possess the official protection of the powers whose nationals were represented in the Council. It cannot be held to fulfill completely the conditions contained in Protocol XVIII of the Congress of Berlin, for that recommendation looked to an official international financial commission, with members appointed by the governments whose nationals held Ottoman bonds. The members of such a commission would have held their mandates from their respective governments, and would have been responsible to them in the first place, and only in the second to the bondholders.

Nevertheless, the Council actually instituted by the Decree of Mouharrem was considered satisfactory by the governments of the powers, who, on being notified of the agreement of December 20, 1881, refrained from exercising pressure with the object of substituting a more official executive organ. However far the Decree may be from fulfilling the requirements of the Berlin Protocol, there can be little doubt that the Turkish Government was moved to dispatch the notes of October 3 and 23, 1880, by the knowledge that this Protocol actually contained a potential diplomatic sanction. These notes did not confine themselves to the elements of the recommendation in the Protocol, for the understanding desired by the Government was to be agreed upon "without any interference whatsoever on the part of the powers," while the kernel of the Berlin recommendation was the "official" character of the commission.

These peculiar characteristics were at once both its weakness and its strength, but probably they contributed more to reinforce than to weaken it. No doubt the bondholders themselves would have preferred it to be endowed with an official international legal sanction. The private nature of the Decree was accepted only because nothing with a more explicit guarantee was obtainable. Yet the governments of the powers never saw fit, until 1919, to attempt to endow it with a more definite sanction, and then only because the functioning of the Council during the Great War was directed towards bolstering up Turkish powers of resistance.[44] Before the Great War, however, the fears of the bondholders because of the incompleteness of the guarantee were never realized, for the Ottoman Government faithfully kept its engagements.

As a matter of fact, the Decree itself contained a provision which passage of the years proved to be as efficient a sanction as might be desired. Article XX provides that "in case the Government suspends or causes the present agreement to cease functioning, the bondholders will regain entirely the fullness of their rights established by the original contracts, insofar as their bonds will not have been redeemed. . . ." The Government, anxious to retain as great a control as possible over the revenues remaining to it, could not think of abrogating an agreement the suspension of which would without doubt prove disastrous, and possibly call into action the Berlin Protocol in all its disagreeable details. The absence of a definite diplomatic sanction caused the Decree to be regarded with respect, by virtue of the very uncertainty of action which might result in case of its abrogation.

An incident occurred in 1896 which has been construed as "internationalizing" the Decree of Mouharrem. Rumors were prevalent in certain quarters of London and Berlin that Russia and France were in disagreement concerning the operation of the Public Debt Administration, and that the Russian Ambassador at Constantinople was advising the Sultan to suppress or modify the Decree of Mouharrem. In order to quiet these rumors, the Russian Ambassador, M. de Nelidof, on December 19, 1896, dispatched the following note to the Sublime Porte:

---

[44] *Infra*, Chapter VIII.

> The Russian Ambassador is instructed to bring to the attention of the Ottoman Government the fact that, if the Porte violates in any way the rights of the Council of the Public Debt, or seizes the revenues that have been ceded to the bearers of Turkish bonds, Russia, in agreement with the other powers, will consider herself obliged to claim the institution of an international financial commission as forecast by Protocol XVIII of the Congress of Berlin, which will be charged to study the financial condition of the Ottoman Empire and the portion of its revenues that could be handed over to its creditors. Inasmuch as under such circumstances and by virtue of a clause of the Decree of Mouharrem the arrangement agreed upon between the Ottoman Government and its creditors would fall to the ground, the Imperial [Russian] Government hopes that the Sublime Porte will appreciate how unfortunate for itself that eventuality could become, and will abstain from any act capable of such a result.[45]

M. Edmond Théry, editor of *l'Économiste Européen*, considers that

> this note is equivalent to the internationalization of the Council of the Debt and of the revenues ceded to the holders of Ottoman bonds. In fact, it is the best thing for which the French holders might wish, for . . . it is beyond doubt that their position is protected from any serious harm, if the prescriptions of the Decree of Mouharrem are strictly observed.[46]

M. Théry does not explain his word "internationalization", but one thing is certain: however illuminating this attitude of the Russian Government may be, it cannot have had the effect of changing the sanction of the Decree from an unofficial potential one, into an official one. The only thing which could have effected this transmutation was the substitution of an official convention for the abrogated Decree, or the sanctioning of the original Decree by a diplomatic act. Neither of these was necessary in the circumstances, and it is doubtful if either of them were possible, unless preceded by a complete political upheaval in the Near East.[47]

---

[45] Nouradounghian, *op. cit.*, Volume IV, p. 541.

[46] *L'Économiste Européen* (Paris), January 8, 1897.

[47] Moreover, in the same year it was Russia that prevented the consideration by the powers of a French proposal to institute a more clearly-defined sanction. At that time the introduction of reforms in the Empire was retarded by the need of money. A scheme was consequently proposed

The Decree of Mouharrem was a private bilateral contract between the Ottoman Government and its creditors; although it must not be forgotten that it possessed semi-official attributes. Its sanctions were contained in Article XX of the Decree itself, and in the diluted diplomatic atmosphere surrounding its application.[48]

It is impossible to discuss the character of the Decree of Mouharrem without speaking of the nature of the control which it instituted. In his *Traité de la science des finances,* M. Paul Leroy-Beaulieu sets forth the necessary essentials of foreign financial control. Such control is set up "by diplomatic acts determining the future conditions of service of a foreign loan, and by the nomination, by one or several foreign powers, of persons of their

---

by France for the reorganization of Turkish finance on the basis of European control. The scheme was to establish, by means of conversions of existing loans, extension of the time of redemption, and the introduction of monopolies, favorable conditions for a large Ottoman loan. This, all the European Great Powers were to guarantee, on condition that the Debt Council, which was at the time composed of representatives of the bondholders of several countries, should be transformed into a representation of the Powers themselves, as in Egypt, and that the future Debt Commission should exercise control over the entire financial administration; in other words, that Europe should, as in Egypt, have the right of interference in Turkish financial matters. This plan fell to the ground in consequence of the opposition of Russia, which was strongly averse to any international control of the government of Turkey. *Annual Register,* 1896.

[48] In consulting various works on the Public Debt, it has been interesting to compare their authors' opinions of the nature of the Decree of Mouharrem. Morawitz, *op. cit.*, p. 231, and Du Velay, *op. cit.*, p. 445, both consider it a contract, and not a unilateral decree of the Turkish Government. Agreeing with these two authorities are Roumani, A., *Essai Historique et Technique sur la Dette Publique Ottomane* (Paris, 1927), p. 113; Delaygue, L., *Essai sur les Finances Ottomans* (Paris, 1911), p. 90; Clerin, G., *Inexécution par un état de ses engagements financières extérieures* (Nancy, 1908), p. 133; Poulgy, *op. cit.*, p. 105; Imbert, H., *Les emprunts d'états étrangers—Recours individuel et action collectif des créanciers* (Paris, 1905), p. 64. But Dupuis, L., *Le contrôle financier de la Dette Publique Ottomane* (Paris, 1908), p. 104; Lacroze, Reynaud, *L'Immixtion financière en droit international* (Paris, 1903), p. 92; and Leroy-Beaulieu, P., *Traité de la science des finances* (2 volumes, Paris, 1912), think of it not as a contract, but as a unilateral act of the Ottoman Government. All of these writers, however, mention the peculiar character of the instrument, while only one, Théry, E., *op. cit.*, p. 39, thinks of it as possessing "une veritable caractère internationale." None of them see in the Public Debt Council the real elements of official foreign financial control, although this depends, of course, in each case upon the type of sanction imputed to the Decree of Mouharrem, and how important is the unofficial approval of the syndicates' delegates by their respective governments. See *infra*, Chapter IX.

own nationality who are charged to supervise the maintenance of the pledges and the regularity of their collection."[49] It is probably taken for granted that official control is meant by this definition; in any case, the two essential elements of official financial control are the sanctioning of the future conditions of service by a diplomatic act, and the official character of the executive body.

It is seen at once that the administration instituted by the Decree of Mouharrem falls short of meeting these requirements. While there has been some disagreement concerning the diplomatic sanctions of the Decree of Mouharrem, there can be no doubt that the members of the Public Debt Council served in an unofficial capacity.[50] Because there were quasi-official sanctions connected with the Decree of Mouharrem, the Public Debt Administration is found to stand half-way between an official financial control and a purely private financial control. Without attempting too exact a definition, it may be termed private financial control possessing international elements.

In this connection the opinions of two authoritative European writers on Turkish financial history are interesting. Morawitz finds the real guarantee of the holders against the breach of the Decree not in Article XX, but in Article XXI.

> In thus pledging itself to communicate the Decree of Mouharrem to the foreign powers, the Ottoman Government certainly has not given the arrangement . . . the compass of a diplomatic convention properly called, in the absolute sense of the term; but it has conferred upon it [the Decree] a sufficiently marked international character for the powers to have at once the right and the duty not to stand by as indifferent and inactive witnesses to any real transgression of the understandings confirmed by the Decree.

Morawitz thinks that this contract, by its nature and by the circumstances in which it was concluded, would be placed under the protection of the powers, even if it were not by express mention placed under the safeguard of international law.[51] The

[49] *Op. cit.*, p. 585.

[50] But cf. *infra*, Chapter IX, p. 224 *et seq.*

[51] *Op. cit.*, pp. 231-2. But Morawitz thinks that express mention does place it under the safeguard of international law. Article XXI (communication to the powers), the preamble (reference to the Berlin Protocol), the completion of the Decree itself as an agreement between the Government and its creditors as promised by the Turkish delegate at Berlin, and

"right" expressed by Morawitz is unquestioned; is not the "duty" very questionable?

Du Velay expresses the opinion that the convention sanctioned by the Decree of Mouharrem "is in fact a veritable *concordat* accorded Turkey by its creditors. . . . It was arrived at between the two interested parties, freely and by common accord, and, with the exception of the reserves expressed concerning the protection of the Decree, without diplomatic interference." But, he continues, "the Decree of Mouharrem, although invested with a private character, is none the less placed under the protection of the powers signatory to the Treaty of Berlin." [52] To an extent the Decree is placed under this protection, in that the powers would have the right to consider measures to be taken in case of its abrogation.

There is a consensus of opinion that a connection exists between the Berlin Congress and the Decree. Opinions vary from one extreme to the other. Morawitz scorns the argument that Protocol XVIII of the Berlin Congress endowed the Decree with an international character, though utilizing the action of the Congress to support the contention that the Decree is placed under the safeguard of international law.[53] Commandant Berger, on the other hand, considers that the powers assumed a more direct responsibility: ". . . They, by their collective representations, have called it [the Decree of Mouharrem] forth, and by their unanimous agreement on this subject expressed at the Congress of Berlin, are constituted guardians of the convention and of the Decree of Mouharrem which ratifies it." [54] In another place he is even more definite in his conviction: "It is more than a moral obligation which the European governments have assumed towards the holders of Ottoman securities; it is a formal engage-

---

the convocation of representatives of its creditors, are ample reasons, in Morawitz's opinion, why the powers did not act in Turkey as they acted in Egypt and in Tunis. *Ibid.* At least one London journal saw in Article XXI the ultimate sanction for the execution of the Decree: "Lastly, as a final security for the observance of the arrangement it is agreed that the Porte is to communicate to the powers the substance of the convention which it has entered into with the bondholders." *Saturday Review* (London) Volume LIII (January, 1883), p. 111.

52 *Op. cit.*, p. 445.

53 *Op. cit.*, p. 55.

54 *Mémoires, Congrès International des Valeurs Mobilières* (Volume IV, Paris, 1900), p. 4.

ment to safeguard their value and the guarantees which were obtained in the creation of the Administration of the Public Debt." [55]

Another French member of the Council, M. de la Boulinière, thus expresses his opinion:

> Although the Administration of the Debt is Ottoman, the presence at its head of an independent Council composed of foreign delegates is sufficient to keep Turkey from violating its engagements; the potential menace of the provisions of the Congress of Berlin . . . could likewise, if necessary, encourage it to respect an institution which Turkey has created in order to escape the commission provided for in the Protocol. Moreover, if it is true that the powers have no cause to intervene to insure the normal working of the prescriptions of the Decree of Mouharrem, and if it is the rôle of the Debt Council to do so, it is no less certain that Turkey had to notify the powers of the same Decree, and that any infraction of its provisions or any violation of the obligations undertaken would justify the immediate intervention of the interested powers, to which the delegates and the bondholders' syndicates would certainly appeal.[56]

The sanctions of the Decree of Mouharrem were in reality more potential than actual in their nature. Under ordinary circumstances they were sufficiently well defined in character to insure the rights of the bondholders and to guarantee the attributions of the Public Debt Council. For over forty years the Ottoman Government made no formal attempt to disengage itself of the obligations assumed under the Decree of 1881. Even in times of stress, unless it was during the Great War, the attitude of the Government was satisfactory. During these forty years the Empire fought five different wars, experienced three revolutions, and on numerous occasions was disturbed by internal difficulties. Under these varied circumstances, the sanctions of the Decree must be recognized as having possessed considerable force. Earlier, opinions cited agree in general that the Decree had sufficiently forceful qualities to meet all ordinary hazards. If these opinions referred to such circumstances as have just been suggested, they must be considered essentially correct. Considered, however, in the light

---

[55] *Ibid.*, (Volume II, 1901), p. 26.

[56] *Notice sur l'importance, les conditions juridiques, économiques, et financiers du capital français en Turquie et sur le rôle de la D. P. O. et l'efficacité de sa garantie* (Constantinople, 1913), pp. 7-8, cited hereafter as *Notice.*

of the unprecedented situation of 1919-23 these opinions are not so weighty. During this period the rights of the bondholders and the position of the Council were drastically altered.

The significant fact to be noted during this period is that the Decree of Mouharrem as the fundamental law upon which the Public Debt rested was all but swept away. The unratified Treaty of Sèvres (August 10, 1920), which had forecast an official debt council under the protection of the Allied powers and functioning with the sanction of an international treaty, had proved a boomerang to its Allied dictators.[57] Three years later at Lausanne a spirited attempt was made by them to sanction the Decree of Mouharrem by confirming it in the treaty between Turkey and the Allies. The dominant argument in the Allied position was thus set forth by M. Barrère, one of the French delegates: ". . . The Debt was an institution the status of which had been defined by the Decree of Mouharrem, and officially communicated to the powers. That status was thus placed under their guarantee." [58]

The Allied powers proposed to constitute themselves the special guarantors, for their own benefit, of a situation formerly conceived to be under the quasi-guarantee of all the signatories of the Treaty of Berlin. The Allied point of view, that the absence from Constantinople during the Great War of the British and French delegates rendered the actions of the Council illegal, had as its necessary conclusion the assumption that in the future the Allied powers themselves would oversee the operation of the situation by sanctioning it with an international treaty. But it can hardly be maintained that this argument of the Allies in 1923 was prompted by the same motives that moved the signatories of the Treaty of Berlin to promulgate Protocol XVIII. Imperialist objects were in view in 1923, while in 1878 the importance of financial control over so-called backward countries was not fully appreciated.

The refusal of the Turkish delegation at Lausanne to allow a clause confirming the Decree of Mouharrem to be included in the treaty was a forecast of the final provisions of the treaty itself. Among the outstanding financial provisions of the Lausanne settlement are these: (1) distribution of the responsibility for the an-

---

57 *Infra*, Chapter VIII.

58 *Parliamentary Papers*, No. Cmd.1814 (1923), p. 553.

nuities and capital of the pre-war Ottoman debt; (2) return of the ceded revenues to the Turkish Government; (3) the provision for the substitution of new revenues.[59] The bondholders were thus deprived of one of their two most important rights under the Decree of Mouharrem, namely, ownership of the ceded revenues. The second important right—administration of the ceded revenues by the Council—has been replaced by the provisions of the 1928 Draft Contract.[60]

This agreement, the negotiation and provisions of which are treated elsewhere in detail, is a document of a legal nature similar to the Decree of Mouharrem. They are both private contracts between a government and its creditors. But the Draft Contract does not possess the inchoate international legal sanctions which were found to contribute so much to the strength of the Decree of Mouharrem.[61] The "international elements" possessed by the latter are lacking in the Draft Contract. Legally, the final sanction for the respect and performance of the clauses of this settlement must be sought in the good faith of the Turkish Republican Government.

---

[59] *Infra*, Chapter VIII, pp. 202-3.
[60] *Ibid.*, p. 204 *et seq.*
[61] *Supra*, p. 99 *et seq.*

Chapter VI

THE PUBLIC DEBT COUNCIL PROVES ITS WORTH

The reduction of the Ottoman foreign debt to fifty-six percent of the outstanding total in 1881 created the initial impression that unnecessary hardships had been visited upon holders of Turkish securities. A comparison of this figure, however, with the fifty-eight percent, which is an average of the issue rates appearing in the prospectuses, shows that only a small net amount was sacrificed. True, the anticipated normal rate of interest (one percent) was low indeed as compared with earlier returns. Nevertheless, the creation of the Public Debt permitted European creditors to envisage the future with tranquillity, firm in their conviction that under normal circumstances interest and amortization charges would be met punctually. Commenting, in 1883, on the provisions of the Decree of Mouharrem, a London review stated that "Impartial people who did not allow their wishes to run away with their reason hardly expected that the Porte would concede as good terms to the bondholders as in fact Mr. Bourke and his colleagues have obtained. . ."[1]

The Council a Success in its Primary Aim

According to the Decree of Mouharrem, the Council received the power to administer, to collect, and to hold in deposit, the revenues resulting from the development of the sources of income ceded to the bondholders. In itself this power would have offered little likelihood of any increase in income. A further provision, however, delegated to the Council the right to introduce such changes and improvements in the regulations governing the exploitation of its revenues as did not overstep existing laws and decrees. Moreover, the Council also received the right to change

[1] *Saturday Review,* Volume LIII (January, 1883), p. 110. The author of this article maintained, moreover, that "it is no secret that it is Mr. Bourke of all the delegates who was most earnest in his efforts to benefit the bondholders. The other delegates were more or less delegates of great financial institutions which had other views besides the wish to obtain something for the bondholders. . . . "

existing legislation concerning any of its revenues, provided a previous agreement concerning the modification had been reached with the Government. These various powers offered to the Council the opportunity of employing its energy and ability to accomplish the utmost improvement of the revenues under its control.[2]

From the point of view of income, the revenue from the salt monopoly was the most important ceded to the bondholders. In 1862, during the negotiations which resulted in the loan of that year, the Government had created this monopoly, and the income therefrom had formed part of the security for the loan. The Turkish Empire is particularly rich in salt, both in rock form and in salt marshes. The development of this revenue, however, presented unusual difficulties. The extensive coastline afforded an excellent opportunity for the introduction of smuggled salt; the absence of railroads, and even of an extensive system of highways, impeded transportation; moreover, the peasant was accustomed to purchase his yearly supply of this commodity at a single transaction, a financial charge which was a serious burden.

---

[2] The regularly-appearing official publications of the Council were the following: *Compte Rendu* (annually since 1882), of a nature to inform interested persons of the administration of the revenues ceded under the Decree of Mouharrem (cited as *Compte Rendu*); *Rapport Annuel sur la Gestion des Dimes, Aghnam, et Revenues Divers* (annually since 1898), calculated to show the administration of revenues collected and applied under contracts "hors décret," particularly kilometric guarantees, (cited as *Rapport Annuel*). The *Procès-Verbaux du Conseil d'Administration*, minutes of the Council meetings, were private (cited as *Procès-Verbaux*). Besides these publications, the British delegate has issued annually a *Special Report on the Ottoman Public Debt* for the information of the British and Dutch holders (cited as *Special Report*). Special publications have from time to time been published by the Council or certain members thereof, the most important of which are the following: *Procès-Verbaux et Annexes de la Commission de 1881;* Berger, L., *Aperçu—Administration de la D. P. O., Son institution, son organisation, et son fonctionnement pendant les seize premières exercises* (Contantinople, 1899) (cited as *Aperçu*); *Décret Impérial du 28 Mouharrem (8/20 Décembre 1881) réglant le service de la Dette Publique consolidée de l'Empire Ottoman, Protocol et Décret Annexe du 22 Djemazi-ul-Akhir 1321 (1/14 Septembre 1903)* (Constantinople, 1919); *Convention du 10/22 Novembre 1879 Décret et Annexes; Note sur l'institution, l'organisation et le fonctionnement de l'Administration de la D. P. O.* (Constantinople, 1912) (cited as *Note*); *Quelques Précisions sur l'Administration de la D. P. O., Ses origines, son statut, les résultats de son activité* (Constantinople, 1924) (cited as *Précisions*); de la Boulinière, J., *Notice; Recueil des contrats d'emprunts conclus entre les gouvernements Allemand et Ottoman au cours de la guerre générale (1915-18) à l'occasion des émissions de papier-monnaie en Turquie* (Constantinople, 1919) (cited as *Receuil des Contrats*); *Billets de monnaie—Receuil de lois, décrets, conventions et autres documents y relatifs* (Constantinople, 1919) (cited as *Billets de monnaie*).

Nevertheless, the Council applied itself to its new task with energy and efficiency. In the 1863 budget the revenue from the salt monopoly was figured at Ltqs. 625,000; in the budget for 1874-5 revenue from the same source was reckoned at Ltqs. 825,000. Although the revenue from salt during the early years of the administration of the Council failed to reach the estimate of the 1875 budget, these estimates were probably much higher than the sums actually realized. The Council's management must certainly be considered as no less efficient than that of the Government; yet not until the year 1898 did the salt revenue surpass Ltqs. 800,000. In 1900 the revenue from this source reached Ltqs. 875,000.

In considering the figures for these last two years an important factor must be mentioned. In 1892 the Council had adopted the policy of developing the export trade in this commodity. In that year the first steps were taken for placing on a productive basis the working of the vast salt deposits on the shores of the Red Sea. On account of its geographical proximity, and of the demand existing there, India was chosen as the best potential market for the disposal of the salt mined from the Red Sea salines. An agent of the Council was dispatched to India to develop the demand for Turkish salt; Commandant Berger, the alternate president of the Council, devoted himself to an extensive study of the conditions of salt extraction, and placed the results of his research at the disposal of the Council. The efforts thus put forward were eminently successful. The revenue from salt exports in 1892 was negligible; gross receipts in 1908-9 amounted to nearly Ltqs. 100,000. Profits in this year were about Ltqs. 12,000, in spite of a severe contest between Liverpool and Spanish salt merchants on the Calcutta market, which led to a heavy cutting of prices.

Similar attempts were made to increase the sale of salt within the Empire. The fishing industry and the cultivation of olives, both of which require large amounts of salt, offered excellent opportunities for the development of domestic consumption. The efforts exerted were handsomely rewarded: the total revenue from salt in 1881-2 amounted to Ltqs. 635,000; in 1907-8 it was Ltqs. 1,075,880, an increase of nearly seventy percent; in 1913-14 the revenue was Ltqs. 1,103,023, exclusive of a war supertax of nearly

Ltqs. 500,000. These increases were not due entirely to the increase in general consumption and export trade; under the pressure of the Council and coöperating with it, the Government had increased its ability to combat contraband, particularly on the southern Black Sea coast, by the purchase and placing in operation of two coast guard vessels.[3]

Similar gratifying returns resulted from efforts directed towards the development of the silk industry. To the Council belonged the revenue from the silk tithe from certain districts contiguous to Constantinople, Adrianople, Broussa, and Samsoun. It was difficult to limit a stimulus to the industry to those particular parts of the country: so the north-central part of Anatolia as a whole profited from the efforts of the Council. In 1885 the Pasteur system of selection of silk worms' eggs for the rearing of silk worms was introduced. An institute of sericulture was established at Broussa in 1888 for free instruction in silk rearing to students from all parts of the Empire. Through 1908 the diploma of the institute had been granted to 919 students; besides, nearly 500 silk growers had passed through the course of instruction. The return of these people to their homes stimulated new interest in improved methods of silk culture. As a result, some sixty million mulberry trees were planted in Turkey between 1890 and 1910, involving the cultivation of some 130,000 acres. New incubating houses and spinning factories were constructed. In the districts administered by the Council the revenue from the silk tithe increased from Ltqs. 17,000 in 1881-2 to Ltqs. 125,000 in 1906-7, the value of the silk crop itself in those regions having advanced over a million pounds. A similar benefit was evident in those regions not under the administration of the Council. Thus the total value of the silk tithes in Turkey increased in the above-named period from some Ltqs. 20,000 to Ltqs. 276,000, and the total value of the crop from about Ltqs. 200,000 to Ltqs. 2,765,000.[4]

The gratifying increases which rewarded the energy of the Council in developing the salt monopoly and the revenue from the silk tithes under its control, were also evident in the other revenues. The indirect taxes, other than the silk tithe, which were

---

[3] Du Velay, *op. cit.*, pp. 177, 318; Caillard, Sir Vincent, article "Turkey, Finance" in *Encyclopedia Britannica*, 11th Edition, Volume XXVII, pp. 430 *et seq.*

[4] Caillard, *loc. cit.*

ceded to the Council, were the stamp tax, the fishing tax, and the spirits tax; in each of these corresponding increases were achieved. The difficulty in extending the application of these taxes was almost as formidable as the Council had experienced with the salt monopoly. For instance, the revenue from the stamp tax arises from the sale of stamps to be affixed to contracts between individuals, to commercial paper, and to the securities of newly-created companies. In Turkey each of these sources presented difficulties to be overcome. The Turks themselves rarely resorted to a written contract when an agreement was reached; only when an agreement with a Greek, an Armenian, or a foreigner was negotiated was something more than a verbal agreement used. The operations of banks formed the most potential source of revenue under the second heading; yet not until 1880 was there any general submission of commercial paper to the demands of the stamp tax. Prior to 1893 nationals of states possessing extraterritorial rights were exempt from the stamp tax. In that year, and according to a decree of March 20, 1894, all foreigners were held to pay this tax. But other provisions, particularly inviolability of domicile, of the treaties granting these rights, contributed to the difficulty of enforcing the 1894 decree. As regards the stamping of obligations of newly-organized companies, insecurity of conditions within Turkish borders prevented a normal increase in the number of such companies. Indeed, the policy of the Government in granting concessions was to exempt the securities of the concessionaire companies from the operation of the stamp tax.[5]

Similar difficulties existed in the legislation concerning wines, beers, and alcoholic beverages. The importer of wine paid import duties amounting to eight percent ad valorem, whereas the native wine grower was held to pay a fifteen percent ad valorem tax to the Government. Such discrimination discouraged the extension of wine growing, and prevented the Council from increasing its revenue from this source. Efforts actually exerted concerned themselves with combating phylloxera, and the Council rendered great assistance to the peasants in attempting to stamp out this disease of the vine. Moreover, the tax on beers and on other domestically-produced alcoholic beverages was likewise fifteen percent, whereas import duties were little more than half this fig-

[5] Du Velay, *op. cit.*, pp. 484-5.

ure. Here the Council used its energy to convince the Government of the wisdom of changing existing legislation, but to no avail.

The tax on fishing in Constantinople and its suburbs was somewhat easier to administer. Fishermen were bound to bring their catches to a central fish market, where they were sold at auction under the direction of an agent of the Council. On the amount realized by this sale, twenty percent was levied for the Council, plus three percent for meeting expenses.

There can be no doubt that the Council was energetic and conscientious in administering the taxes which came under its control. Every modification which could be effected without going beyond the legislation controlling these taxes, was introduced. The records of the Council, the yearly reports, and all the official literature of the Public Debt Administration abound with evidence of the efforts made by the Council to increase the revenues and extend their application throughout the country. Some of the existing difficulties have been indicated. Nevertheless, a steady increase occurred in the value of the revenues from the stamp tax, spirits tax, and fishing tax. In the twenty years following 1882 the stamp revenue nearly doubled, increasing from less than Ltqs. 140,000 to Ltqs. 240,000 in 1902. The spirits tax increased during the same period from Ltqs. 178,000 to Ltqs. 278,000. The fishing tax, although considerably smaller in amount, showed a comparable increase. In the same twenty years it rose from Ltqs. 23,000 to Ltqs. 50,000.[6]

The receipts from the tobacco monopoly was also one of the revenues of the Council. According to the Decree of Mouharrem, the Government would not oppose the exploitation of the salt or tobacco monopoly *en régie,* but previous agreement with the Government was necessary. The Council chose to develop the salt monopoly under its own direction. But the exploitation of the tobacco revenue was farmed to the *Société de la Régie Cointércsée des Tabacs de l'Empire Ottoman,* according to an agreement of May 27, 1883, between the promoters of this company, the Public Debt Council, and the Government.[7] The concessionaires were

---

[6] *Ibid;* also pp. 501 *et seq.*

[7] Young, *op. cit.*, Volume V, pp. 189-247; Du Velay, *op. cit.*, pp. 502-15. During its first ten years the *Régie* paid an average dividend of 15.40 francs per share; in 1900 the price of the shares on the market was 313.12 francs. Théry, E., *Les finances ottomanes* (Paris, 1911).

the Crédit Anstalt, of Vienna, the banking house of S. Bleichröder, of Berlin, and the Imperial Ottoman Bank. The proposals presented by this syndicate had the support of the Council. The following statement is taken from the Council's report of 1882-83:

> From the beginning, the Council would have proceeded to remedy the contraband situation, if it had not been approached concerning a proposition which had for its purpose the transformation of the present system, substituting therefor a "*régie cointéresée.*" The proposals which have been made to us [the Council] include advantages of the highest order. We have accepted them, not, however, without having changed them in certain details; and, strengthened by the rights conferred on us by the Decree of Mouharrem, we have supported with our recommendations the representations which the group seeking the concession has made at the Sublime Porte.[8]

According to the terms of the contract, the company paid to the Council an annual rental of Ltqs. 750,000. The Public Debt and the Government were also to benefit according to a fixed scale in the profits above this sum plus the charges necessary to insure an income of eight percent on the paid-up capital.

Thus far the indirect contributions and the revenue from the salt and tobacco monopolies have been considered. There were certain other fixed annuities which were also ceded to the Council, one of which was the surplus of the Cyprus revenues. The Turkish Government had ceded this revenue in the belief that there would be a surplus in the revenues of this island. Its occupation by the British, however, in accordance with the convention of June 4, 1878, and the administration of its revenues by the latter, removed any of its surplus revenues from the control of the Turkish Government, because the surpluses were applied by England to reimbursing the sums paid out for interest and amortization of the 1855 loan (which had received Cyprus revenues as security) when the suspension of the service on the debt occurred in October, 1875. Thus, after 1878 Turkey received no revenue from Cyprus. But by Article VIII, section 6, of the Decree of Mouharrem, an annual payment of Ltqs. 130,000 was to be made to the Council, in case the surplus of Cyprus revenues was not at its disposal. Until 1890 this amount was paid yearly

---

[8] *Compte Rendu*, 1882-83, p. 12.

by endorsing drafts on the customs; the same procedure was followed after that year, but the amount of the annuity was reduced to Ltqs. 102,596, the reduction being justified by the Government by the contention that the former sum was in reality more than the excess of the Cyprus revenues. The decreased annuity was accepted with reserve by the Council.[9]

The revenue due the Council from Eastern Roumelia proved a most difficult one to realize, and the negotiations concerning it extended over a period of fifteen years. It is unnecessary to go into them in detail. It should be mentioned, however, that the Constantinople Conference of December, 1876, in granting a degree of autonomy to this province, stipulated that a portion of the budget should be devoted to the payment of the public debt. The Treaty of Berlin sanctioned this provision, and the commission which was directed to determine the sum for which Eastern Roumelia would be responsible, fixed it at Ltqs. 240,000. This annuity was, however, too heavy a charge; the Roumelian assembly contended that the average income on the basis of which it had been calculated was too high, and reduced it to Ltqs. 180,000. The payments on this amount were very irregular, and in 1887 the Council and the Roumelian provincial assembly sanctioned a convention fixing the annual payment at Ltqs. 130,000, and agreed on the means of liquidating the arrears. The payments on the annuity as thus determined were scrupulously kept until 1894, when the Bulgarian Government, having purchased the Roustchouk-Varna railway from its owners, contended that the credits to the Turkish Government which the former owners had ceded to the Bulgarian Government should be used in liquidating the annual payment to the Sublime Porte. The difficulty was partially smoothed over by Commandant Berger, the president of the Council, who settled the contested point as far as the Public Debt Council was concerned. The payment of the annuity on the terms of the 1887 convention was resumed; but it was agreed that three monthly instalments should be retained each year by the Bulgarian Government until the credits of the former owners of the railway were liquidated. The proclamation of Bulgarian independence on October 5, 1908, necessitated the negotiation of a new convention, by virtue of which the Council was authorized to retain the

[9] Du Velay, *op. cit.*, pp. 467-9.

amount of the annuity out of the surplus of certain revenues and tithes which the Council collected for the Government.[10]

In another place it has been noted that the Congress of Berlin recognized the claims of the bondholders concerning the payment to be applied to the Ottoman debt by those parts detached from the Empire. Articles IX, XXXIII, and XLII, of the Treaty of Berlin deal with this subject, treating specifically the responsibilities of Bulgaria, of Montenegro, and of Serbia. Article X of the convention of 1881 between Greece and the Ottoman Empire lays down a similar responsibility for Greece. But in spite of numerous protests from the bondholders and repeated suggestions from the Council, neither the Turkish Government nor the representatives of the other signatory powers showed themselves disposed to settle these points. The determination of these portions of the debt, and the negotiation of conventions for the payment of the charges thereon would have benefited the bondholders materially, as, by the Decree of Mouharrem, any sums paid to the Porte under these headings were the property of the Council. The Decree also ceded the Bulgarian tribute to the bondholders, but, until it was fixed, the Imperial Government agreed to replace it by the payment of Ltqs. 100,000 from the tobacco tithe.[11]

There remain but two revenues to be considered. It will be remembered that the Council was to enjoy any surplus resulting from the upward revision of commercial treaties; likewise, if a general application of the law on shops and stores produced a revenue greater than that accruing under the income tax law, the surplus belonged to the Council. Unfortunately for the bondholders, the Government showed itself tardy in proceeding to the

---

[10] *Ibid*, pp. 469-72; the text of the 1908 convention is in *Report of the Council of Foreign Bondholders* (London) 1911-12, p. 371. In return for the waiving by Russia of its claims to forty of the seventy-four annuities of the 1877 war indemnity still outstanding on January 1, 1909, Turkey renounced its claims to any rights flowing from Article IX of the Treaty of Berlin regarding the Bulgarian tribute, the Bulgarian contributive portion of the public debt, the arrears in the annuities of Eastern Roumelia, and its property rights in the Oriental railways situated in Eastern Roumelia and seized by the Bulgarian Government. *Russo-Turkish Convention of St. Petersburg of December 8, 1909. Nouveau Recueil Général*, 3me Série, Volume IV, pp. 54-55.

[11] The proportional shares supposed to have been borne by Bulgaria, Montenegro, Serbia, and Greece, have not been assumed by these countries. *Report of the Council of Foreign Bondholders* (London), 1926-27, p. 420.

accomplishment of the second of these.[12] As for the first, it was only in 1907 that new commercial treaties were finally concluded. In the meantime, the Supplementary Decree of September, 1903, had intervened, defining new conditions under which the Government was to profit from surplus revenue of the Council. Moreover, the consent of the powers to the revision of these treaties was secured for the sole purpose of devoting the revenue from the three percent surtax to the initiation and administration of reforms in the *vilayets* of Macedonia.[13]

This discussion of the revenues and of the difficulties accompanying the efforts to expand them suggest certain unusual accomplishments of the Council.[14] At times, of course, the Government had opposed plans offered by the Council to increase its income. Such obstruction was encountered when the Council attempted to persuade the Government to modify legislation concerning the spirits tax. A similar attitude on the Government's part was manifest in the matter of enforcing the law on shops and stores. Moreover, in reducing the income substituted for the excess of Cyprus revenue, the Imperial Government had followed an arbitrary course.

Notwithstanding the difficulties encountered, the administration of the ceded revenues by the Council produced noteworthy increases in the gross receipts. For purposes of comparison five-year averages will be convenient. The first period produced an average annual gross revenue of Ltqs. 2,339,749; for the following period this figure was Ltqs. 2,328,444; for the five years from 1892 to 1897, Ltqs. 2,503,261; for the period immediately prior to the conclusion of the Supplementary Decree (1903), the average annual gross revenue was Ltqs. 2,538,042. From 1902 to 1907 a considerable increase may be noted, the average annual

---

12 "Although having participated in an unofficial capacity only, we [the Council] have the satisfaction of having lent useful support in the negotiations between the Porte and foreign governments" concerning the modification of this law. *Compte Rendu,* 1882-83, p. 15. But the characteristic feature of the Decree of Mouharrem, namely, that all surpluses of the ceded revenues were the property of the bondholders, so impeded these negotiations that the Council never realized any revenue from this source.

13 *Infra,* Chapter VII.

14 But the material presented here is not intended to be exhaustive. For more comprehensive treatment, consult Young, *op. cit.;* Du Velay, *op. cit.;* Heidborn, A., *Les finances ottomanes* (4 volumes, Vienna, 1912) and *Manuel de droit publique et administratif de l'Empire Ottoman* (2 volumes, Vienna, 1908).

receipts being Ltqs. 3,060,643. This increase arose chiefly from the more efficient application throughout the Empire of the new stamp law. Another contributing factor was the development of the salt revenue; likewise the general revenue situation had improved, because of better facilities afforded by the Imperial Government. The figures for the periods subsequent to the promulgation in 1907 of the new customs convention are as follows: from 1907 to 1912, Ltqs. 4,527,539; from 1912 to 1917, Ltqs. 4,035,789; from 1917 to 1922, Ltqs. 9,887,482; and for the period 1922 to 1926, Ltqs. 4,362,564. The operation of the three percent customs surtax naturally increased the gross revenue of the Council, but the Government profited from the balance over fixed charges for interest and amortization purposes.[15]

A comparison of these figures shows a general improvement in the expansion of the income from the Council's revenues. In large measure this must be attributed to the honesty and efficiency of the Administration. Although the large majority of the employees were Ottoman subjects, both Moslems and Christians, regular payment of adequate salaries practically wiped out bribery and graft within their ranks.[16] Thus the Council was freed of one of the factors which had previously corrupted the tax-collecting organization of the Imperial Treasury. Furthermore, the Decree provided that "the Imperial Government will coöperate, with the means at its disposal, in collecting the ceded revenues in all parts of the Empire." The resulting coöperation between the Administration and the forces of the Government decreased the volume of smuggling and the trade in contraband. Similarly, this coöperation resulted in the collection of taxes in certain provinces which, on account of geographical inaccessibility or local insubordination, had heretofore failed to forward revenue receipts to the Treasury.

---

[15] *Reports of the Council of Foreign Bondholders* and *Comptes Rendus*. The last three figures are hardly comparable with the others; the effects of the Great War and the Greco-Turkish War, such as the decline in imports, modified legislation, fluctuation in the value of the Turkish paper pound, etc., introduce too many extraneous factors to allow any real comparison.

[16] In 1886, out of a total of 3040 employees, 2719 were Moslems, 266 Orient Christians, and 55 Europeans; in 1901, the figures were 4843, 4471, 317, and 55 respectively. The total number of employees in 1915 was 5278, while, as a result of the transfer of the Public Debt agencies to the authority of the Turkish Republican Government, the total figure for 1923 was 906. *Rapport Annuel*, 1886-87, 1901-2, 1923-24.

Were the revenues of the Council sufficient to meet the charges on the reduced debt? In spite of the failure to execute the provisions of the Treaty of Berlin which had been inserted for the benefit of the bondholders, the revenues proved ample for interest and amortization charges. The flexible interest provisions of Article XI of the Decree of Mouharrem meant that the annual outlay for this charge might vary from year to year.[17] The revenues ceded by the Government were estimated, however, to yield annually one and one-quarter percent on the debt, or Ltqs. 1,463,133, plus the charges on the Priority Bonds, amounting to Ltqs. 590,000. During the first three years of its administration, the Council applied the whole of its net revenue of Ltqs. 6,100,000 to the payment of one percent interest, one-quarter percent amortization and the Priority Bond charges.

Deficits of Ltqs. 7,200 and Ltqs. 12,500 were experienced, however, in the years 1886-87 and 1887-88 respectively. Credit balances were realized following these years, however, and not until the period of the Great War did further deficits occur. In fact, balances for the period 1888-1902 amounted to over a million pounds. In the years 1894, 1900, and 1902, the reserve fund for raising the rate of interest above one percent exceeded the sums necessary for making a distribution of a supplementary one-quarter percent interest.[18] Such a distribution was made on the coupon due September 1, 1903, although the Council's right to pay this supplementary distribution was contested by the Government.[19] Moreover, the Supplementary Decree was concluded at this time, fixing the total charges to be met from the Council's revenues at Ltqs. 2,157,375. Annual surpluses above this figure were divided between the Government and the Council in the proportion of seventy-five percent and twenty-five percent respectively.[20]

The redemption of the bonds by the sinking and reserve funds proceeded according to schedule, and by 1903 twenty-two percent of the outstanding bonds, including all of Group I, had been redeemed.[21] Prior to 1903 the low interest rate kept the quotations far below par; nevertheless, between 1886, when conversion of the

---

[17] *Supra*, Chapter V, p. 93.
[18] Young, *op. cit.*, Volume V, p. 85.
[19] *Infra*, pp. 120-1.
[20] *Infra*, pp. 172-3.
[21] Young, *op. cit.*, Volume V, p. 85.

old bonds was finally terminated, and 1898, when Group I was completely redeemed, the price of the bonds in this Group on the London exchange advanced from 24 to 67.[22] The harmonious situation created between the Council and the Government by the Supplementary Decree of 1903, and the increased desirability of the bonds of the Unified Converted Debt, were reflected in their course on the London exchange; in September, 1903, the quotation was 86.37, while in October, 1906, the price was 93.50.[23]

Two Important Divisions of Opinion

The Government contested the right of the Council, under the terms of the Decree of Mouharrem, to proceed to the distribution of an extra one-quarter percent interest on the bonds, when the amount accumulated was sufficient for that purpose. It was agreed that the point should be arbitrated according to the provisions of Article XIX of that Decree. Accordingly, a *compromis* on the question of the increase in the rate of interest was reached on March 2, 1903. The point to be decided was: "In conformity with the provisions of the Decree and, according to the accounts, is, or is it not, necessary to distribute one-fourth percent interest to the bondholders, in addition to one percent?"

The two arbitrators named by the Government were Djelal Bey, Minister of Public Instruction, and M. Beernart, former President of the Belgian Council of Ministers. The persons named by the Public Debt Council were M. Caillaux, former French Minister of Finance, and M. Ador, former Vice-President of the Swiss Federal Council.

After deliberating on the point at issue, the arbitrators divided evenly, and, in accordance with Article XIX and the *compromis,* an umpire was appointed. Lord Alverstone, Lord Chief Justice of England at the time, accepted the rôle, and on July 18, 1903, handed down the following decision:

> As from September 14, 1903, and as long as the funds at their disposal for the payment of interest, whether arising

[22] Between 1886 and 1903 the bonds of Group II fluctuated in price between 12.50 and 54. Groups III and IV were less desirable; between the same dates the courses of these bonds were 13 and 30, and 13 and 28 respectively. Quotations are from the London *Economist* and the London *Statist.*

[23] Block, Sir Adam, *Special Report,* 1905-6, p. 10.

> from the annual sums actually received by them or from existing or future reserve of accumulated fractions, permit, the Council of Administration ought to distribute to the bearers of the bonds interest at the rate of one and one-fourth percent per annum.[24]

As a matter of fact, Lord Alverstone's decision did not profit the bondholders, for the Supplementary Decree of September, 1903, intervened.[25] The rate of interest on the bonds was raised to four percent, and the Government was permitted to share in the profits of the Administration.

Another article of the Decree of Mouharrem became the subject of contention, but not between the Council and the Government. The Council itself divided on the important question of its presidency. It will be remembered that, according to Article XV of the Decree, the presidency during the first five years was to alternate annually between the English and the French delegates. This provision was due to the number and considerable importance of the Ottoman bonds held in England and France. If the situation was to change at the end of that period, the Council was to elect its president. The Council divided on the interpretation of the words "essential modification."

It appears that the Rome Chamber of Commerce was the first to voice the desire that the presidency rotate annually among the members of the Council, or that it be elective. During the summer of 1892, the Italian and German delegates, Marquis Guiccioli and Dr. Lindau, prepared a project embodying this idea, and on October 10 of that year laid it before the Council. The Council did not discuss the proposition until the following March, however, when it declared itself incompetent even to examine the proposal that the presidency should rotate among the entire Council membership. Concerning the second part of the proposition, the proposal that the presidency be elective, the Council, "in stating that it knows of no document showing the existence of an essential modification, and that the contrary is well known, declares itself equally incompetent to make any inquiry on that point." The Council was of the opinion that the responsibility of proving that such modification had occurred rested with the Rome

---

24 *Procès-Verbal*, July 18, 1903, *Annex*.

25 *Supra*, Chapter V, p. 98.

Chamber of Commerce. In case it were found to exist, the different syndicates should establish its authenticity, and should inform the Council thereof, in order that the Council, in agreement with the Government, might proceed to the election as provided for in Article XV.[26]

There the matter seems to have rested for some time. Not until March 14, 1898, was it again brought up for consideration. On that date Dr. Lindau made a motion, which was adopted, that two members of the Council should form a commission to inquire into the question of whether "essential modification" had occurred. In making the motion he was presenting his own point of view, as well as those of his Austrian and Italian colleagues. As a result of this decision, Marquis Guiccioli and M. Auboyneau, who had been appointed to make the investigation, presented their report to the Council on November 3, 1898, and on November 7 this report was submitted to the syndicates for their consideration. The action of the syndicates was exceedingly slow. On March 11, 1899, as a result of further observations by Dr. Lindau, the Council decided that during the first meeting after January 13, 1901, the policy of the Council would be decided. The German delegate was impatient, however, and brought the subject on the *tapis* again on March 15, 1900. The debate in the Council was finally held on October 22, 1900.

In the eyes of its protagonists, the question of the presidency must have assumed large proportions, for the minutes of this meeting are voluminous. The arguments of the German, Austrian, and Italian delegates evoked stiff opposition on the part of their British and French colleagues. Although the political importance of the presidency was not discussed, it is an interesting and, perhaps, significant fact, that the division of the Council on this important point followed the political line-up of Europe. However, the German Ambassador at Constantinople in 1913, Baron von Wangenheim, stated in a dispatch to Bethmann Hollweg, that "the question of the presidency as raised by us at that time [1892-93] was more a question of prestige" than of anything else.[27]

---

[26] *Procès-Verbaux*, October 10, 1892, and March 14, 1893.

[27] *Die Grosse Politik des Europäischen Kabinette* (40 volumes, Leipzig, 1919-24), Volume XXXVII, p. 873, von Wangenheim to Bethmann Hollweg, October 20, 1913.

For the present purpose the important point is that after long and tedious debate, the Council finally decided to arbitrate the question. On the proposal of the Council, the French and German syndicates named M. Jules Roche, and Dr. Heilborn, of the University of Berlin, to submit to the Council the names of three persons from which the arbitrator was to be chosen. These names were submitted on April 12, 1901, and M. Ador, Vice-President of the Swiss Federal Council, was chosen.[28]

M. Ador's arbitral sentence was rendered in a report to the Council under date of February 9, 1902. According to the arbitrator the issue involved the interpretation of three separate points: first, interpretation of Article XV of the Decree of Mouharrem; second, meaning of the words "number and importance" appearing in Article XV, (i. e., should the division of the bonds between the different countries be considered on the basis of "nominal" or of "real" value?); third, decision of the point whether, in considering the matter of the presidency, Ottoman bonds held in Holland and Belgium should be added to those held in England.

In view of the prestige and influence attached to the office of president of the Council, and also of the importance attributed to the question by the German delegate and the German Government in 1913 and 1914, M. Ador's interpretations of these points are extremely interesting.[29] He deemed that "essential modification took place if the number and importance of the bonds held in England and France is less than the number and importance held by other countries represented on the Council." The "number and importance" of the bonds was to be determined by "their denomination, their nominal value, and the special security attached to them from the point of view of their redemption." Finally, "the bonds held in Belgium must not be added to those held in England for the purpose of determining the presidency." [30]

---

[28] *Procès-Verbaux*, October 22, 1900, and March 18, 1901.

[29] *Infra*, Chapter IX, pp. 232-3.

[30] *Procès-Verbal*, February 17, 1902, *Annex*. In a communication to the Council dated July 31, 1901, the Council of State "claimed for the Government the exclusive right to interpret the Decree of Mouharrem . . . Essential modification means that the original proportion must be turned around, that is, the greatest part of the bonds must have passed to countries represented by other delegates [than the English and French], and the smallest part must remain in French and English hands." In the eyes of the Government no arbitration was valid to settle a difference which divided the Council. To this contention the Council reserved its rights. *Ibid.*. September 16, 1901.

The decision of M. Ador presented a rational interpretation of Article XV of the Decree of Mouharrem, but his arbitration did not pretend to establish the exact percentage of bonds held in each country. The award did contain, however, a table showing such percentages for the year 1885. French citizens held forty percent while bearers of British nationality possessed twenty-nine percent of the total. Ottoman, Belgian, and Dutch subjects each held roughly seven percent, while between them the bearers of German, Italian, and Austro-Hungarian nationality retained barely nine percent.[31]

It was extremely difficult to establish these percentages when the bonds changed hands daily in the stock markets of Europe. At this time, however, the statement in the minutes of the Council for March 1, 1893, presents a true, if somewhat general, appraisal of the situation. In that place it is stated that it was "common knowledge" that no essential change had taken place. As a matter of fact, English and French bondholders have always held the majority of the bonds. Indeed, in 1914, fifty-eight percent were held by French citizens, but by that time Germany had increased her holdings to nearly thirty-three percent, while bonds in English hands were less than five percent of the total.[32]

Support of Foreign Railroad Enterprise

The Council was not content to function strictly within the limits laid down for it by the Decree of Mouharrem. Composed of energetic Europeans, at an early date it showed itself solicitous of the economic development of the Empire. Its activities in encouraging and developing the salt monopoly and the silk industry suggest the comprehensive scope of reform and improvement of which it was capable. It was in another field, however, and one quite outside the confines of its original functions, that the Council manifested its breadth of interest. Under the ægis of the Public Debt Administration railroad construction in Turkey received its greatest impetus.

It is unnecessary to inquire in detail concerning the development of railroad construction in Turkey. It is sufficient to say that the need was great; the poverty of the country was due in

31 *Procès-Verbal*, February 17, 1902, *Annex*.
32 Poulgy, *op. cit.*, p. 160.

large measure to the lack of means of rapid communication. The interior towns were connected neither with one another nor with the seaports. This circumstance not only retarded economic development, but also added greatly to the difficulty of defending the Empire.

European promoters who had constructed lines in Turkey before 1875 underwent many difficulties with the Government in the matter of tariffs, securities, back accounts, and protection of their property. The rude jolt which in 1875 shocked holders of the Government's securities, discouraged further the persons with capital already invested in railroads, as well as those who possessed ideas concerning future development of rail communication. The fact was that immediately after the default foreign capitalists had little or no confidence in the integrity of the Government. The establishment of the Administration of the Public Debt in 1882 had renewed some of the earlier enthusiasm concerning economic regeneration of Turkey by means of railroad construction. The credit of the Empire had been improved, important revenues were in the hands of the Public Debt for the exclusive benefit of the bondholders, and the Council itself was consolidating its position as an important economic factor in the Empire.

The Administration of the Public Debt was, in fact, admirably fitted to perform the functions which foreign promoters found lacking in the Government itself. The two primary demands were: an agency in which perfect trust could be reposed, and the coöperation of an administration which was capable and efficient. In the opinion of European investors the Government possessed neither of these attributes. But the Public Debt, also from the viewpoint of western Europe, did possess them; its support and coöperation were therefore necessary.

The Council was greatly interested in the economic development of the Empire. The income from its revenues would increase more rapidly if transportation were made easier and further markets opened by a network of railways. The interests of the bondholders, which were the first concern of their representatives, would be served by the improvement in communication methods; the credit of the Empire abroad and the consequent enhancing of the bonds on the exchanges, would be a normal result of economic regeneration. It was to the obvious advantage of the Council and the bondholders for the former to be guided by a liberal and progressive economic policy.

It is an uncertain point whether the original stimulus to railroad construction which followed the institution of the Council in 1882 came from the Council itself, from the Government, or from foreign promoters and capitalists. As is noted above, the obvious position of the Council would be to encourage such a policy to the utmost. In fact, Sir Vincent Caillard, who was one of the first British delegates, is of the opinion that "the Council suggested that it supervise the collection and administration of the tithes of the districts to be traversed by a proposed railway." [33] His opinion should receive due consideration, for he was the alternate president of the Council, and a person who was himself interested in railroad projects in the Empire. A recent author confirms this point of view: ". . . the Public Debt Administration recommended to the Sultan that certain revenues of his Empire should be set aside for the payment of subsidies to railway companies." [34]

The Sultan himself, however, is known to have possessed ideas on the policy of railroad construction. He was definitely in favor of it, for, although it would mean the infiltration of western political concepts and economic principles, the advantages to the country from the economic and strategic points were far greater.[35] But in the report of one of the meetings of the Council, it appears that "in the future the Council will be unable to administer any further tithes appropriated by the Government as kilometric guarantees or for any other purpose, without being consulted in sufficient time to reach a previous agreement with the Government and the concessionaire." This indicates that officially at least the Council had not been consulted concerning railway construction prior to being informed by the Imperial Commissioner of the intent

[33] Caillard, *loc. cit.*, p. 437. But cf. Depuis, L., *Le contrôle financier de la Dette Publique Ottomane* (Paris, 1908), p. 90, where it is stated that "it was M. Theodore Berger, director of the Ottoman Bank and president of the French syndicate interested in purchasing the Haidar Pasha railway, who had the happy idea that the Council of the Public Debt should administer the tithes" assigned as railway guarantees. The author was assured in a personal interview with Sir Vincent that it was he who first made this proposal, and that the Council adopted it as a definite policy under his presidency.

[34] Earle, E. M., *Turkey, the Great Powers, and the Bagdad Railway* (New York, 1923), p. 19.

[35] Ali Vahbi, *op. cit.*, *passim.*

of the Government, and this would seem to be confirmed by the minutes of the two meetings in 1888 when the Council was informed of its new functions under the concession which had just been granted to Dr. Kaulla for the extension of the Haidar Pasha-Ismidt line to Angora by way of Eski-Shehir.[36]

The position occupied by the Public Debt, the type of men composing it, and their well known interest in railroad enterprise, contribute to the belief that we must look beyond the official presentation of the situation. It may, therefore, be concluded that all three of the agencies mentioned above, the Council, the Sultan, and foreign promoters, were simultaneously interested in pushing a policy of railway construction, each for a different reason. The Council's primary reason was in the interest of the bondholders; but does it seem unlikely that personal financial reasons may partially explain the Council's zeal in furthering foreign railway enterprise? Would not the fact that several Council delegates were simultaneously members of the directing boards of these foreign-controlled railways further confirm this impression? The Sultan's interest was the development of trade and commerce within his empire, and the promotion of means of defence. As for the concessionaires and promoters, they hoped to add to the prosperity of the country because it would increase profits on their investments.

In any event, whatever may have been its official point of view, the Council accepted the new functions which were conferred upon it. On April 26, 1888, the Imperial Commissioner informed the Council of an *iradé* which had just been issued, stipulating the conditions for the construction of railways in Asiatic Turkey. Article VI of a subsequent administrative ordinance defined the function which the Council assumed. This provision was reproduced almost verbatim as Article XXIX of the convention of September 27, 1888, between the Imperial Government and Dr. Alfred Kaulla, representing the *Deutsche Bank*, awarding to the group which he represented the concession for the extension of the Haidar Pasha line to Angora. As this is the first railroad concession in which the Public Debt Council figures, and as the article of this convention agrees closely with similar articles in subsequent agreements, it may be quoted here:

---

[36] *Procès-Verbaux*, March 13, 1893, April 26, October 22, 1888.

The Imperial Government guarantees to the concessionaires an annual gross revenue of 15,000 francs per kilometer constructed and in operation; in the case of the operating receipts being less than this amount, the following procedure will be followed to make up the figure of 15,000 francs annual gross revenue per kilometer of railroad constructed and in operation:

During the adjudication of the tithes of the *sandjaks* of Ismidt, Erthogroul, Kutahia, and Angora, through which the line runs, an agent of the Public Debt Administration must be present, and the promissory notes which the successful bidders are bound to furnish for the value of the tithes resulting from this adjudication shall be made payable to the order of the Public Debt Administration's agencies in the above-mentioned *sandjaks,* and shall be paid exclusively to them. The amounts which the Imperial Government agrees to pay annually to the concessionaires to complete the kilometric guarantee mentioned above will be taken out of this sum, and will be paid by the Public Debt Administration, and the balance will be forwarded by it to the Imperial Treasury.[37]

For twenty years subsequent to 1888 the Council assumed this function whenever a new concession was granted by the Government. By the year 1907 this function of intermediary between the concessionaire and the Government was being fulfilled for the following railway enterprises: Salonica - Constantinople (since 1894); Salonica-Monastir (since 1892); Smyrna-Cassaba and extensions (since 1894); Haidar Pasha-Angora and Eski Shehir-Konia (since 1888 for the former, 1894 for the latter); Bagdad (since 1903 for the first section, since 1908 for the second and third); Damascus-Hama and extensions (since 1897). The extent and the importance of the Council's coöperation is evident from this list; the first two of these lines were situated in European Turkey; the Anatolia and Bagdad lines traversed the whole of the Anatolian peninsula from the Bosporus to the Amanus mountains, and thence across the deserts of Mesopotamia toward Bagdad; the Damascus-Hama line with its extensions served the Syrian seacoast and the hinterland. This imposing array testifies to the confidence and trust placed in the Administration of the Public Debt. It is a question whether any of these enterprises

---

37 *Ibid.,* October 22, 1888.

would have been undertaken had it not been for the existence of the Administration of the Public Debt.[38]

The function of administering kilometric assignments was bound to raise disputes between the Government, the Council, and the interested railway companies. However willing the Government may have been to welcome the influx of foreign capital under the stipulation that the Government's pledges should be placed in the hands of a neutral third party, it was not willing that the interpretation placed upon this function should be one-sided. Moreover, the Government may have recognized the close relationships between the members of the Council and the directors of the railways and the financial establishments interested in their exploitation. In any event, from the date of the assumption of this new rôle by the Council, there was a running battle with the Government, continuing for years, as to the exact limits within which it was legitimate for the Council to defend the interests of the railways while carrying out its mutual pledge to the Government and the railways themselves as regards the collection of the assignments. On a later page this interesting part of the problem will be considered; for the present, three examples of the Council's interpretation call for examination.

As the result of an administrative change in the *sandjak* of Erthogroul, certain villages which had formerly contributed to the pledges of the Anatolian railway now formed part of the *sandjak*

---

[38] The importance of this side of the Council's activities is evidenced by the creation in 1898 of a separate department of "Tithes, Taxes, and Different Revenues" for the special purpose of centralizing the accounts for the different railways, and of turning over the proper sums to them. In a letter of December 22, 1898, to the Ottoman Bank and the interested railway companies the president of the Council announced the creation of this department. "This is a special department designed to procure, as much for the Imperial Government as for the financial establishments and railway companies, the maximum production from the tithes assigned to the different loans and kilometric guarantees, the administration and collection of which are confided to the Public Debt Administration. Profiting from its ten years' experience, the Council desires, as far as it is able, to perfect a service which, although producing satisfactory results for those interested, nevertheless still shows certain defects in its functioning." *Procès-Verbal*, December 17, 1898. A member of the Council was to be asked twice yearly to act as the directing head of this department with powers and attributes defined in a code of regulations The institution of this separate department for administering functions assumed by the Council outside the Decree of Mouharrem indicates the vast extension of its powers, and the increasing economic importance which was being attached to the Administration.

of Broussa, where the tithes were pledged to the service of a Government loan. In deciding its policy, the Council, in July, 1893, laid down the principle that, according to Article XXIX of the convention of October 4, 1888, the Council "in administering the tithes assigned to the Anatolian railway, acts only as the mandatary of the Government, and, as a consequence, it must accept the changes which the Government deems it necessary to make in the administrative divisions of the Empire, without judging whether these changes are of a nature to prejudice third parties. . . . Also, if the Government thinks it necessary to change the boundaries of a *sandjak* in which the Public Debt administers the tithes for the account of a third party, the Council must function on the basis of this change, clearing itself by informing the interested third party of the modification. If this party deems it wise to protest to the Government, the responsibility of so doing rests upon it. As regards the Public Debt, it will only conform to the resulting solution, without taking part in the debates." [39]

In July, 1899, another related point was raised, during the settlement of which the Council asked the opinion of its legal adviser concerning its duty to the Damascus-Hama line. On January 28, 1899, the latter had agreed to cede to a group of banks, of which the Ottoman Bank was one, its annuity of Ltqs. 33,000 from the Government. The Ottoman Bank and the Council had agreed for this sum to be paid to the former. At this point the Government intervened and "invited the Council not to pay any of the service on this Ltqs. 33,000 until further notice." The minutes of the Council of July 17, 1899, contain the opinion of its legal adviser: "The Administration is the common mandatary of the Imperial Government and of the Damascus railway for the execution of a provision defined in their convention. The Public Debt has accepted this mandate. The principal obligation imposed consists in doing everything in its power to collect the assigned tithes; to apply annually from the receipts of these tithes the sum necessary for the service on the annuity; to pay this service directly to the aforesaid company, and to hold the remainder, after deducting expenses, at the disposal of the Government. The Government can no more give orders to withhold the necessary sums from the company for the service of its annuity than the company has a right to demand

[39] *Procès-Verbal,* July 27, 1893.

that the Debt refrain from paying the surplus to the Government. The sole desire of one of the contractors, lacking the consent of the other, can not relieve the Debt of the obligations which it has assumed." [40]

Again, in 1905, the Council, during the course of a disagreement with the Government concerning the modification of the system for the collection of the tithes, saw fit to speak in no indefinite terms of its obligations: ". . . In effect the Public Debt is only a third party to the contracts concluded between the Imperial Government and the financial establishments and railway companies, and the signature which it has affixed to these contracts, for the purpose of lending the support of its guarantee to the contractors, binds it definitely only as the administration charged with the management of the assigned revenues. In this connection the Council has the right and the duty to see that the contracts in question are rigorously respected, as it can administer the revenues which have been confided to it by third parties, according to the provisions of the conventions, only as long as these conventions shall not have been revised as the result of a general agreement among the contracting parties. . . ." [41]

These examples indicate the Council's interpretation of its position. The terms of the contracts might reasonably have been interpreted legally whenever the rights of one party were alleged to be injured. Or the Council might have been less zealous in its interpretation of its position, had the interests of the bondholders and of the members of the Council themselves been less closely related. As a matter of fact, in the many disputes which arose between the Government, the Council, and the concessionaires, the Government usually found itself at considerable disadvantage, as the interests of two of the parties usually coincided, leaving the Government to fight its battle alone. Moreover, the ability, the resources, and the prestige, of the Council were such that, under a given set of circumstances in which the Government sincerely thought its interests would be served by altering the status quo, the obstruction offered by the other two contracting parties, with the possible threat of a diplomatic sanction in the background, was too formidable for the Government to overcome. Of course, it is

---

[40] *Ibid.*, March 23, May 4, July 6 and 27, 1899.

[41] *Ibid.*, July 24, 1905.

not contended that a flagrant breach of an important point in an agreement should have been passed unnoticed by the Council. All that is meant is that the prestige of the Council in Europe, achieved as a result of its administration of the revenues ceded directly to its charge, and the coincidence of interests of the railways, banks, and the members of the Public Debt Council, placed the Government at a serious strategic disadvantage in its dealings with foreign companies.

Proof of the unity of interest existing between the Council and the Anatolian Railway is afforded by reference to an incident which occurred in 1901. At that time the Board of Directors of the railway was considering the extension of the Bagdad line beyond Konia. The debate concerned the manner of delivery to the Board of the special assignments destined to guarantee the payment of the kilometric guarantee accorded by the Imperial Government. "The problem of realizing the value of these assignments . . . without overburdening the present state of the Government's budget cannot be solved by the Anatolian Railway alone. For the accomplishment of this object the efficient coöperation of other more powerful agencies will be necessary."[41a] Of the other more powerful agencies the P. D. A. was the most important. At that period Dr. Lindau and Commandant Berger, the German and French delegates to the Council, were among the board members of the Anatolian Railway.

It cannot be denied that it was to the advantage of the railway companies already named to include in their boards of directors one or more members of the Public Debt Council. To be sure, the strictly legal provisions of the contracts to which the Council was a party might have been zealously carried out if the contrary had been the case. The company in question would have been assured of the moral support and prestige which the Council enjoyed. Moreover, the Council itself, fully aware of the difficulties inherent in administering Turkish revenues, would have been able to fulfill its duties under the contracts without any of its members sitting on a board of directors. The prestige of the Administration and of its Council had been gained through its integrity and efficiency, based on regular payment of salaries, payment of a living wage, dispensation of justice in disputes among

41a *Annual Report of the Anatolian Railway Company*, 1901, p. 7.

employees, and the application of sound principles of finance. It can hardly be contended that the Council's prestige would have suffered had it assumed the position of "mandatary for the Government and for the concessionaire," without representatives of the mandatary possessing functions in the concessionaire companies. The contrary was the case, however; some of the members of the Council possessed distinct interests in the future of the railways.

Versatile Council Members

Shortly after the organization of the Anatolian Railway Company in 1888, Sir Vincent Caillard, the British delegate to the Council, was elected to the board of directors, a position retained by him until 1897, when he resigned both offices. Sir Vincent's successor in the Council, Major Sir Edward Fitz Gerald Law, also succeeded him on the board of directors of the Anatolian Railway Company. The delegate of the German bondholders in 1888, Herr A. Goescher, was likewise elected a director of this company; he resigned from the Council, however, in August, 1889, at which time his successor in the Council, Herr Herman Gerlich, was elected to fill the post on the board of directors vacated by Herr Goescher. In 1899, Dr. Rudolf Lindau, who, in 1891, had followed Herr Gerlich as German delegate on the Council, was elected a director; his successor on the Public Debt Council, Dr. Karl Testa, who had been elected by the German syndicate to that post in 1902, also replaced his predecessor on the board of the Anatolian Railway Company. When Dr. Testa died in 1911, he was succeeded on the Public Debt Council by Herr Charles Bunz; Herr Bunz took Dr. Testa's place on the Anatolian Railway board.

When Major Fitz Gerald Law resigned from the Council of the Public Debt in March, 1900, the British delegate who succeeded him, Sir Henry Babington-Smith, was not elected to the Anatolian board; but the alternate president of the Council, Commandant Léon Berger, the French delegate on the Council since 1887, assured the presence of a second Council delegate on the Anatolian Board, when he was elected a director in June, 1901. From that date until his death in 1909, Commandant Berger proved himself a staunch defender of the interests of the Anatolian Railway. In fact his interest in Turkish railroads was not confined to the Anatolian line; from an early date he was president of the Constantinople board of the Salonica-Constantinople line, the Smyrna-Cassaba and extensions line, and the Damascus-Hama line in Syria. His death, however, did not deprive these companies of active assistance from the Public Debt Council; M. de la Boulinière, who followed Commandant Berger's immediate successor in the Council, M. Arsène Henry, was elected to the Anatolian board in 1909. Nor did the Salonica-Monastir line and the Bagdad line lack zealous defenders on the Public Debt Council. Dr. Testa, already mentioned, was president of the Constantinople board not only of the Anatolian line, but also of the Salonica-Constantinople and the Bagdad lines. When it was organized in 1903, the Bagdad company had members of the Public Debt Council on its board in the persons of Dr. Testa, Commandant Berger, and Hamdy Bey, the latter the delegate of the Ottoman bondholders. Count d'Arnoux, the director-general of the Public Debt Administration, was likewise a member of the Bagdad board of directors, as was his successor in the Debt, M. Léon Pissard. This recitation of the members of the Council who were also members of one or more boards of the foreign-directed railways operating in the Ottoman Empire might be extended. The above list is sufficient proof, however, that the railways themselves realized the advantage of possessing representation in the Council of the Public Debt Administration. To make the interests of the railways those of the Public Debt Council was the surest means of guaranteeing the necessary coöperation.[42]

During the years following 1888 several instances can be cited in which the Council was solicitous of the interests of the railroads. One of the most frequent complaints was that the Government had not proceeded to auctioning the tithes in the districts where they were pledged as kilometric guarantees. Thus, in December, 1894, the Council received a letter from the director-general of the Salonica-Monastir railway and the Anatolian line, Dr. von Kühlmann, in which he complained that "the greatest part of the tithes assigned to the kilometric guarantee has not been auctioned." He begged the Council "to intervene at the Imperial Treasury in order that the latter may fulfill the conditions of the

[42] *Annual Reports of the Anatolian and Bagdad Railway Companies, passim,* and *Procès-Verbaux, passim.*

conventions." The Council, "heedful of its own responsibility in the complete execution of the conventions and of protecting the interests in question, promises to study the matter."

In December, 1895, however, the same companies together with the Smyrna - Cassaba and Salonica - Constantinople lines, the *Deutsche Bank* and the Ottoman Bank, again protested to the Council against the infraction of the conventions by local government authorities. The Council recognized the legitimate basis of the protests, and complained to the Government.

On October 15, 1896, the above-named railroads dispatched a letter asking that the Council should retain provisionally the proceeds of the tithes over which there was litigation between the Government and the railroads, a request which was granted. On June 3, 1897, Dr. Lindau, the German delegate, made a strong speech in the meeting of the Council in which he agreed with the numerous complaints of the railroad companies, and thought the Council should take some action to decrease the accounts in arrears. On June 7, 1900, letters were received from the directors of the Salonica-Constantinople and Smyrna-Cassaba lines, concerning the tithes of certain villages which had been transferred by the Government to the account of the *Evkaf,* the Government Ministry of Religious Foundations. A solution was suggested by the railway companies; the Council, "agreeing with the opinion of the railroad companies, and appreciating their concern in this matter, begs the Imperial Government to take into consideration the rights of these companies, and the different interests involved.[43]

A situation which arose during the summer of 1901 illustrates perfectly the advantage to the railroads of having representation in the Public Debt Council. Three railroad companies, the Smyrna-Cassaba, the Salonica-Constantinople, and the Damascus-Hama lines, had made earnest requests both to the Council and to the Government that the balance due on guarantees for the year 1900 be paid before their annual meetings. There was also a question which concerned the Council as the representative of the holders of the Government's securities: an unpaid balance due the Council from the customs. The Minister of Finance informed the Coun-

---

[43] *Procès-Verbaux,* December, 1894, December, 1895, October 15, 1896. June 3, 1897, and June 7, 1900.

cil of the Government's inability, due to extraordinary expenses, to meet these demands on time. He requested the Council, therefore, to complete the sums due the railways, and guaranteed that the Council would be reimbursed out of surpluses from other pledged revenues.

At this point Commandant Berger explained how the Finance Minister came to make these proposals. The financial condition of the Treasury was extremely difficult. The Public Debt Council and the interested railways "were going to be obliged to employ diplomatic methods, if, after a collective representation to the Minister of Finance, the claims of all the interested parties were not satisfied." In an interview with this minister, the French delegate, in his capacity as member of the Council, emphasized the necessity of at least meeting the unpaid balance of drafts on the customs. This, the minister agreed to do; Commandant Berger, still in his capacity as member of the Council, promised the minister to do what was possible to persuade his colleagues to accede to the Government's other request concerning the arrears due the railroads.

In deliberating on the question, the Council decided that the income from the assigned revenues during the remainder of the year would be sufficient to meet the balances due the Smyrna-Cassaba and the Damascus lines. It decided to accede to the Treasury's request thus far; there would be insufficient remainder, however, to warrant the Council's meeting the arrears due the Salonica-Constantinople company. But this possibility had been foreseen by Commandant Berger, and he had obtained the promise from the Minister of Finance, confirmed by the Imperial Commissioner to the Debt Council, that the tithes from two additional *sandjaks,* Damascus and St. Jean d'Acre, for the following year, would be endorsed to the order of the Council. If the necessary *iradé* to effect this endorsement were forthcoming before the annual meeting of the Salonica-Constantinople railroad, the Council would meet the arrears due this company. But the Financial Commission, in spite of the confirmation given the figures of the Council concerning the arrears, contested their accuracy, and refused to accede to the requests of the Ministers of Finance and Public Works. Commandant Berger, this time in his capacity as president of the Salonica-Constantinople company, pursued the question by several interviews with the above-named ministers. During the course of one interview, when the position of the Imperial Financial Commission was recognized as final, the Finance Minister suggested the exchange of certain irrecoverable vouchers for tithes of the year 1900 against an equal number of recoverable vouchers for the following year.

Finally, in a meeting of the Council on July 29, the date of the annual meeting of the Salonica-Constantinople company, the president of the Council, Mr. (later Sir Henry) Babington-Smith, recommended that the Council accept the proposal of the Minister of Finance. The Sultan himself had signified, both to the Debt Council and to the French and German Ambassadors, the authenticity of the proposed exchange of vouchers, and the Council met on time the arrears due the Salonica-Constantinople company. The mention of the French and German Ambassadors in the minutes of the Council meetings, the energetic manner in which Commandant Berger, as member of the Council, was able to keep that body *au courant* concerning his negotiations, as president of the company, with the imperial ministers, show the usefulness of a board president who also sat as a member of the Council. The intransigence of the Imperial Financial Commission manifested the repugnance of a part of the Government to alienate future revenues as railway pledges.[44]

When their troubles were brought to the attention of the Council, Commandant Berger always showed himself capable of defending the interests of the railways with which he was connected. In August, 1903, the Imperial Commissioner presented an order from the Grand Vizier to the Minister of Finance stating the substance of an *iradé* directing that the tithes of the *sandjaks* of Damascus, Acre, and Hama should be assigned as guarantee for the Rayak-Hama section of the Damascus-Hama line, "in conformity with the consideration given this subject by the Finance Ministry and Commandant Berger." But the subsequent explanation of the arrangement made to the Council by the Imperial Commissioner was different from the interpretation of Commandant Berger. The French delegate "asks for the floor in order to declare that the Government is wrong in representing him as having consented to the proposal that the charges of the

[44] *Ibid.*, June, July, and August, 1901.

Damascus-Hama railway be insured this year by means of the tithes of only three *sandjaks*. In the name of the Damascus-Hama railway company, he protests against this interpretation of his requests and affirms that he has always claimed and still claims the tithes of the four *sandjaks* assigned by the convention. . . ." In the Government's opinion, the tithes of the three *sandjaks* were more than sufficient to meet the charges for guarantees.[45]

In the German delegate, Dr. Testa, the German-directed railways in Turkey possessed as ardent a defender as did the French-directed lines in Commandant Berger. In the Council's meeting of January 30, 1905, the Imperial Commissioner presented the observations of the Finance Ministry on the incorporation into the imperial domains of a large farm in a region where the tithes were assigned as guarantee to the Anatolian railway. The Department of the Civil List had claimed from the Council the restitution of certain sums which had been paid by the tithe gatherers from the district in question. The Council countered with the demand that a new pledge of similar proportions be handed over by the Government to replace the tithes from the farm recently incorporated into the imperial domains. The Ministry of Finance responded that inasmuch as the tithes of this region had always produced a surplus, there was no cause to assign other pledges. At this point in the remarks of the Imperial Commissioner, Dr. Testa "took the floor in order to declare that the reason invoked by the Government for refusing the compensation destined to make up the loss to the Anatolian railway company . . . will not be admitted by the Council either in fact or in law." He proceeded to elaborate this argument, with the result that "the Council, fully in accord with Dr. Testa on this point, makes the most express reserves to the position of the Government, and asks the Imperial Commissioner to bring them to the attention of the Minister of Finance."

On March 23, 1905, M. de Janko, the Austrian delegate and representative of the Tithes Section of the Public Debt Administration in the meetings of the railway conference, informed the Council that the claims of the Anatolian railway and similar claims of the Smyrna-Cassaba line had been considered at a recent meeting. The representatives of the railways repeated their argu-

---

45 *Ibid.*, August 6, 1903.

ment of being unable to accept any diminution of the pledges, no matter how small it might be, and "renewed, in this connection, the just observations made by Dr. Testa in the meeting of January 30." With a zealous defender of their rights in the Council itself, and another member acting as *liaison* between the Council and the conference of the railway companies, the latter were assured that their claims would be supported by a body enjoying the greatest influence and thoroughly in touch with the smallest details. Commandant Berger himself was president of the railway conference![46]

Mention has already been made of the collision between the Government, the Council, and the railway companies and banks, which occurred during the summer and fall of 1905. The occasion was the Government's desire to make a change in the system of collecting the tithes in some of the Anatolian provinces. The decision of the Grand Vizier to proceed to make the desired change came as the result of an examination of the budget for the following year, and after the new system had been tried out in certain sections of Macedonia.

The first clash arose in July, when the Council was notified that the Ministry of Finance had transmitted to the governors and officials of the Anatolian provinces concerned the necessary administrative orders for the change. The president of the Council, Mr. (later Sir Adam) Block, considered this action of the Finance Ministry as contradicting the contents of a dispatch of July 1 from the Imperial Commissioner to the effect that

> the system of collecting the tithes on the basis of the average of five years, to be applied this year in the provincial capitals of the three European *vilayets,* having been provisionally executed as an experiment, can have no infiuence on the basis of the system of collection [existing elsewhere], and, as a consequence, in case of its subsequent extension, deliberations thereon will take place in accordance with the conventions

with the railways and banks.

The fears of the president of the Council were quieted, however, after an interview with the Grand Vizier, Ferid Pasha, in which Mr. Block was joined by M. Deffes, director-general of the

[46] *Ibid.,* January 30, 1905, and March 23, 1905.

Ottoman Bank, Commandant Berger, representing the Smyrna-Cassaba and Salonica-Constantinople railways, and M. Huguenin, representing the Anatolian, Bagdad, and Salonica-Monastir railways. To the observations of these gentlemen the Grand Vizier responded that "the action of the Finance Ministry was premature and that the extension of the new system in Asia Minor could not take place before next year, even if the Government, after the experiment actually in progress in Macedonia, should decide to proceed to this extension."

This much of the incident is related to the Council in its meeting of July 24, 1905, during the course of which Commandant Berger "as president of the railway conference, declares that that assembly has charged him to thank the Council for its intervention with the public powers, and the efforts it is still making to have the conventions respected." There is something of comedy in the minutes of the meeting where it is stated that "the Council [composed almost entirely of persons directly interested in the organizations in whose behalf he had acted] unanimously approves of the actions of its president and thanks him for them."

The observations of the Council on this question had been submitted to the Finance Ministry, which had brought them to the attention of the Imperial Financial Commission. The opinion of the senior member of this Commission was that "the only object of the conventions . . . is to make it impossible for the income from the tithes of the designated localities to be deviated from their assignments, and to insure their payment to the agencies of the Public Debt . . ." The Government itself had the right to determine the method of taxation, and its administration. Neither the Public Debt Administration nor any of the interested banks or railways was admitted as possessing the right "to consider this [new] system of collection as not conforming to the provisions of the conventions." The Council made most express reservations on this interpretation.

In the Council records of October 16 the story of the incident is brought up to that date. Commandant Berger read into the minutes a voluminous defence of the railways' interests which he had uttered at a meeting of the railway conference. On this occasion he was acting, of course, as president of the boards of the railways which he represented in the conference. He had been asked by the conference to communicate his remarks to the Debt Council; but the members thereof (of whom Commandant Berger was one) reserved their right "to bring the facts and arguments contained in Commandant Berger's exposé, as well as the memorandum prepared on this subject by the President of the Public Debt Council [Mr. Block], to the attention of their respective embassies." After reading to the Council his exposé of the situation, Commandant Berger asked his colleagues to consider the declarations of the railway conference.

He did this on the double ground that

> as delegate to the Council of the Public Debt, he must have a particular interest in the credit of the Empire, which concerns the French bondholders to such a large extent, at the same time that, as president at Constantinople of the boards of three railways, he cannot remain indifferent to the danger which menaces the considerable capital invested in the industries of Turkey by the savings of all countries.

Dr. Testa, the German delegate, approved without reserve the explanation and observations of his French colleague. He was of the opinion that a difficult situation would be created if the Government persisted in its contentions. "As German delegate to the Public Debt Council, and as president, at Constantinople, of the Anatolia, Bagdad, and Salonica-Constantinople railways, he was not afraid to state, in asking Said Bey [the Imperial Commissioner] to note his words, that the Government's thesis, when it is known in Berlin, will produce the most disagreeable impression. . . ." The British delegate and president of the Council, Mr. Block, also shared the opinion expressed by Commandant Berger. With Dr. Testa and Commandant Berger, Mr. Block "feared that the permanent application of the financial experiments of the Government, without previous agreement [with the banks and railways], would produce a painful repercussion in Europe."

The explanations of the Imperial Commissioner did not diminish the opposition of the Council. Mr. Block disagreed with Said Bey's contention that the "Council, whose rôle is limited to the collection [of the revenues], has no right to protest against the exercise of the Government's prerogatives" to introduce changes into the tithes system. According to Mr. Block, the Council's "rôle is not limited to a simple collection; it has a share in the management of the tithes through its agents, who are part of the local commissions in which the auctions and other operations relating to this tax are decided. The Council even contends that it is not only a right but also a duty for it to place the Government on guard against the difficulties which this question will raise, for its president has signed the conventions which are now the object of the debate." It is perhaps unnecessary to add that Commandant Berger upheld this argument. He added: "If the bearers of the railway and other bonds were injured by the application of the new tithe régime, they would have the right to appeal to the Administration, which, as mandatary of their interests, would, by weakness or inertia, have compromised them."

But in this meeting the Council did nothing more than renew the reserves which it had already formulated. It seems that the policy of the Government to extend the new system to the Anatolian provinces had been postponed. In a meeting of November 4, 1907, the Council was informed, however, of an intended extension of the new system of collection to the European provinces. Inasmuch as the districts involved did not contribute to the pledges administered by the Public Debt, the Council limited itself to receiving the notification of the Imperial Commissioner. But "the Council hopes that the Government will not proceed to the general extension of the system . . . even in case the results of the new attempt are satisfactory. The preceding experiences seem to the Council so enlightening that even in the face of the most favorable forecasts, these new results could not weaken them." [47]

[47] *Ibid.*, July 24, October 16, and November 4, 1905. The question of abolishing the ceded revenues and modifying their administration was discussed in the meetings of the 1881 Commission. When the pertinent article of the draft settlement was being debated the foreign representatives desired to qualify seriously this right of the Government. Among the qualifications desired were: restriction of the Government's sphere of action to certain of the ceded revenues; previous agreement with the Council, its consent being dependent upon unanimity; and previous substitution of a revenue of similar proportions for the tax which the Government proposed to suppress. Under pressure of the Imperial Commissioners the final wording of this section of the Decree of Mouharrem (Article IX, Section 8) was: "If the Government desires to suppress the tithes, the fishing tax, or the spirits tax, . . . it shall have the right to do so, on condition that the suppressed taxes be replaced by other revenue of equal magnitude, and with the consent of an absolute majority of the Council . . ." *Procès-Verbaux et Annexes de la Commission de 1881*, pp. 117, 121-24.

While the question of modifying the revenues ceded to the Council is con-

In relating these illustrative incidents it has not been considered necessary to inquire into the justification of the policy of the Council, nor into the validity of the Government's contentions. The purpose has been rather to present a number of instances in which the policy of the Council coincided with the interests of foreign financiers.

The statement has been made that "the Public Debt Administration controlled Ottoman financial policy and exercised its control in the interests of European bankers and investors." [48] It seems that the instances appearing above bear out this statement; the opposition of the Council in 1905 to the desire of the Government to change the basis of collecting the tithes is an excellent example of the manner in which this control was exercised. To show this the more fully, further details of this incident may well be presented.

It will be recalled that the system of collecting the tithes was open to grave abuses. No doubt great improvement had been accomplished in this connection since the uncontrolled corruption prior to the days of the Public Debt Administration. Yet even as late as 1905 the Government itself realized the grave objections and difficulties which were present. In an effort to remedy the situation, the Government proposed to introduce a different system.

For many years there had been followed the system of farming the tithes, that is, leasing their collection to a tithe farmer, when the price offered was equal to or higher than the price of the preceding year. This was the system which had been in effect when most of the railway contracts were signed. In the case, however, of a bid being lower than that realized the preceding year, the tithes were collected in kind, gathered into warehouses, and dis-

---

nected only by analogy with that of changing the method of administration of tithes assigned as kilometric guarantees and for the service of loans, the debates in the 1881 Commission anticipated the difficulty which would be encountered should the Government elect to embark on such a course. The opposition of foreign interests, together with the partisanship of the Council in the dispute with the Government in 1905, agree closely with the points raised by the Government in the debates of the 1881 Commission. The actually static quality of contracts between the Government and foreign interests (in spite of clauses providing for alteration) was a serious hindrance to any attempt of the Government to bring its administrative methods into line with modern principles of government.

[48] Earle, *op. cit.*, p. 11.

posed of when a favorable price was obtainable. The railroad companies had consented to this type of administration in the cases where farming was inconvenient or impossible. The Government proposed to abolish the collection of this tax by either of the above methods, substituting therefor a collection in cash by the agents of the Treasury, on the basis of the annual average for the five preceding years.

In desiring the introduction of the latter method, there seems no reason to believe that the Government was motivated by a desire other than to correct inherent abuses. Certainly it seems impossible to presume that there was any thought of disengaging itself from the obligations assumed under the conventions with the railway companies and the Public Debt Administration. The Government felt that its obligation was discharged in maintaining the pledged revenues intact, in keeping them from being alienated to other destinations, and in permitting the income therefrom to be paid over to the companies. It did not admit the right of any outside agency to dictate the type of administration that should be followed in the collection of its revenues. If, in its opinion, the obligations assumed under the conventions could be just as effectively discharged under a different system of administration, it had a sovereign right to introduce that system.

To these contentions the Public Debt Administration and the railroad companies and banks interposed strenuous objections. The basis upon which the conventions had been concluded was that the agents of the Public Debt Administration should intervene officially in the farming of the revenues, should receive the vouchers signed by the Treasury officials, and should realize on these vouchers the sums necessary for the payment of the pledges to the concessionaires. To introduce a system where the tax was dischargeable directly by the taxpayer and in cash destroyed the nature of the tax entirely. This would deprive the Public Debt's agents of their functions under the conventions. The whole basis of the argument was that the contracts were being modified by the unilateral action of the Government, without having reached a previous agreement with the other two parties. Such a situation, the Council contended, had been envisaged in the conventions themselves, and the Government in deciding to introduce the new system was acting beyond its rights.

To analyze either of the points of view sketched above or to determine which of them is the better founded in law is unnecessary.[49] From the European point of view it is obvious that the nature of the conventions was altered. On the other hand, some validity may be attributed to the Government's contention. Also, from the standpoint of results obtained (the new system had already been tried out in certain districts of the European provinces with results which, in the opinion of the Debt Administration, were disastrous), it may be admitted that the Public Debt Council was in a better position than the Government to judge whether or not the interests of the railroads and the banks were injured. But these observations avoid the crux of the matter. The important fact is that a Government policy, conceived in the interests of the Government and the country, and in its opinion causing no injury to the rights of organizations established within its territory, was definitely sidetracked by the opposition of the Public Debt Council as the agent of the interested parties. It may be contended that the provisions which the Government considered obnoxious could have been removed by arriving at a previous agreement with the other parties. This may be admitted in theory, but in practice the Government had experienced many instances where it was necessary to obtain the consent of more than one party to a contract. In every case this had been accomplished only with the greatest difficulty, after long and tedious negotiations, and not infrequently with some loss of prestige and *amour-propre*. The negotiations between the Imperial Government and the European powers for a revision of the customs treaties, obtaining the powers' consent to raise import tariffs from eight to eleven percent, were started

[49] They are summarized here from extended arguments appearing in the Council minutes. The Council was extremely zealous in defending its point of view. Voluminous briefs, one dealing with the legal nature of the situation, and another with the economic side of the case, were drawn up for presentation to the interested parties, the foreign embassies, and the Ottoman Government. It is impossible to determine the real reason which forced the Government to postpone the introduction of the *"système forfaitaire."* The Sublime Porte was engaged at this time in dealing with Europe concerning the increase in customs duties, another point intimately related to the rights of the Public Debt Council, and connected at the same time with the larger political question of Macedonian reform. It is not impossible that the Government, in the face of delicate negotiations of a more important character than the question of administration of the tithes, felt it would be better to realize one of these projects rather than run the risk of losing everything as a result of the protracted and unyielding attitude of Europe.

in the 1880's and concluded in 1907. The experiences of the Government in endeavoring to extend the application of the stamp tax and income tax laws to foreign residents were almost as long drawn out. The support which foreign embassies brought to railway companies and financial establishments during this period would undoubtedly have been persistent and effective if the Government had undertaken to arrive at a "previous agreement" with the interested parties. The prolongation of such negotiations would have led either to the abandonment of the Government's policy, or to permission to alter the contracts in exchange for further economic concessions, which would have still deeper intrenched foreign interests in Turkey. In any event, the influence of the Public Debt Council was too formidable to be overcome; the attempt of the Government was defeated, and the rights of foreign companies were upheld.

Now mention should be made of a transformation in the Council's conception of its functions as third party to the conventions between the Government, banks, and railway companies. Reference has been made to an example which occurred in 1893, when the Council considered its obligation discharged by "informing the third party of the modification" which the Government had made in a province where certain revenues were pledged to a third party; this notification was made "without judging whether these changes are of a nature to prejudice" the third party; the Public Debt "will only conform to the solution which results" from negotiations between the Government and the other interested party "without taking part in the debates."

Contrast this with the idea expressed in 1899: ". . . the principal obligation imposed [on the Debt Council] consists in doing everything in its power to collect the assigned tithes." Or compare the conception of its duties as defined in 1893 with this statement made in 1905: the Council "has the right and the duty to see that the contracts in question are rigorously respected." Surely the statement of the alternate president of the Council in July, 1905, "if the bearers of the bonds were injured . . ., they would have the right to appeal to the Administration which, as mandatary of their interests, would, by weakness or inertia, have compromised them," is a different conception from the statement of 1893 mentioned above![50]

---

[50] *Supra*, pp. 130-1.

AID FOR THE OTTOMAN GOVERNMENT

Besides the functions of the Council under the Decree of Mouharrem, and its position as a third party to railroad contracts, its importance in the Turkish Empire was enhanced by a simultaneous extension of this second function to include contracts for new state loans negotiated between the Government and certain foreign banking houses. This duty of the Council has been already implied when, in instances cited, reference has been made to railway companies *and* banks. The principle was the same: in the same way that the president of the Council would become a party to a contract between a railway company and the Government to collect the income from the revenues assigned as pledges for a kilometric guarantee, he would assume a similar obligation when the Government desired to float a new loan, and designated the P. D. A. to collect the revenues assigned to meet the interest and sinking fund. This duty of the Council to the banks was as important as its obligation to the several railway companies. In fact, the close relationship between railroad construction and government financing, which characterized the German railroad enterprises in Turkey, was due almost entirely to the Public Debt. Its position as mandatary for the Anatolian Railway Company, in collecting the tithes of the districts through which the railway passed, was considerably enlarged when, under the Bagdad concession of March 5, 1903, it accepted a somewhat similar obligation, on the basis of which 11,000 francs of the 15,500 francs kilometric guarantee took the form of an annuity to be capitalized as a four percent state loan.[51]

[51] Caillard, *loc. cit.;* Earle, *op. cit.*, Chapter IV. The government loans for which the Council agreed to collect the assigned pledges were the following: five per cent. 1888 for 60,000,000 francs with the Deutsche Bank, converted to four per cent. in 1903; four per cent. 1890 for 113,625,000 francs (Osmanié) with the Ottoman Bank; five per cent. 1896 for 74,380,000 francs with the Ottoman Bank; four per cent. 1903 for 54,000,000 francs (Bagdad, first series) with the Deutsche Bank; four per cent. 1901-1905 for 120,606,000 francs with the Ottoman Bank; four per cent. 1905 for 60,000,000 francs (armaments) with the Deutsche Bank; four per cent. 1909 for 108,000,000 francs (Bagdad, second series) with the Deutsche Bank syndicate; four per cent. 1909 for 119,000,000 francs (Bagdad, third series) with the same syndicate; four per cent. 1908 for 108,355,000 francs with the Ottoman Bank; five and one-half per cent. 1913 for 35,000,000 francs (docks and arsenals) with the National Bank of Turkey; five per cent. 1914 for 775,000,000 francs with a French railroad syndicate. The total nominal capital of this series of loans is 1,627,966,000 francs, or Ltqs. 81,398,300. Ravndal, G. B., *Turkey, A Commercial and Industrial Handbook*, United States Government Report (De-

While the opinion of the Council as to its function under these various contracts is, in general, that already set forth, the reader will be interested in the further quotations referring to specific loans. When the contract for the 1896 loan was discussed in the Council, the following statement was included in the minutes: ". . . the intervention of the Council in the present contract . . . has as its object to lend to the Imperial Government . . . assistance limited to the mandate of control, collection, and division of the assigned revenues to the proper destination." In 1901, when the loan of that year was negotiated, "the Council declares that its mandate will be limited to the conditions announced for the administration of the 1896 loan."[52]

An interesting example of the manner in which the Council interpreted these functions is afforded by an incident in 1911 and 1912 concerning the 1888-1903 loan from the *Deutsche Bank*, known as the "fisheries" loan. The reason for its name is that the revenue to meet the interest and sinking fund was largely drawn from the taxes on the fishing industry in those parts of the Empire where this revenue was not already ceded to the Council by the Decree of Mouharrem. In December, 1911, considerable difficulty was experienced in the collection of certain supplementary portions of this general tax in the province of Bagdad. The Council of State decided to abolish these taxes. Inasmuch as they formed part of the pledge to the *Deutsche Bank* for this loan, their suppression diminished to this extent the returns from this tax in the province of Bagdad. On being informed of the action, the *Deutsche Bank* uttered a denial of the right of the Government to proceed to this suppression without a previous agreement with the Public Debt and itself. But the Council, in examining this letter, discovered that the Bank did not say whether it would bring its claim to the attention of the Government, or whether it counted on the Public Debt to undertake the protest. The president, Sir Adam Block, thought in the second case "the Council has no right to intervene. Charged with the execution of certain contractual clauses, it can only see that no harm is done to them, and, in case of transgression, notify the interested party of this fact. . . ." The Council agreed with its

partment of Commerce, Trade Promotion Series, Number 28) (Washington, 1926), p. 214.

[52] *Procès-Verbaux*, March 20, 1896 and December 5, 1901.

president's view, and persisted in its opinion when the interests of the *Deutsche Bank* were taken up by Mr. Gunther, director general of the Bagdad railway. He maintained that "it is incumbent solely upon the Public Debt to initiate the presentation to the Government of the proposals intended to solve the differences concerning the changes to be introduced into the loan contracts."

Apparently there was a clear difference of opinion concerning the function of the Public Debt Council. But, inasmuch as the *Deutsche Bank* had suggested a means of overcoming the difficulty with which the Council was in accord, "the president does not believe it necessary to insist on this divergence of opinion, . . . and proposes that the solution advanced by the *Deutsche Bank* be recommended to the Minister of Finance." By the aid of the German delegate, Herr Pritsch, who explained the point of view of the *Deutsche Bank,* and by the latter's instructions to the management of the Anatolian Railway to support the steps taken by the Council, the matter was settled to the satisfaction of both the *Deutsche Bank* and the Council. But the Council, in ultimately acceding to the request of the *Deutsche Bank,* tacitly admitted the joint interest involved.[53]

There is another function which the Public Debt Council undertook to perform. We have seen how the Council's importance was increased by the addition of new duties under railway contracts and government loans. The acceptance of these new obligations resulted from the requirements which foreign promoters considered necessary for the safety of their money. Although the Council may have acted under official government instigation, it can hardly be conceived that the heavy drains on the Treasury, and the administration of the assignments by the Public Debt, would have occurred had the original stimulus not arrived from some outside source. But in the collection of certain revenues at the direct request of the Government, the latter acted entirely on its own initiative. Thus it happened that in 1888 the Council was requested to collect the surtax of one and one-half percent on the silk and tobacco tithes for the account of the Government, to be handed over to the Agricultural Bank and the Ministry of

---

[53] *Ibid.,* December 21, 1911, January 18, February 29, March 28, and April 15, 1912.

Public Instruction. In 1890 the collection of the valonia (acorns used in tanning) and opium tithes was requested of the P. D. A. Beginning with 1898, a new one-half percent surtax was introduced by the Government on all tithes assigned as pledges for kilometric guarantees, and for service on the 1890 and 1896 loans. The collection of this surtax was likewise confided to the P. D. A. Although this further extension of the Council's functions is a testimony of the Government's opinion of the integrity and usefulness of the Debt Administration, the importance of the revenues collected under this heading cannot be compared with those under the railway and loan contracts.

Again, in April, 1907, a considerable extension of the Council's functions resulted from the conclusion of a new customs convention with the European powers. The powers delegated to the Council the duty of collecting the three percent customs surtax, which was the main object of the new treaties. But the importance of this new duty is so great as to call for discussion in a later chapter.[54]

Confining our attention for the present to the revenues administered under the Decree of Mouharrem, those administered by the Council as third party to railroad and loan contracts, and finally those administered for the Government's account, we may inquire what portion of the revenues of the Ottoman Empire, in the aggregate, came under the control of the Public Debt Administration. To answer this query accurately, we should have at our disposal exact figures for the total revenues. These are practically impossible to obtain. We have seen in what chaotic condition the finances were prior to 1882, and since that date the budgets of the Empire have been little more reliable than before. But the revenue for 1874-5 was officially estimated at twenty-two million pounds (Turkish). When the autocratic government of Abdul Hamid was overthrown in 1908 and the Young Turks took over the reins, a sincere attempt was made to draw up a budget which would accurately reflect conditions. Djavid Bey's budget for 1910-11 was just under twenty-six million pounds (Turkish). Striking an average of these two figures we arrive at a figure which, albeit approximate, will nevertheless allow a comparison. Against the average of twenty-four million pounds we can com-

[54] *Infra*, Chapter VII.

pare the revenues under the control of the Debt Administration. Its reports show that, for the year 1898, the total revenues of the Administration accruing to it under the Decree of Mouharrem were two and a quarter million pounds (Turkish); it also collected Ltqs. 545,000 to be applied to government loans outside the Decree, Ltqs. 760,000 to apply to railroad guarantees, and Ltqs. 75,000 for the Government's account. The total of these revenues is Ltqs. 5,630,000, representing 23.46 percent of the total estimated average revenue of twenty-four million pounds. For the period 1882-1898 the percent would probably be somewhat lower; but, after 1898, owing to the stimulus given to railroad construction and also to the rôle of the Public Debt in government financing, a larger percentage of the Empire's revenue was collected by the P. D. A. On that basis, to say that the Council controlled a quarter of the Turkish revenue may be accepted as approximately accurate.[55]

But considerably more significant than the percentage of the revenues controlled by the Council, is the fact that the liquid resources of the country were in its hands. We have seen how the indirect taxes were ceded to its control by the Decree of Mouharrem; how the development of rail communication brought the tithes of the districts traversed by the railways under its control; how subsequent government loans increased the proportion of the Empire's tithes which it administered; and how certain revenues were collected for the Government's account.

If Turkey tried to increase her revenues by stimulating sources not already pledged to foreign interests, she found herself faced with difficulties on all sides. Her right to increase import duties could be exercised only with the consent of the European powers. If she attempted to extend the application of a new stamp law or of the income tax, she met the opposition of the same countries, who claimed exemption for their nationals under the Capitulations, or qualified their consent by demanding the modification of legislation which was deemed injurious to foreign commercial or financial interests. The tax on realty and the military exoneration tax were incapable of any substantial increases. The income from posts and telegraphs, the only important monopoly unpledged, could be

[55] Du Velay, *op. cit.*, pp. 317-18; Caillard, *loc. cit.*; *Comptes Rendus, passim*; *Rapports Annuels, passim.*

improved only with difficulty, in a country where a largely agricultural population has its interests centered in local affairs. The foreign creditors of Turkey enjoyed the best revenues of the country, and those most capable of improvement.

In point of fact, the credit of the Empire rested largely on the prestige of the Public Debt Council. As in the days prior to 1882, European confidence rested on the Ottoman Bank, so in latter years, foreign investors placed their confidence in the Administration of the Public Debt as a European-controlled institution, rather than in the Government. However ready to use the Public Debt as an agency to build up the country, the Government itself possessed potential qualities capable of improvement under disinterested stimulus. There was stimulus indeed, but hardly disinterested. The railway and financial projects, in behalf of which such valiant support was exerted by the Council, were primarily business enterprises, having the development of the country for the native population only as a secondary motive.

The only substantial difference between the foreign money which went into Turkey before 1875 and that which followed the institution of the Administration of the Public Debt is in the security which the funds invested during the latter period possessed. The motive in the two instances was the same: profit for the promoters. The credit of the Empire undoubtedly profited from the prestige of the Public Debt; likewise the security of foreign capital was increased, risks reduced, and profits enhanced. So important was the development of the Council's control of resources outside the Decree of Mouharrem that, for the year 1898, revenues collected under this heading surpassed by over a million pounds the revenues collected by virture of its functions under the Decree. According to a recapitulation on March 1, 1923, "Hors Décret" loans administered by the Council amounted to over 56 million pounds (Turkish), while Decree Loans were less than this figure by over ten million pounds. The Ottoman Government, on the other hand, administered a total of but twenty-five million pounds.[56]

From a practical viewpoint, the Administration of the Public Debt was more important as a factor in the development of the country by foreign capital than as the safeguard of the remnants

[56] Ravndal, *op. cit.*, p. 214.

salvaged from the speculative period prior to its institution. It had grown from an organization set up primarily to watch over the interests of the bearers of pre-Decree government bonds into the watch dog of contemporary foreign capital intent on the economic exploitation of the country. The opening-up of the Ottoman Empire to Europe and the world was accompanied by the realization of profits whose production was assured by the interposition of the Public Debt Council.

Chapter VII

FUNCTIONING FOR OFFICIAL EUROPE

During its first twenty years the Public Debt had steadily consolidated its position as the most important financial organism in the Empire. But in 1907 the Debt received a more important function to discharge, the semi-official duty of collecting, as agent of the European powers, the three percent customs surtax which resulted from the conclusion of a new customs treaty.

Prior to this date the Council had acted in a double rôle as the representative of the bondholders and as a department of the Imperial Government. Both of these activities brought the Debt into supplementary spheres of action. Its position as representative of the bondholders was widened to include the interests of other foreign investors and financiers. As a department of the Government the Council's position was extended to the use of its prestige to obtain better terms for the Porte in borrowing in Europe, and to collect new revenues for its account. Although from the point of view of its status as a department of the Imperial Government the actions of the Council were always official, from the standpoint of foreign organizations its activities were always private. We have seen how the Public Debt worked hand in hand with the railways and banks; what more natural than that it should receive a mandate from their respective governments to discharge the duty of collecting the surtax?

While the addition of this new duty to the functions of the Council came about as the result of a complicated situation, three important factors may be isolated calling for detailed consideration. Those factors are (1) the demand of the European powers for reform in Macedonia; (2) the poverty of the Ottoman Government and its request for an increase in customs tariffs; and (3) the right of the holders of Ottoman Government bonds to the increased revenue resulting from an upward revision of the customs treaties.

Reform in Macedonia

The portion of the Ottoman Empire known as Macedonia was composed of the three *vilayets*, or provinces, of Salonica, Monastir.

and Kossova. The problem of reform in this area dates back to the Treaty of Berlin, in which the Sultan had agreed to the introduction of certain measures designed to improve conditions. The reforms had never been accomplished to the satisfaction of the powers, but no one of them had been willing to put pressure on the Sultan for fear of starting a serious quarrel between Russia and Austria, since both of them claimed special privileges. Therefore, the conditions in these provinces had continued deplorable, due in part to the abuses in the system of tithe collection, in part to the fact that the inhabitants of the territory were a heterogeneous lot, part Moslem, part Christian, all intensely nationalistic and capable of being stirred to fever heat.[1]

Our particular interest goes back no farther than 1902, when the financial situation of the provinces was recognized as one of the most important of the conditions demanding attention. M. Steeg, the French Consul General at Salonica, had for a long time interested himself in the reform projects and in the essential requisites for any satisfactory solution. One of his dispatches to M. Delcassé, dated October 28, 1902, emphasized the difficulty in the administration caused by the system of tithe collection. Most of the tithes were farmed out to influential officials, who, according to the report, abused their power. The tithes were mostly assigned as kilometric guarantees, and were paid to the Public Debt Administration. M. Steeg felt that "a regulation requiring that Administration to collect these revenues in kind would undoubtedly be sufficient to put an end to these intolerable abuses." On December 15, 1902, M. Steeg outlined the reforms which seemed to him essential. He emphasized the necessity of some real financial organization in the provinces, without which "he found it illusory to hope for any improvement whatever." He deemed it necessary that each *vilayet* have a budget, that expenditure and revenue be closely watched by an efficient organization, and that the revenue of the district be expended within the local areas where it originated, in order that these parts of the country might benefit, instead of diverting it to Constantinople for the use of the central Government. He suggested that the P. D. A. and the Ottoman

[1] For a statement of the elements in the Macedonian situation, see Brailsford, H. N., *Macedonia, its races and their future* (London, 1906).

Bank might be useful agencies to put into effect a new financial organization.[2]

The part of M. Steeg's report which referred to the financial reorganization was embodied substantially in the proposals for reform presented by the Russian and Austrian Ambassadors to the Sublime Porte on February 21, 1903:

> In order to insure the regular working of the local administration, a budget of receipts and expenditures shall be drawn up for each *vilayet,* and the revenues of the province, which are to be checked by the Imperial Ottoman Bank, shall be assigned in the first place to the requirements of the local administration, including the payment of the civil and military salaries. The mode of collecting the tithes shall be altered, and the system of farming them out in bulk shall be abolished.[3]

Lord Lansdowne, British Secretary for Foreign Affairs, accepted in principle the Russian and Austrian program on February 17, 1903, and notified Sir Nicholas O'Connor, the British Ambassador, to support its presentation to the Porte. The French and Italian Ambassadors likewise supported the program, and because of this almost united front of the great powers, the Imperial Government accepted the note as the basis of Macedonian reforms.[4]

During the next two years, however, the attention of the Ottoman Government and of the powers was devoted to another point of the Austrian and Russian program, namely, the reorganization of the *gendarmeric.* It was not until early in 1905 that an *aide-mémoire* from the Russian and Austrian Ambassadors called the attention of the Sublime Porte to the financial reorganization. Under this pressure the Government on March 7, 1905, came to an agreement with the Imperial Ottoman Bank concerning the method of receiving the tithes and paying the expenses of the three *vilayets.*[5] The other powers, thus confronted with a *fait accompli*

---

2 *Livre Jaune, Affaires de Macedoine* (1902) Dispatches 32 and 48.

3 *Parliamentary Papers,* No. Cmd. 1467 (1903) Dispatch 7.

4 *Ibid.,* Dispatches 1, 5, 6 and 63.

5 *Ibid.,* No. Cmd. 2759 (1906) Dispatch 4. This partial adhesion of the Porte to the demands of Russia and Austria was considered by Sir Edward Grey as placing the greatest amount of influence concerning Macedonian financial reorganization in the hands of these two powers. He was pleased to find that they did not contest the right of the other powers to be represented in this reorganization, a right which Great Britain had reserved in her approval of the Murszteg Program of February 21, 1903. See *supra.*

as far as the finances of the provinces were concerned, considered this arrangement as unsatisfactory. In commenting on it to Lord Lansdowne, Sir Nicholas O'Connor said: ". . . the arrangement eliminates all mention of foreign control, thereby depriving it of the only security or safeguard that its terms will be properly complied with, and leaving its execution entirely to the discretion of the Ottoman authorities."[6] The opinion of the British Ambassador was shared by the governments of the other powers; in a collective note of May 9, 1905, the foreign ambassadors accepted the agreement of March 7 with the Ottoman Bank only on the condition that the four powers other than Austria and Russia (who already had civil agents in Macedonia) should each appoint a financial delegate to confer with the Russian and Austrian civil agents, the financial commission thus formed to have authority "to supervise the execution of the financial reforms . . . and to insure the observance" of the agreement with the Ottoman Bank.[7]

The international financial commission, upon the appointment of which the approval of the powers was contingent, in reality was appointed and started to function only in October, 1905. On July 13, 1905, the Porte refused to accept this qualification of the approval, and, when the powers proceeded to appoint the members of the commission, the Imperial Government refused to recognize these appointments (August 29). When the delegates actually assembled at Uskub in October and began conferences with the civil agents of Russia and Austria, the Porte remonstrated against this infraction of its sovereignty, but to no avail. In the face of the intractable attitude of the Imperial Government, the powers on December 5 proceeded to an international naval demonstration, during the course of which the islands of Mytilene and Lemnos were occupied. On December 16 the Porte finally recognized the international financial commission.[8]

Whatever may have been the authority of this commission, the poverty of the Government and the delay in meeting its obligations under the agreement of March 7 were severe handicaps. Sir Nicholas O'Connor realized the seriousness of the situation, but

[6] *Ibid.*, Dispatch 50, March 8, 1905.
[7] *Ibid.*, Dispatch 162.
[8] *Ibid.*, No. Cmd. 2816 (1906) Dispatches 9 and 49.

did not think the Government would be able to carry out its obligations unless it was able to uncover a new source of revenue. M. Steeg, who had been appointed as French delegate on the commission, notified M. Pichon on April 7, 1907, that a deficit of Ltqs. 40,000 was to be noted at the end of the second financial period, and added that the commission itself was of the opinion that sufficient revenue should be provided to balance the budget. To this extent both Sir Nicholas and M. Steeg were favorable to the proposal to raise the customs duties. But M. Steeg added,

> the Imperial Government seems to consider itself wholly relieved of the financial obligations assumed under the agreement of March, 1905; it considers itself as covered by the declaration, many times repeated, that it will be impossible for it to meet the budgetary deficit of the three provinces as long as the powers will not consent to the collection of the three percent customs surtax.[9]

Turkey Proposes a Tariff Increase

The proposal to raise the customs duties was a new loop in a thread which had been unravelling for years. The limitation on import duties was one of the restrictions of the Capitulations, originally granted to France, but in recent times extended to all the powers that had commercial relations with Turkey. Inasmuch as the Porte had a separate treaty with each power enjoying this privilege, Turkey's right to raise its customs tariffs was dependent on an agreement with each of these powers, permitting its exports to become subject to a higher duty. Most of these agreements were due to expire in the 1880's, and in new conventions their ad valorem basis had been replaced by specific duties.[10] Although

---

[9] *Ibid.*, No. Cmd. 3455 (1908) Dispatch 8; *Livre Jaune, Affaires de Macedoine* (1906-7) cited Dupuis, *op. cit.*, pp. 95-102.

[10] The policy of the Ottoman Government at this time was outlined briefly by Bertram Effendi to the 1881 Commission: (1) Abolition of the export tax of one per cent. ad valorem; (2) Suppression of the transit tax of one per cent. ad valorem; (3) In regard to those imports subject to eight per cent. ad valorem duties, adoption of the following measures: (*a*) Certain articles to be placed on the free list; (*b*) Certain articles to be subject to a tariff of three per cent. ad valorem; (*c*) Maintenance of the then existing scale of eight per cent. for a third category of goods; (*d*) Specific duties, not to exceed twenty per cent., for all other objects imported into the Empire. *Procès-Verbaux et Annexes de la Commission de 1881*, p. 111.

negotiated, these conventions had not been ratified and therefore were not operative. In the absence of other agreements the former treaties remained in force.

The need of money to carry on Macedonian reform being most evident within the district itself, it was Hussein Hilmi Pasha, the Inspector General of the provinces, who suggested to the British and French Consuls General at Salonica on January 24, 1905, that the import duties be raised from eight to eleven percent.[11] The proposal was made in more official form some three weeks later in a memorandum from Musurus Pasha, the Turkish Ambassador in London, to Lord Lansdowne.[12] It appears that this proposition was put forth as a counter-proposal to the Austrian and Russian *aide-mémoire* to the Sublime Porte of January 17, 1905, a reminder which resulted, as we have seen, in the March 7 agreement with the Ottoman Bank. Lord Lansdowne's answer of February 27 was the most important reply which the Ottoman Government received from the identical request concerning customs duties which had been sent to the other powers. In reality it formed the basis for the negotiations which finally culminated in April, 1907, in the signature of the new treaty. Lord Lansdowne's letter had such important bearing on subsequent negotiations that its principal provisions are included here.

The British Secretary for Foreign Affairs said that the British Government would first have to be convinced of the accuracy of the estimates on which had been based the proposal to meet the Macedonian deficit by the desired increase in duties. Moreover, it would have to be satisfied that the Imperial Treasury was receiving as much as might reasonably be expected from the application of the then existing tariff laws. The regulations concerning chemical analysis of imported materials and concerning mining rights would have to be revised. The estimated yield from any increase in duties would probably be insufficient to meet the budget deficit; but

> it seems in any case indispensable that there should be a definite assignment of the proceeds of the increased duties (after payment of the obligatory twenty-five percent to the Administration of the Public Debt) to some competent authority entrusted with the collection and control not only of these

[11] *Parliamentary Papers*, No. Cmd. 2759 (1906) Dispatch 9.
[12] *Ibid.*, Dispatch 25.

> funds but of the local revenues which they are intended to supplement.

Lord Lansdowne added that, inasmuch as sixty percent of the foreign commerce of Turkey was with the British Empire, it was extremely important for British interests to be satisfied concerning the disposal of the surplus from any increase in the customs duties.[13]

The viewpoint of the other European powers toward the proposal of the Ottoman Government was more conciliatory than the attitude of Great Britain. Germany had already signified her consent;[14] Russia and Austria were willing to agree to the increase of tariffs; France would follow in Britain's footsteps; Italy could hardly be expected to hold out when agreement had been reached among the other powers. Although it seemed somewhat easier to meet the demands of these other powers, even here some qualifications were made to a general consent. Austria and Russia likewise agreed that some guarantee was necessary that the revenue from the increased duties would be properly assigned. It is an interesting fact, however, that the representatives of these two powers continued to ask a more conciliatory attitude on Great Britain's part. This was due, no doubt, to the privileged position that their civil agents already occupied in Macedonia. They could afford to pose as friends of the Sultan in the face of extravagant British demands, as long as their position in Macedonia remained secure.[15]

---

13 *Ibid.*, Dispatch 39. Lord (then Sir Edward) Grey, who, as Lord Lansdowne's successor, concluded the negotiations, defends British policy in Macedonia in these words: "Our motive was disinterested . . . Our activity in protesting against Turkish misrule diminished our influence and was therefore adverse to British commercial interests in Turkey . . . Humanitarian feeling in Britain and the persisting sympathy for Christian populations under Turkish rule was so strong that British policy and material interests were overborne by it . . . Not one of the other powers was disinterested; not one of them believed that Britain was disinterested. Each was conscious of some political motive of its own, and they all invented some political motive that was attributed to us." Grey, Viscount, of Fallodon, *Twenty-five Years, 1892-1916* (2 volumes, New York, 1925), Volume I, pp. 166-7.

14 As far back as 1890 Germany had negotiated a new customs convention with Turkey in which the Sublime Porte was recognized as having Germany's permission to increase tariffs without limit, provided agreement to this effect could be reached with the other powers. In the absence of this agreement the 1890 convention never came into force.

15 *Parliamentary Papers*, No. Cmd. 2759 (1906) Dispatches 20 and 38.

It will not be necessary to include here the story of the negotiations concerning the trade and commercial demands of the powers. These were their *quid pro quo,* and even their consent to the increase demanded absolute guarantees. The "competent authority" which Lord Lansdowne considered indispensable was found to exist in the Administration of the Public Debt, and to its particular rôle we now turn our attention.

Although the original proposal concerning the increase in tariffs was made in January, 1905, it was not until a year had passed that serious negotiations were again undertaken. The Turkish Government exchanged a series of notes with Lord Lansdowne and his successor, Sir Edward Grey, but the concessions which the Porte was willing to make fell far short of the necessary demands laid down by Lord Lansdowne on February 27, 1905. Moreover, the Turkish Government may have concluded to make use of the international financial commission, hoping that its presence would alleviate the budgetary difficulties of the three provinces. But the Imperial Government was in continuous financial straits; the local revenues of Macedonia were insufficient to meet expenditures, and the necessary supplements would have to come from Constantinople. The insistence of Sir Nicholas O'Connor on the increasing gravity of the situation stimulated the British Government to a reconsideration of the question, and the Turkish Government was finally brought to the realization that far-reaching concessions were necessary if the desired increases were to be forthcoming. In the end it agreed that the whole of the revenues resulting from the customs revision should be cared for by the Public Debt.

In a note from Sir Edward Grey of January 31, 1906, Sir Nicholas was instructed to determine if the necessary assurances concerning the use of the revenues for the three percent surtax would be undertaken by the Public Debt Council.[16] The British Government, which had originally thought of the international financial commission as the most convenient agent to which should be delegated the duty of discharging this function, finally became convinced that the Debt Council was the only organization really capable of undertaking the task. This change of opinion is made clear by the contents of a dispatch of February 20, 1906, from M. Paul Cambon, French Ambassador in London, to M. Rouvier.

---

[16] *Ibid.*, No. Cmd. 3455 (1908) Dispatch 7.

The French Foreign Minister was informed that one of the conditions of the British Government was

> that an effective control be exercised over the collection and use of the funds coming from the surtax. . . . Nevertheless, it is evident that the financial commission recently constituted in Macedonia possesses neither the power nor the necessary personnel for the requisite inspection of the entire customs administration of Turkey, and, as a result, His Majesty's Government is of the opinion that the collection of the surtax must be confided to the Administration of the Ottoman Public Debt.

In a note of March 8, M. Cambon added: ". . . The procedure proposed by the British Government consists in choosing the Debt as agent charged to insure the collection of the three percent customs surtax . . . according to the conditions demanded by the powers, and to have this project presented to the Sultan by the Debt itself . . ." M. Cambon added his personal opinion that he thought "it would belong to the Administration of the Public Debt to insure the execution of the conditions imposed by the powers for the increase of customs duties." [17]

The British Ambassador presented the attitude of his Government to the Grand Vizier, Ferid Pasha, in an interview on February 20. The Imperial Government did not relish the idea of a foreign organization interfering in the administration of its customs. Ferid Pasha was "clearly opposed to any measure which could have the character of a European control of the customs or the finances of the Empire." He refused to admit that "the coöperation of the Public Debt can be claimed in order to insure the collection of the surtax." He admitted, however, that "the Ottoman Bank, whose collaboration had been so useful in the reorganization of Macedonian finances, could be called to exercise a surveillance over the collection of the customs duties . . ." The opposition of the Grand Vizier was weakened by the insistence of Sir Nicholas on the viewpoint of his Government. On February 26 he reported to Sir Edward Grey that "I informed the Grand Vizier that, in the view of His Majesty's Government, the surveillance by the Public Debt Administration constituted the most effectual means of securing the proper collection of the proposed

---

[17] *Livre Jaune, Affaires de Macedoine* (1906-7) Dispatches 7 and 16.

increase, and that they regarded the establishment of this control as a condition upon which their consent to the surtax will be made dependent." The following day he reported that "the Grand Vizier has expressed his willingness to discuss with the Ottoman Public Debt the claim of that body to control and encash the surtax." [18]

At this point the Debt Council entered into the negotiations. After informing the Grand Vizier on February 26 of the demands of the British Government, Sir Nicholas reported:

> I propose to request Mr. Block to lose no time in presenting their case to the Grand Vizier, and I feel confident that the support given the proposal by the action of His Majesty's Government will contribute very materially to an understanding being arrived at which will afford to the public and to British commerce ample security that the surplus revenues derived from the increased duty will not be misappropriated to purposes other than those for which it is intended, or to objects which are not consonant to British interests.

On February 27 he reported that "I have advised the president, Mr. Block, at once to approach His Highness [the Grand Vizier] on the subject." [19]

On March 1, 1906, the increase in the customs duties was first considered officially by the Council. The president, Mr. Adam Block, built up a strong argument favorable to the Council's right to the care of the revenue. He based his contention on the financial section of the note of October 3, 1880, from the Sublime Porte to the powers, and on Article VIII, paragraph 3, of the Decree of Mouharrem, whereby the Government ceded "the surplus of customs receipts resulting from a modification in the tariffs in the event of a revision of the commercial treaties." Article XVI, paragraph 2, provided that "the Council will have the care of this revenue." Moreover, Article III, paragraph 2, of the Supplementary Decree confirmed the assignment to the Council of all the revenues ceded to the creditors by the Decree of Mouharrem, "including the increases to be obtained in the customs receipts in consequence of the revision of the treaties of commerce and of the modification of the customs tariffs as is provided in the Decree

---

[18] *Ibid.*, Dispatch 8; *Parliamentary Papers*, No. Cmd. 3455 (1908) Dispatches 19 and 22.

[19] *Ibid.*, Dispatches 19 and 22.

of Mouharrem." To these arguments Mr. Block added the conviction of the Council "that the Government is free to dispose of its part of the surplus of the receipts of the Public Debt." But "it is evident that any division of the surplus of the receipts can only be made at the closing of the accounts of all the ceded revenues and after the payment of interest and sinking fund on the Debt is assured." Moreover, "any division of any revenue whatsoever before its entire encashment by the Administration of the Debt will be contrary to the formal dispositions" already mentioned. The president also thought fit to add that "it would be unjust to pretend that the Government can be released from its obligations by an agreement with the Council concerning the value of the twenty-five percent of the surplus of customs receipts to which it was entitled and by payment to the Council of the sum agreed on." [20]

The position of the Debt as developed by Mr. Block was greatly strengthened by the official support given to it. The German and Austrian Ambassadors considered the rights of the Council as "incontestable"; the Russian and French Ambassadors agreed with the Council's contentions, and Sir Nicholas O'Connor "presumed that his Italian colleague would follow with the other powers." In the proposed assumption of this new function by the Council, the French Government saw something more than the Council's legal rights. M. Rouvier, on March 9, forwarded a dispatch to M. Boppe, French chargé d'affaires at Constantinople, in which he told the latter that he had "pointed out to Paul Cambon . . . that if, in order to guarantee the destination of the surtax to Macedonia, the powers think it possible to make the Sultan accept the intervention of the Public Debt in the collection of the customs, nothing would conform more to French interests." [21]

The powers were united in the conditions on which they would consent to the increase. These were made clear to the Sublime Porte in a collective note of May 28, 1906, section two of which concerns itself with the employment in Macedonia of the proceeds of the surtax. The powers demanded an "effective guarantee" to fulfill this provision, a phrase which Sir Edward Grey considered

---

[20] *Procès-Verbal*, March 1, 1906.

[21] *Parliamentary Papers*, No. Cmd. 3455 (1908) Dispatch 24, Sir Nicholas O'Connor to Sir Edward Grey, March 7, 1906; *Livre Jaune, Affaires de Macédoine* (1906-7) Dispatch 17.

as not sufficiently explicit. He would have preferred that the Debt be specifically mentioned in the note, but gave his consent to the actual wording on the condition that by "effective guarantee" the Administration of the Public Debt was meant. The answer of the Ottoman Government was sent on June 21. As far as the customs surtax was concerned, the substance of this answer had been decided on by the Council of Ministers on June 8: "To pay over twenty-five percent of the customs surtax to the Public Debt, on the condition, however, that the collection would be made directly by the agents of the customs service." The Government considered that its obligation to the Debt Council was discharged in turning over to it twenty-five percent of the revenue accruing from the application of the new surtax, inasmuch as under the Supplementary Decree, Article VII, "the surplus of the ceded revenues is to be divided between the Imperial Government and the Public Debt Administration at the rate of seventy-five percent for the former and twenty-five percent for the latter." [22]

Yielding to Europe's Demands

The divergence between the point of view of the Council, which had been transmitted by the Imperial Commissioner to the Government after the meeting of March 1, and the position of the Government itself, as contained in the reply to the collective note of May 28, is striking. On July 2, the British Ambassador said that the proposal of the Government was "absolutely inadmissable." The Council considered the terms of the Government's proposal as "contrary to the provisions of the Decree of Mouharrem and the Supplementary Decree," and decided that "it was impossible

[22] *Parliamentary Papers,* No. Cmd. 3455 (1908) Enclosure in Dispatch 38; dispatch from the Imperial Commissioner contained in *Procès-Verbal,* July 19, 1906. The statement of this natural desire of the Government merely reiterated the position taken by Wettendorff Bey, one of the Imperial Commissioners on the 1881 Commission, where, in the meeting of September 15, 1881, he pointed out "the necessity of a special clause [in the proposed settlement] relating to the transfer to the Council of the sums arising from any future increase in customs duties . . . the administration and collection of which must always be made by agents of the Treasury." *Procès-Verbaux et Annexes de la Commission de 1881,* p. 36. Although this statement was accepted in principle by the foreign commissioners (*ibid.,* p. 37), there is no mention of this fact in the Decree of Mouharrem, Article VIII, Section 3, where the increase in customs tariffs is treated. There is, nevertheless, a statement as follows: "The method of guaranteeing to the bondholders the revenue mentioned in Section 3 . . . will be the object of special regulations."

to give its approval" to the Government's thesis. As far as the powers were concerned, the Public Debt and the Ottoman Government would have to come to an agreement concerning the rôle to be played by the former in the collection of the surtax. These two parties must reconcile the two points of view.[23]

It may be questioned whether the Government really considered it likely that an agreement with the Council was possible on the basis of the collection of the surtax by the Government customs officials. Even if the Council would have been satisfied with this basis, the powers themselves would never have given it their approval. But the powers were willing to entrust these negotiations to the Council, because they were aware of the fact that, in its dealings with the Government, the Council had always insisted on an ample interpretation of its rights. In this case, the rights of the Council and the interests of the powers coincided. On the other hand, the Government probably put forth its contention for the purpose of bargaining. It can hardly be blamed for this, inasmuch as its freedom of action was already considerably limited by the functioning of the Council, a limitation which would be increased if the Council were to act as the agent of the powers. But it was impossible for the Government to persist in its contention. The demands of the powers were too well defined, and the Council's intention to make its rights respected was too well known, for the Sublime Porte to hope for a compromise favorable to its point of view.

The Council was notified of the Government's decision on August 2, when the Imperial Commissioner announced the following action of the Council of Ministers: "The entire receipts from the three percent surtax can be remitted to your Administration." The observations of the Council concerning the details of verification of the accounts were approved by the Ministers. The Commissioner, in thus notifying the Council of the Government's modified position, formally accepted the proposals of the Debt for the control and collection of the surtax. Commandant Berger was delegated to confer with the customs officials in order to define the relations of the agents of the Public Debt with the customs service on the basis of the agreement concluded with the Government.[24]

---

23 *Parliamentary Papers*, No. Cmd. 3455 (1908) Dispatch 38.

24 *Procés-Verbal*, August 2, 1906.

The termination of the debate between the Council and the Government concluded this phase of the negotiations. But there was a second point on which the coöperation of the Public Debt was desired. It will be remembered that Lord Lansdowne, in his reply of February 27, 1905, to Musurus Pasha, expressed doubts concerning the ability of the receipts from the application of the surtax to make up the whole Roumelian budgetary deficits. On the basis of the imports into Turkey, the surtax would yield annually approximately Ltqs. 600,000, in addition to the twenty-five percent which belonged to the bondholders under the Supplementary Decree. But the deficit in the Roumelian budget was estimated by the Inspector General of the provinces at some Ltqs. 800,000. If the reform project was not to be continually handicapped by budget deficits, an extra 200,000 pounds would have to be found. Now, the Council collected many of the Empire's revenues other than those ceded to the bondholders. The gross receipts from the revenues administered by the Council for purposes "outside the Decree" always showed an annual surplus over the gross demands, although the requirements for the service on individual loans, or railway guarantees, sometimes had to be met from this surplus. According to the contracts, however, the surplus, after meeting the various demands, was to be turned over to the Government. Here was another source of revenue which was under the administration of the Council, and it might be possible to persuade the Council, with the consent of the Government, to meet any deficit in the Roumelian budget, should there be one, up to a certain amount.

M. Constans, French Ambassador at Constantinople, undertook to act for the powers in this respect, and proposed to his colleagues that the Public Debt be asked to meet any remaining deficit up to Ltqs. 250,000. "My proposal was unanimously accepted, and each of my colleagues should insist that his delegate at the Public Debt support it. President Berger, for his part, will certainly support it." [25]

In the meantime the representatives of the powers had drawn up a second collective note in answer to the Porte's proposals of June 21. This was submitted to the Government on September 30, and Sir Edward Grey's concern over the omission of a direct reference

---

[25] *Livre Jaune, Affaires de Macedoine* (1906-7) Dispatch 37.

to the Public Debt in the earlier note was remedied. The question of an effective guarantee was defined, and the proposal of M. Constans was likewise included:

> In order to insure the fulfillment of the above condition [an effective guarantee], the Ottoman Public Debt shall undertake to pay over in its entirety to the Roumelian budget the portion reverting to the Imperial Government out of the proceeds of the customs surtax. This undertaking shall further provide for the Debt to make good annually the deficit in the said budget to the amount of 250,000 pounds (Turkish).[26]

The French Ambassador's suggestion was brought to the unofficial attention of the delegates to the Council, and its inclusion in the collective note left the Government no alternative. On December 6, the Imperial Commissioner presented the request of the Government that the Administration guarantee the budget deficit up to 250,000 pounds. The importance of the decision was recognized. Mr. Adam Block thought that "before giving an answer to this request of the Porte, each member of the Council ought to be convinced that the Council shall never fail to fulfill its part of an undertaking which will be registered and taken cognizance of in all the chancelleries of Europe." The Council decided to agree to guarantee the 250,000 pounds for the Macedonian budget in case of deficit, reimbursing itself under instructions from the Porte, out of the tithe surplus, which, it was thought, would almost certainly suffice; if it did not, the Government and the Debt Council would agree on some source from which to meet the deficiency. Mr. Block tried to secure the surplus of the ceded revenues as a second guarantee, but met with the opposition of all his colleagues. The final decision of the Council was taken on December 10 by a vote of five to one, Mr. Block refusing his consent before obtaining the approval of the bondholders whom he represented. He urged that this decision, which would bind the Council before the powers for seven years, was one of the most important it had ever taken.

The formal engagement undertaken by the Council was embodied in a letter from Commandant Berger to Said Bey, the Imperial Commissioner, under date of December 17, 1906:

---

[26] *Parliamentary Papers*, No. Cmd. 3455 (1908) Enclosure in Dispatch 95.

In accordance with your verbal request of today's date, I have the honor to confirm to you by the present note the terms of the decision taken by the Administrative Council of the Ottoman Public Debt relative to the request of the Ministry of Finance to guarantee in some measure, from the year 1907-8, the settlement of the deficit of the three Roumelian *vilayets*.

The Council of the Ottoman Public Debt undertakes to place annually to the credit of the budget of the three Roumelian *vilayets* the portion accruing to the Imperial Government out of the proceeds of the customs surtax recently decreed as long as this surtax shall be in force.

The said Council also undertakes to meet annually the deficit in the above budget, should there be one, to the amount of 250,000 pounds (Turkish) as long as the whole of the proceeds of the *"revenus divers"* actually assigned shall continue to be made over to it by the Imperial Government.[27]

The obligations assumed by the Council were clearly defined in this letter, but several months elapsed before the Government had persuaded the powers that the other demands contained in the collective note of September 30, 1906, had been fulfilled. Finally, the question arose as to what form the agreement concerning the surtax and the new function of the Council would take. This phase of the problem was discussed by M. Pichon in a dispatch of December 17, 1906, to M. Constans, the French Ambassador:

It would be a real advantage to obtain the acceptance of the principle that the agreement sanctioning the adhesion of the powers to the customs increase should take the form of a diplomatic act or a bilateral agreement. . . . It will be important that this act should refer very explicitly to the arrangement which will be entered upon with the Ottoman Public Debt and the Ottoman Bank concerning the guarantee of the assignments.[28]

The French point of view prevailed, and the agreement took the form of a diplomatic act. The prolonged negotiations were finally concluded by the signature on April 25, 1907, of a commercial treaty between Turkey and the representatives of France,

[27] *Procès-Verbaux*, December 6 and 10, 1906; *Parliamentary Papers*, No. Cmd. 3455 (1908) Dispatches 104 and 105; *Livre Jaune, Affaires de Macedoine* (1906-7) Annex to Dispatch 56.

[28] *Ibid.*, Dispatch 55.

Italy, Germany, Great Britain, Austria-Hungary, and Russia. The most important provision is in Article I:

> All goods imported by land or sea into the Ottoman Empire at present subject to the eight percent duty ad valorem shall pay as soon as the present agreement comes into force . . . a duty of eleven percent ad valorem.

The part played by the Public Debt Administration is described in Article VI:

> The portion which by virtue of existing laws shall remain at the disposal of the Imperial Ottoman Government out of the sums encashed on account of the customs increase shall be devoted exclusively to the financial requirements of the three Roumelian *vilayets*. In accordance with the undertaking given by the Council of the Ottoman Public Debt Administration by a letter dated December 17, 1906, addressed to the Imperial Commissioner on the Public Debt, the sums mentioned in the preceding paragraph shall be placed annually to the credit of the budget of the three *vilayets* of Roumelia by the Administration of the Ottoman Public Debt. The collection and payment of these sums shall be made in conformity with the agreements arrived at between the Sublime Porte and the Public Debt Administration.

Article VII provides:

> In conformity with the undertaking given in the same letter of December 17, 1906, the Public Debt Administration shall make good annually the deficit, should there be one, in the budget of the three Roumelian *vilayets* to the amount of 250,000 pounds (Turkish).[29]

But the difficulties between the Public Debt and the Government which characterized the negotiations from the beginning persisted throughout the attempts to arrive at an agreement for the collection and payment of the sums in question. The Government customs administration desired to retain as many of its prerogatives as possible; the Council, on the other hand, insisted on obtaining sufficient control of the necessary operations to make its function real and not illusory. The resulting compromise is found in the instructions given by the Public Debt to its agents

---

[29] *Parliamentary Papers,* No. Cmd. 4469 (1909).

in the customs houses; these instructions were agreed on by the Council and the customs administration on June 24, the day before the convention with the powers became effective.

The duties of the Public Debt agents are defined in Article I:

> The agents of the Public Debt Administration delegated to the Imperial customs administration will receive from the central banking offices of the Administration of the Indirect Taxes the three percent of the eleven percent duty received by the customs authorities, this tax being realized by right of import duty, according to the treaties and conventions and according to the customs laws in force, on merchandise subjected to an eight per cent duty, and in the provinces the Public Debt agents will receive the three percent from the cashiers at the provincial customs agencies. The seventy-five percent of the sums resulting from this customs surtax of three percent and banked by the Public Debt will be put in the coffers of the Ottoman Bank by the Administration of the Public Debt in order to cover the budget deficit of the three Roumelian *vilayets* and will be used to balance this same budget.

In Article III is given the control over the accounts:

> In order to record and calculate the surtax of three percent, the above-mentioned agents will examine and verify whenever necessary all the records relative to the collection and encashment of the said tax.

In Article IV is set forth the method of remittance:

> The sums realized from the three percent customs surtax by the agents of the customs will be remitted as received against a receipt and to the account of the Public Debt to the agencies of the Ottoman Bank wherever this institution has branches. In the localities where there are no agencies of the Bank the money will be delivered to Public Debt agencies also against receipts. The accounts of the receipts and the monthly encashments will be balanced during the first week of the following month.

The limitations on the activities of the agents are presented in Article II:

> The agents of the Public Debt must not interfere in any way either in the functions of the customs agents or in the affairs relating to the customs services. No intervention can be made with the regulations followed until now for prohibiting the importation into the Empire of harmful books

> and writings, of arms, inflammable articles, and explosive materials. If, while exercising their dutes, these agents become cognizant of errors or omissions which might be prejudicial to the production of the three percent surtax, they will have done their duty by notifying their Administration.[30]

The returns from this surtax are worthy of note. The first year of its operation produced revenue of over half a million pounds (Turkish), and from 1908-9 until 1913-14, the returns amounted to over a million pounds annually. With the advent of the Tripolitan and Balkan Wars of 1911-13, and the Great War from 1914-22, the operation of this surtax was seriously affected by the sharp decline in imports, and also by the unilateral action of the Imperial Government in changing the customs tariffs without the consent of the powers. Thus, on September 18, 1914, the customs duties were raised to fifteen percent; a further increase to thirty percent was initiated on May 18, 1915; and on September 1, 1916, specific duties were substituted for ad valorem duties. From June, 1907, to May, 1915, the surplus of duty over eight percent was encashed by the Council, according to the terms of the agreements with the Government. When the duty was raised to thirty percent, the Government proceeded to requisition fifteen percent of the tax in kind, and refused to the Council any share in this levy of goods, allowing the Administration seven percent of the fifteen percent levied in cash, that is, the difference between the original eight percent and fifteen percent.

After the introduction of specific tariffs, the Government decided to pay fifty percent of the total duty to the Debt, but in 1917 changed this decision and consented to pay only the residue of the duty after deduction of a sum equivalent to eight percent of the daily receipts calculated on the value of the goods. The Public Debt agents who had been delegated to the customs administration in June, 1907, were withdrawn at the request of the Government on October 22, 1914. From this date on, their function of verifying the accounts was performed by inspectors who came every month for this purpose. With the conclusion of the Great War, however, and the occupation of Constantinople by Allied forces, the Council on October 25, 1919, decided to reinstate its permanent agents at the customs houses. In April, 1923, this

[30] *Procès-Verbal*, June 24, 1907, *Annex*.

function of the Council was again interrupted by the action of the Angora Government, which encashed the surplus for its own account, and was permanently terminated by the negotiation of new commercial treaties at Lausanne.[31]

The Significance of Surtax Control

The acceptance of the function of collecting the customs surtax and of applying it to the credit of the Roumelian budget constitutes the most important alteration of the Council's character since its institution. Its position toward the bondholders was unchanged; the Decree of Mouharrem and the Supplementary Decree were not altered. In fact, the conclusion of the commercial convention of 1907 finally put into effect certain provisions of these Decrees which, although of potential value to the bondholders, had lain dormant for many years. Furthermore, the position of the Council towards the Government, the railway companies, and banks was not affected. The many railway contracts and loan agreements to which the Council's president had affixed his signature were legally as binding as before. As far as its former functions under the two Decrees and the railway and loan contracts were concerned, the responsibility of the Council remained the same. The collection of the customs surtax was in no way connected with the Council's previous obligations.

In fact, it had assumed a new function, and a function the like of which it had never before discharged. The two Decrees and the contracts to which it was a third party could in no way be considered diplomatic agreements. The Decrees were not negotiated between two governments, but between the Ottoman

[31] *Reports of the Council of Foreign Bondholders* (London) 1907 to 1914; Block, *Special Report*, 1915-16-17, pp. 12-13; *Procès-Verbaux*, October 15 and 22, 1914, October 25, 1919. The Treaty of Lausanne specifically recognizes the abolition of the Capitulations, *Parliamentary Papers*, No. Cmd. 1929 (1923) Articles XXVIII and LXXI, and the commercial treaty of 1923 between the Allied powers and Turkey is the first one wherein Turkish sovereignty in commercial matters is more fact than fiction. Text in Martens, *Nouveau Recueil Général des Traités*, 3me Série, Volume XIII, pp. 412-22. Article I provides that customs duties on imports into Turkey from the contracting states shall be on the basis of the specific duties which came into force on September 1, 1916. Provision is made for the periodic revision of these rates according to the relative appreciation or depreciation of the Turkish paper pound in comparison with its value in July, 1923. The duration is for five years. (Articles II and XVIII).

Government and the Council, representing the syndicates of bondholders, the latter organizations enjoying no status in international law. Even less could the railway and loan contracts be considered as possessing an international legal sanction. But the convention of 1907 and the articles therein which defined the function of the Council endowed the latter with the performance of a function which did possess an international legal sanction. Perhaps it cannot be called a positive sanction. It is inconceivable that the Council would deliberately recede from the obligations into which it had entered towards the powers as well as towards the Ottoman Government. But it is conceivable that the Imperial Government might one day have so acted as to render impossible the Council's ability to discharge this duty. In such a case, it is firmly believed that a sanction would have been invoked to dissuade the Government from such action. The manner in which the powers resorted to coercion when the Imperial Government failed to recognize the delegates of the Macedonian financial commission has been detailed. The sanction invoked to compel the Government to accept a policy which the powers believed to be for the good of the Ottoman Empire could as easily have been brought into action to persuade the Government to desist from a unilateral policy which the powers considered as infringing treaty engagements. Clearly, the Council was acting as the agent of the powers, and under their protection. The word "agent" was actually used by Sir Edward Grey in discussing the demands of the British Government with the French Ambassador, M. Paul Cambon.[32]

The probability of this statement is strengthened by an analysis of the Council's function and its position as "third party" between

[32] *Supra*, p. 162. The popular belief at the time was that the Council in fact possessed a "control" on the operations of the Customs. The German delegate, Dr. Testa, desired that this belief be dissipated. He "has heard from different quarters that certain persons are hostile to the interference of the Public Debt in the operations of the Customs. These persons consider the participation of the Administration in encashing the surtax as a 'control' exercised over the operations of the customs service. He believes that the rôle of the Public Debt has been misunderstood; it is in no way a question of control, if by that word one means 'control of expenditure.' The duty of the Administration is to make a verification of the revenues." Dr. Testa thought it "advisable to explain this difference in order to clear up any misunderstanding and to correct a misleading interpretation." *Procès-Verbal*, April 29, 1907. On another occasion Dr. Testa took the opportunity to reiterate the necessity of impressing on the public his conception of the exact character of the Council's new function. *Ibid.*, May 13, 1907.

the Ottoman Government and the powers. The need of money for reform in Macedonia was evident. The reforms, although promised twenty-five years previously, would, no doubt, have never been undertaken had it not been for the pressure exerted by the powers of Europe. The reform project, however necessary to improve the conditions of the inhabitants of the three European provinces, was so considered not so much by the Sublime Porte as by the powers. Without going into the details of the policies of the individual powers, it is well known that Russia and Austria had political axes to grind in Macedonia. The attitude taken by each of the other powers toward Macedonia was largely determined by the policies of these two. Humanitarian motives perhaps influenced the great powers; the adhesion of Great Britain, France, Germany, and Italy to the proposals brought forward by Russia and Austria in 1903 was also undoubtedly influenced by political considerations. The reform project possessed a political coloring, therefore, and the administrative details of this reform created the need of money which local resources were unable to meet. The supplementary sums would have to be supplied by the central Government, and its poverty was notorious.

Although the Sublime Porte had desired for many years to raise its tariffs on imported goods, the particular reason for abandoning its attempt to substitute specific tariffs was the need of the money to meet Macedonian requirements and the belief that the powers would consent more readily to an ad valorem increase than to specific duties. The important consideration is, however, that Turkey was led to request the permission for an ad valorem increase because she needed money to supplement the insufficient local resources in Macedonia required to effect a reform project desired by the powers. The extra revenue collected from the surtax would not alleviate her financial difficulties except in a given area, and that area the one where the powers were interested in reform.

In order to secure the execution of the plan, the powers demanded an "effective guarantee" that the customs surtax would be assigned to the proper object. For this purpose the Public Debt was admirably fitted. From the viewpoint of efficiency and probity, the demand of the powers that the effective guarantee should be found in the Council was probably well-grounded.

However effective might be the intervention of the Debt it provided the necessary element to complete the fabric of fiction which surrounded the whole question of Macedonian reform and the customs surtax. It meant the effective control of the collection and application of the proceeds from the surtax by the Public Debt Council. It closed the circle of illusion.

For illusion it was! The desire of the powers for Macedonian reform compelled the Porte to accept the intervention of an organization directed by nationals of the powers to insure the proper functioning of a customs convention the benefit of which to the Turkish Government was indirect, in that the customs agreement enabled the Porte to comply with the demands of the powers. For the illusory value of this consent, the Turkish Government also paid in another coin: it had to introduce reforms in its internal legislation and administration which the powers demanded for the benefit of their commerce and industry. The Public Debt, in accepting the invitation to act as the agent of the powers, aided them in extracting double pay from the Ottoman Government; in return the Porte received the shadowy value of the powers' consent to revise the customs duties.

The opposition of the Council to the desire of the Imperial Government to introduce a new system of tithe collection has been noted in another place. To this example of the fusion of interests of the railroads, banks, and the Council, must be added the example of the Council as the agent of the powers. In this capacity the Debt proved the harmony of interest existing between itself and the powers, a harmony in which the Government's discomfort was the only discord.

CHAPTER VIII

FORTUNES OF WAR AND PEACE, 1908-28

The life of the Administration of the Ottoman Public Debt under the provisions of its two organic decrees can be divided roughly into two parts: the twenty years following 1882, a period in Turkish history of relative calm, seriously interrupted only by the Greco-Turkish War of 1897; and a second period of roughly the same duration subsequent to 1902, a period of strong contrast to the first. Events of first class importance followed one another in quick succession. After a few years of comparative quiet immediately following 1903, the Young Turk revolutions of 1908-9 were followed in 1911-12 by a disastrous war with Italy which detached the provinces of Tripoli and Cyrenaica. Almost simultaneously with the conclusion of peace with Italy, the allied Balkan nations opened hostilities, and, in the course of the two Balkan Wars of 1912-13, definitely wrested from the Sultan four-fifths of his territories in Europe.

There came, in 1914, the entrance of Turkey into the Great War on the side of the Central powers. This struggle was concluded four years later by the Armistice of Mudros and the occupation by Allied forces of strategic points in the Ottoman Empire. The Nationalist movement, however, under Mustapha Kemal Pasha, prolonged hostilities against Greece, the proxy of the Allies, and in 1922 drove her armies out of Anatolia. In the following summer the Treaty of Lausanne, negotiated between the new Angora Government and the Allied powers, replaced the unratified Treaty of Sèvres, and peace was reëstablished.

WEATHERING THE YOUNG TURK REVOLUTION

The important event in the beginning of the second period was the delegation to the Council of the collection of the customs surtax, detailed in the preceding chapter. Hardly had the Council assumed this new function when the political foundations of the Empire were rudely shaken. In July, 1908, and April, 1909, occurred the revolutions engineered by the Young Turks, and a limited monarchy under a constitution was substituted for the autocratic government of Abdul Hamid. In harmony with the progressive principles voiced by the Young Turk leaders, the new régime continued to coöperate loyally with the Council in its labors. This fact is borne out by a statement made in September, 1908, to the Council by the Minister of Finance:

> Appreciating the services rendered to the credit of the Empire by the Council of the Public Debt Administration, the Imperial Government is glad to be reassured of its coöperation. Sincerely desirous of respecting all obligations undertaken, the Government is certain that the members of the European exchanges will continue to participate in the peaceful and economic development of the country, and relies upon the Council of the Debt to acquaint Europe with the loyal intentions of the constitutional régime.[1]

In his Special Report for 1907-8, Sir Adam Block expressed his conviction of the sincerity of the new Government:

> It is determined to make a thorough and searching examination of the financial situation, and is prepared to place the results before the public. This is to be followed by radical changes in the financial administration. The Porte is also convinced of the necessity of developing the economic resources of the country and of taking immediate measures for the promotion of industry and commerce.
>
> But it remains to be seen what material proofs of sympathy Europe is prepared to give. Were it possible to concede to Turkey its commercial independence, the financial situation would immediately assume a different aspect. . . . Turkey is today barred from raising its tariffs and is thus precluded from enjoying the right accorded to all independent states of increasing its revenues by indirect taxation.[2]

The activities of the Ministry of Finance justified the hopes which had arisen for the improvement of conditions existing in the administration of the finances of the Empire:

> The first necessity was to ascertain the real and exact situation, without any attempts at concealment. This had been done, and in a remarkable and able statement made in

[1] Quoted in Block, *Special Report*, 1907-8, p. 75.

[2] *Ibid.*, pp. 73, 75-6. Mr. Block was knighted shortly after the successful conclusion of the customs convention in April, 1907. See *supra*, Chapter VII.

> the Chamber of Deputies, the present Minister of Finance placed before the nation a faithful exposé of the case, and produced for the first time in the financial history of Turkey a budget which may be taken as correct and authentic.[3]

Thus did the British member and president of the Council, Sir Adam Block, pay tribute to both the policy and the ability of Djavid Bey, who subsequently (1922) became Ottoman member of the Public Debt.

The difficulties to surmount were enormous, but the new broom swept clean. The new régime undertook to establish equilibrium in the budget; retired or discharged large numbers of useless servants in the royal palaces; returned the revenues of the Civil List to the use of the State; undertook the reorganization of all departments of the government; and engaged foreign experts to assist in this process. It was in the interest of the Young Turk Government itself as well as that of the nation as a whole that these reforms should be successful, and there was no lack of enthusiasm in the manner in which they were undertaken.[4]

As a matter of fact the position of the P. D. A. towards the Government showed few signs of being modified because of the advent of the Young Turks to power.

> Taking into consideration the remarkable and successive changes in Constantinople since July, 1908, which, for a time at any rate, paralyzed the executive throughout the provinces, where the peasant class at the outset sadly misinterpreted the meaning of the words "liberty" and "constitution," it is a matter of satisfaction that the revenues of the Debt Administration should have suffered so little.[5]

As far as the Debt is concerned, the change from autocracy to constitutional government was accompanied by the minimum of inconvenience.

Politics in the Background of the Council's Activities

If the almost uninterrupted period of revolution and war from 1908 to 1922 was disastrous for the Empire, it was no less destructive in its effect on the Debt Council. The enviable position

---

[3] *Ibid.*, 1908-9.
[4] See Earle, *op. cit.*, pp. 220-1.
[5] Block, *Special Report*, 1908-9, pp. 7-8.

which it had built up during its first two decades was due to efficient management, genuine interest in the economic regeneration of the Empire, and abstention from activities which might in any way have been termed political. In his Special Report for 1905-6, Sir Adam Block cited the opinion of Lord Fitzmaurice:

> That commission [the Council] was not a body which took a certain amount of money and handed it over to certain bondholders. No doubt that was its first origin and what called it into existence; but gradually, owing to the great skill of the financiers who had control of its operations, it had been entrusted with the collection as well as the administration of several other revenues, and the taxes which it collected with the consent of the Ottoman Government had gradually gone on increasing.[6]

The continuation of this position was dependent upon one factor: its continued abstention from political activities. The extension of its functions in 1907 to include the control of the surtax marked the entrance of the Council as an official body into the political arena. This act greatly increased the prestige and influence of the Council. In Europe its powerful hold upon the Ottoman Empire was more than ever recognized. But when the Council thus allied itself more with the European powers than with the Ottoman Government, its activities impressed themselves on the European as well as on the Turkish public as less economic and more political in character than heretofore. The activities of the Council in discharging functions not delegated to it by the two organic Decrees have been shown to be more important than those connected with the administration of the ceded revenues.[7] These supplementary functions were linked to operations whose success or failure increased or diminished national influence and prestige of the European powers: the transition of the Bagdad railway enterprise from a financial and business venture into an expression of German imperialist expansion; the hot scramble between the German group headed by the *Deutsche Bank* and the French group under the Ottoman Bank for the privilege of floating Ottoman Government loans. Whether or not conscious of the significance of these activities, the Council, in associating

---

[6] *Ibid.*, p. 10. From 1906 to 1908 Lord Fitzmaurice was Parliamentary Undersecretary of State in the Foreign Office.

[7] *Supra*, Chapter VI, p. 152.

with them, laid itself open to serious criticism. The coincidence of the interests of the Council, of the European powers, and of both banks and railways whose direction was European, may have been natural; but the fact remains that a policy which drew these interests closer together was always considered by their supporters to be for the benefit of the Ottoman Empire. This meant extending the influence of non-Turkish agencies, the increased prestige of European commerce, finance, and industry, and the consolidation of Europe's privileged position under the Capitulations.

If the duties of the Council under the 1907 convention increased its prestige in official and unofficial Europe, it also strengthened the impression among educated and liberal Turks that the Council, although composed of representatives of European bondholders' syndicates possessing no official connection with their respective governments, was in fact the semi-official agency of the European governments whose nationals composed it. This opinion was expressed to the author on a number of occasions in interviews with Turks of many professions.[8] Even the present Turkish Government is quoted as being of this opinion:

> It is the wish of Angora that in the future this body [the Council] should represent not the governments of which the bondholders are subjects, but the bondholders themselves.[9]

Whether the quotation states a fact may be disputed, but the state of mind which prompts it cannot be doubted. During the fifteen years which followed 1907 several incidents occurred which contribute to this belief. The clause of the Nationalist Pact of 1920 which opposed restriction of Turkish development in financial matters, the position of the Turkish delegation at Lausanne, and the attitude of the Turkish Republican Government concerning the future position of the Council, were due, more than to any other cause, to the firm conviction that the delegates to the Council were in fact, if not in law, clothed in an official mantle of European

[8] Although they recognized the beneficial aspects of the Council's administration, it was felt, whether rightly or not, that the customs convention of 1907 placed an official stamp of approval on the Public Debt, and that henceforth not European bondholders' syndicates, but European governments were back of the Council's membership. See *infra*, Chapter IX, pp. 224 *et seq.*

[9] *The Near East and India* (London) August 11, 1927, p. 181.

governmental favor. To this reason is also due the destruction in 1922-23 of the prestige and position of the Council, which was at its zenith in 1907.[10]

In regard to the composition of the Council, the Turco-Italian War and the Great War created unprecedented situations. Before 1911 the Ottoman Government had never been at war with a government one of whose nationals held a seat in the Council. The situation had not been envisaged in the Decree of Mouharrem. There was nothing in this contract which determined the action to be taken by the Turkish Government in such a circumstance. No doubt the Council, as the executive organ of a department of the Turkish Government, was considered capable of functioning at all times, in war as in peace, and even in the case of a war with a power like Italy, or any other great power, possessing a national sitting in the Council. It remained to be seen, therefore, what action the Government would take in such an event.

The case of the Italian delegate, Marquis Theodoli, during the Turco-Italian War, is unique. On October 18, 1912, the Imperial Commissioner communicated a dispatch to the Council from the Minister of Finance, containing the notification of a decision of the Council of Ministers:

> In consideration of the state of war, wherein it is inadmissable that Italian subjects occupy public and official positions, the Grand Vizier directs that the functions of Italians in the service of the Public Debt Administration be terminated, with the exception of the delegate of the Italian bondholders.[11]

As concerns the P. D. A., this dispatch executed an official order of a week previous, by virtue of which all Italian subjects residing in the country were expelled. But in this earlier order as well, an exception had been made in favor of the Italian delegate. This exception created an anomalous situation. The directing organism of a department of the Ottoman Government contained a subject of Italy with whom Turkey itself was at war. In view of the peculiar prestige and influence enjoyed by the

[10] For the text of the Nationalist Pact (in French and in English), see Toynbee, A. J., *The Western Question in Greece and Turkey* (London, 1923), pp. 207-10; for an insight into the Turkish position at Lausanne, see *Parliamentary Papers,* No. Cmd. 1814 (1923) *passim.*

[11] *Procès-Verbal,* October 18, 1912.

members of the Council, the confidence and trust of the Ottoman Government in retaining the Italian delegate must be admired.

Unfortunately, however, this trust was misplaced. On September 26 the Italian delegate had informed the German Ambassador, Marschall von Bieberstein, that "Italy had to seize Tripoli, inasmuch as the balance in the Mediterranean had been disturbed by the Franco-German agreement about Morocco." [12] Personal activities of which this statement to the German Ambassador must be an example were considered by the Ottoman Government as "incorrect" and Marquis Theodoli was compelled to leave Turkish territory.[12a]

As his term of office was due to expire on March 1, 1913, the Rome Chamber of Commerce, by which the Italian delegate is nominated, postponed the designation of his successor until that date. The situation, which was disagreeable to all concerned, was aggravated by the ill-considered action of the Rome Chamber, which reëlected Marquis Theodoli for a term of five years. Possibly this was its mode of expressing its confidence in the former delegate, but it was an action which could not be accepted by the Turkish Government. In assuming this position, the Government again acted in a worthy spirit, making clear to the Italian syndicate, by means of the Council, that it could not recognize the validity of the Rome Chamber's letter from M. Tittoni addressed to the Council, inasmuch as in thus notifying the Government of the election of a delegate to fill the vacated seat, the Italian syndicate had not acted according to the provisions of the Decree of Mouharrem. The displeasure of the Government resulting from the step taken by the Rome Chamber of Commerce was con-

---

[12] *Die Grosse Politik,* Volume XXX, Number 10838, p. 59. ". . . the Italian delegate, who has in general no bondholders' interests to represent, uses his position for the furtherance of other objects." *Ibid.* See also Baron von Wangenheim's estimate of these political activities of Marquis Theodoli and of the interests of his successor, Commandant Nogara, *Ibid.,* Volume XXXVII, Number 15267, p. 888. In the fall of 1913 it was revealed that Commandant Nogara had carried on negotiations with the Turkish Government for the concession of a railway line to connect the seaport of Adalia and the town of Burdur, the southeasterly terminus of the Aidin railway. Dominian, L., *The Frontiers of Language and Nationality in Europe* (New York, 1917) p. 251. Marquis Theodoli subsequently became Italian Minister for the Colonies, and is now (1929) Chairman of the Permanent Mandates Commission of the League of Nations.

[12a] *Procès-Verbal,* November, 1912.

veyed to the latter by calling to its attention the breach of a technicality.[13]

Although the former incumbent of the position was *persona non grata* to the Turkish Government, the Minister of Finance, in a dispatch of April 2, 1912, considered that "in spite of the continuation of the state of war between Italy and Turkey, the Ottoman Government sees nothing to prevent the Italian bondholders from electing a new delegate." The Finance Ministry requested the Council to notify the Italian syndicate of the Government's position. The susceptibilities of the syndicate may have been injured by the Turkish Government's refusal to accept the reëlection of Marquis Theodoli; or it may have been deemed unwise to utilize the opportunity afforded by the good faith of the Turks; in any event, Marquis Theodoli's successor was not designated until after the conclusion of peace in October, 1912. On December 3 the syndicate proceeded to nominate Commandant Nogara, who took his seat in the Council for the first time at its meeting of December 19, 1912.[14]

The Financial Link of the Turco-German Alliance

The policy of the Ottoman Government towards the Italian delegate in October, 1911, was duplicated by its policy towards the British and French delegates three years later. Hostilities between Turkey and England and France broke out in October, 1914, but there was no attempt made by the Ottoman Government to evict Sir Adam Block and M. de la Boulinière, the British and French delegates on the Council. Both, however, chose to leave Turkey. The French delegate on November 5 made known to the Council that "the present circumstances oblige him to leave Turkey for a period of undetermined length." Thus, from November, 1914, until April, 1915, the Council was composed of the German, Austrian, Italian, and Turkish delegates. Commandant Nogara, the Italian delegate, left the country on Italy's entrance into the war. From April, 1915, until November, 1918, the policies and activities of the Council were directed by the German, Austrian, and Turkish delegates. The presidency dur-

[13] *Procès-Verbal*, April 22, 1912.

[14] *Ibid.*

ing this time was held by the senior delegate, Hussein Djahid Bey, who represented the Ottoman holders.

The important point is that the exit from Turkey of the delegates who were Allied subjects was undertaken on their own initiative and responsibility, the Government having taken no coercive measures to expel them. Theoretically, at least, the Allied delegates might have remained in Constantinople for the duration of the war. Practically, of course, such a course would have been attended with insurmountable difficulties. The struggle between the Allies and the Central powers differed essentially from the war between Turkey and Italy. To be sure, the status quo in November, 1914, was favorable to Turkey and the Central powers. The bitterness of the war would sooner or later have rendered untenable the presence in Constantinople of the Allied delegates. Realizing this, the Government permitted time to work in its favor, a policy which speedily proved effective, and changed the Council of the Public Debt into the financial link between Turkey and her two powerful allies. If the Decree of Mouharrem contained no provision applicable during the Turco-Italian war, its insufficiency was even more marked during the Great War.[15]

Thus shorn of its Allied elements, the Council lent its influence to the Ottoman Government in prosecuting the war. The most important service which it rendered was in its intervention in the issue of paper money, an operation which could probably not have achieved the success it did without the coöperation of the Council. The Ottoman Government was in dire need of money, and it turned to its allies, Germany and Austria, who signified their willingness to come to its aid. Two contracts of April 20 and May 1, 1915, the first with the German and the second with the Austrian Government, secured for the Turkish Ministry of Finance the use of advances amounting to about six and a half million Turkish pounds. These were the first of a series of seven contracts entered into during the following three and one half years, representing in all some Ltqs. 190,000,000.[16]

[15] *Ibid.*, November 5, 1914.

[16] *Recueil des Contrats*, pp. 5, 7 *et seq.* Before the intervention of the Public Debt in the issue of paper money, the German Government had approached the Ottoman Government with a project for establishing German control of the Ottoman Bank. The Turks opposed this idea, particularly the Minister of the Interior, Talaat Bey. It was then that Djavid Bey suggested the intermediary rôle of the Public Debt.

In the meantime the Turkish Government had sounded the Constan-

These advances were not placed at the direct disposal of the Turkish Government. They were used as cover for as many issues of paper money. It was to this operation that the Public Debt Council gave its support. At the request of the Government, the Council on March 25, 1915, decided to assume the obligation of repayment in specie of the paper money issued in accordance with the first advance from the German and Austrian Governments. The Council intervened in a similar capacity in the other issues. Its obligation under the original decision was secured by gold deposits in Berlin and Vienna banks made to the account of the Public Debt Administration by the German and Austrian Governments and were for a value equal to the issue of paper money. For the following issues, however, the responsibility of the Council was engaged on coverings of German treasury bonds repayable at intervals distributed over eleven years. The undertaking assumed by the Council was real; the bills of the different issues bore the signature of the president of the Council, Hussein Djahid Bey, and were known by the public as "Debt bills."[17]

In thus utilizing its prestige, the Public Debt gave to the Ottoman Government the most important aid of which it stood in

---

tinople board of the Ottoman Bank concerning the possibility of using its privilege of bank note issue to aid the Government in its distress. This, the Ottoman Bank refused to do. On December 23, 1914, it abandoned, for the duration of the war, its monopoly of bank note issue delegated to it by Article IX of its concession. The way was thus clear to consummate Djavid Bey's suggestion to utilize the Public Debt.

In the early days of the war, the Ottoman Government had thought of seizing the revenues ceded to the Public Debt, but the opposition of the German Government had caused this idea to be abandoned. The Council was aware of this desire of the Government, and this knowledge, together with a concurrent realization of the disastrous effects which would result if it were successful, contributed to persuade the Council to assume the new function of aiding in the issue of paper money. (For most of this information the author is indebted to an interview with Dr. Ziemcke, of the German Foreign Office, who was in the Constantinople Embassy during the war). The letter of the Ottoman Bank, in which it abandoned its privilege of note issue, is cited in Article XII of the convention between the Public Debt and the Government for the first issue of paper money. *Billets de Monnaie*, p. 12.

[17] *Procès-Verbal*, March 25, 1915; *Recueil des Contrats; Billets de Monnaie*. It was not without considerable persuasion that the Government finally obtained from the Council its consent to act in the third and subsequent issues. The technical details involved, the necessity of a greatly increased staff, and finally some apprehension concerning the wisdom of the financial policy of the Government, caused much questioning on the part of the Council. In the end, however, it consented to act as in the first two issues. *Procès-Verbaux*, February 10 and 28, and March 9, 1916.

need, namely, the means of providing resources for carrying on the war. It was an action that shows how completely the Council was dominated by the desires of the Government as an ally of the Central powers. Its policy in respect of the paper money was one which was definitely favorable to the Government in its prosecution of the war, and the aims of the Turkish Government coincided with those of its allies.[18] The Italian delegate, Commandant Nogara, was still in Constantinople as a member of the Council, Italy not yet having entered the war, when the important decision of March 25, 1915, was taken. The decision was unanimous, Commandant Nogara associating himself with his German, Austrian, and Turkish colleagues.

As might have been expected, this action of the Council drew forth vehement protests from the British and French delegates and the delegate of the Ottoman Bank. On May 15, 1915, Hussein Djahid Bey laid before the Council a letter which had been received from M. de la Boulinière. The French delegate considered that

> the intervention of the Administration of the Ottoman Public Debt in an operation of this kind is absolutely incompatible with the mission confided to the Council by the bondholders. If this Administration, at the request of the Ottoman Government, has intervened on several occasions to control the collection of revenues assigned by the Government as pledges for certain loans, it should not be called upon to guarantee the availability in cash (*disponibilité effectif*), after the completion of the war, of deposits made outside Ottoman territory, in foreign countries in which it possesses no means of control.
>
> Moreover, it cannot be admitted that such a transformation of the financial rôle attributed to the Council up to the present can be effected without the consent of the syndicates; it is even less possible that the members of the Council present at Constantinople should override the express protests of those of their colleagues whom the present state of affairs has forced temporarily to leave Ottoman territory.

[18] But representatives of the House of Bleichröder and of the Deutsche Bank with whom the author discussed this question in Berlin, believe that in functioning in this capacity the Council was more solicitous of its own position, both at the time and in the future, than it was of aiding the Government in its prosecution of the war. See Commandant Nogara's opinion, *infra*, p. 188. The coincidence of interests is, however, remarkable.

M. Steeg, the delegate of the Ottoman Bank, and Sir Adam Block, the British delegate, expressed protests in similar letters.[19]

This opposition was met by the unanimous opinion of the other members of the Council that the new function which the Administration had been called upon to fulfill was not incompatible with its powers. Hussein Djahid Bey recognized that the Council assumed obligations which had not been forecast by the Decree of Mouharrem, but at the same time thought that "these engagements are absolutely and in reality covered by the Ottoman Government." Moreover, the protests of his colleagues had been received after the decision of the Council had been taken. Herr Pritsch, the German delegate, while admitting that unanimity was desirable in deciding on a measure of this character, was equally convinced that "protests of the English and French delegates can have no influence on the attitude of the Council, which has conformed to the demands of the situation." In his opinion, inasmuch as the English and French delegates were subjects of states at war with Turkey, "they must be considered as being opposed to any measure which would be for Turkey's interest. This means that in any question that affects the interests of the Government at the same time as those of the bondholders, but without prejudicing the latter, the Council of the Debt is obliged not to allow itself to be influenced by the declarations which the English and French delegates have made." Commandant Nogara, the Italian delegate, shared the point of view of his colleagues. In his opinion, "the decision taken by the Council to lend its coöperation to the financial operation undertaken by the Government is based on the same principles followed up to now by the Council in similar situations of the Government, although the form of this assistance may be considered different." He was convinced that "the aid given by the Council does not injure the interests of the bondholders. On the contrary, it is of a nature to maintain, if not to increase, the prestige of the Administration in the country, something that is of considerable moral advantage." The opinion of the Council's legal adviser was taken: "In accepting this new mission, the Council has not pledged the bondholders of the Debt as forecast by the two Decrees any more than in previous participations in the financial operations of the Government; this accept-

19 *Procès-Verbal*, May 15, 1915.

ance has no effect either on the application of the ceded revenues or on the employment of the reserve funds." The Austrian member of the Council was absent from this meeting; but as the opinion of those members present was unanimous, the Council decided to receive the protest, but not to modify the decision taken on March 25, 1915.[20]

Two other policies of the Council during the war period agitated its members who were subjects to the Entente powers. Early in 1915 the Council decided to suspend, for the period of the war, the redemption and payment of interest on securities belonging to Allied subjects and forming part of the loans whose service was confided to the administration of the Council. In May, 1918, in order to subscribe to the Ottoman internal loan, the Council considered as redeemed, bonds of the Unified Debt of a value of Ltqs. 700,000, which had been bought before the war with the proceeds of the Tripolitan indemnity, and deposited in Paris.[21]

With this situation in mind, we can consider the circumstances in which the German and Austrian delegates were expelled from Turkey. Article XIX of the Mudros Armistice of October 31, 1918, provided for the expulsion of all German and Austrian subjects from Ottoman territory. Informed of this provision through the daily press, the Council, still composed of the Turkish, German, and Austrian delegates, assembled on November 21 to consider the situation. The president, Hussein Djahid Bey, thought that a general application of this provision would not interfere with the position of the German and Austrian members of the

---

[20] *Ibid.*

[21] The Treaty of Lausanne, which concluded the Turco-Italian War of 1911-12, contained provisions for the annual payment by the Italian Government of a sum representing the capitalization at four percent of an amount corresponding to the average annual receipts over the three-year period immediately preceding the war from the revenues accruing to the Debt Council from the provinces of Tripoli and Cyrenaica. The payment was to be made to the Council, and on no account was it to be less than two million Italian lire. Article X. *Nouveau Recueil Général*, 3me Série, Volume VII, p. 10. This revenue, the realization of which was obtained by the Council with no administrative expense, should, in the opinion of M. Eugène Borel, have been applied to extraordinary redemption of the bonds of the Unified Debt. If such a policy had been adopted and executed, the Council could in truth have been said to have possessed the greatest concern for the well-being of Turkish interests, as the day when the ceded revenues could be released from foreign control would have been brought appreciably nearer.

Council, inasmuch as their special status was defined by the Decrees forming the organic law of the Administration of the Public Debt. This position had never been contested by the Ottoman Government, and for that reason, he thought, could be even less opposed by the powers signatory to the armistice. He recalled the circumstances during the Turco-Italian War in which the Italian delegate had been excluded from the general application of the law expelling Italian subjects. He also cited the fact that during the Great War, the Government had taken no steps to expel the French and British members of the Council, and that their exit from the country had been voluntary. Basing his argument on these facts, in which he was naturally joined by his colleagues, the president proposed to communicate to the Ottoman Government, by means of the Imperial Commissioner, a letter containing the point of view of the Council. It was also decided to communicate this position to the English and French admirals, Sir Arthur Calthorpe and Admiral Amet, and to acquaint the various syndicates with the Council's action. The Imperial Commissioner was begged to employ all his influence with the Government to obtain a favorable result.[22]

Unfortunately for Dr. Zahn and Count Wickenburg, before the next meeting of the Council on November 27, the support they had received from Hussein Djahid Bey as president of the Council was compromised by the arrival in Constantinople of Sir Adam Block, who, as British delegate, immediately took up the duties of president of the Council. The mandate conferred on the president at the meeting of November 21, to acquaint the English and French admirals with the Council's contention, thus devolved not on the Turkish delegate, but on Sir Adam Block, who, accordingly, discharged this duty.

Upon the refusal of the Ottoman Government to recognize the special character of the delegates under the Decree of Mouharrem, the German and Austrian delegates on November 27 demanded a special meeting of the Council. The communication of this decision of the Sublime Porte did not mean that the Government had failed to put forth an effort in favor of the delegates in question. The Government and the Imperial Commissioner did everything in their power to persuade the Allied High Commissioners to make

22 *Procès-Verbal*, November 21, 1918.

an exception in favor of Dr. Zahn and Count Wickenburg, but without result. The decision of the Government, therefore, merely recognized the status quo, and was probably dictated more by necessity than by any other considerations, inasmuch as its attempt to influence the Allied High Commissioners signified its real desire in the matter. The two delegates renewed their protests. Dr. Zahn considered that

> It is the duty of the Council to formulate its most express protests. In effect, the measure taken against the German and Austrian delegates constitutes a grave violation of the Decree of Mouharrem, which is recognized by the interested powers. It compromises the composition of the Council as provided for in the Decree by making it impossible for its members of German and Austrian nationality to exercise their functions. Taken at this moment this measure deprives the Council of the quorum necessary for its decisions. It is even more flagrantly in opposition to the legal and factual position of the Council, inasmuch as during the present war, the Council and each of its members has worked without prejudice to safeguard not only the common interests of all the bondholders, but also the special interests of different groups of bondholders and others interested, without distinction of nationality.

Sir Adam Block was unable to share the opinion held by his German, Austrian, and Turkish colleagues. His argument was extremely simple:

> It is not a question here of a violation of the formal terms of the Decree of Mouharrem pertaining to the prerogatives of the members of the Council. No relation exists, in fact, between the Decree of Mouharrem and the armistice concluded between the Ottoman Government and the Entente powers and the United States of America, a treaty which possesses a purely political and military character.

He added that the German and Austrian delegates retained complete liberty to protest against the measure of expulsion concerning them; but "the Council can only file these protests."

Dr. Zahn added this parting observation:

> If, at the moment of signing the armistice, the negotiators of that document had envisaged the prerogatives of the members of the Council as recognized by the Decrees, there can be no doubt that these negotiators would have taken into con-

> sideration the special character devolving upon the members of the Council from these Decrees. Once notified of the privileges of the Council, the representatives of the Entente powers would not have failed to address their respective governments for a solution of the question.[23]

These energetic protests of the persons involved and of the Imperial Government were ineffective. The particular clause in question was applied by the Allied High Commissioners, with no exceptions in favor of the two Council members, and they were forced to leave Turkey. The Ottoman Minister of Finance made a final attempt to effect a solution favorable to the German and Austrian members, an effort in which he tried to enlist the aid of the Council. But, with the departure of the members in question and the consequent domination of the Allied point of view in the Council's deliberations on the question, the proposal was speedily rejected:

> Considering, since the return to Constantinople of the British delegate, that this matter has been treated in accordance with the clauses of the armistice, the Council considers it today as wholly and definitely settled.

After this date, December 16, 1918, the matter was not raised again.[24]

---

[23] *Ibid.*, November 27, 1918.

[24] *Ibid.*, December 16, 1918. To argue that the expulsion of the German and Austrian delegates was due to the pro-Turk and pro-German activities of the Council during the war may be rationalization. Such an argument seems possible, however, from the facts available. German officials who were connected with the Public Debt at the time, and officers of the German syndicate, maintain that the expulsion was entirely a political act, as do Dr. Ziemcke of the German Foreign Office, Sir Adam Block, and Sir Vincent Caillard. These experts, nevertheless, are reluctant to connect the "political" quality of the expulsion with the important aid rendered the Ottoman Government by the Council during the war. This hair-splitting seems to avoid the point at issue, namely, that the Council in 1918 was no longer the same type of organization that it had been in its early years. Prior to the Great War it had proved itself a valuable and potent ally with all the European powers in their dealings with Turkey. During the war it had so functioned, but exclusively for the Turco-German alliance. Upon the successful conclusion of the struggle, therefore, the Allied governments could no longer envisage the possibility of Austro-German membership. Sir Vincent thought their expulsion an unwise act, as it tacitly recognized the possibility that the Council, as an economic organization, might at the same time be a basis upon which political influence rested. It would be interesting to know to what extent the Allied delegates on the Council used their considerable political influence to maintain intact the composition of the Council as constituted by the Decree of Mouharrem.

THE SHACKLES OF SÈVRES

To the majority of those who held Ottoman bonds and to their champions, the Allied powers, the conclusion of the Great War brought high hopes. The opportunity was at hand, so the bondholders believed, to consolidate their ownership of the ceded revenues. Moreover, in their opinion, this was the occasion to strengthen the position of the Council. In order to attain these objectives the defects in the sanctions of the Decree of Mouharrem were to be remedied by the provisions of an international treaty. Indeed, for a time it seemed that these aspirations were to be realized. In coöperation with partisans of the bondholders [25] the Allied powers drafted and then imposed upon the vanquished Ottoman Empire the humiliating Treaty of Sèvres, August 10, 1920. The financial clauses of this treaty provide the superstructure of the financial control which the Allies proposed to exercise over Turkey;[26] the foundation, of many years' standing, was found to exist in the Administration of the Ottoman Public Debt.

In the future, so Article 246 of the treaty provided, the Council was to be reorganized to include only the delegates of the British, the French, and the Italian bondholders, and the representative of the Imperial Ottoman Bank. Thus constituted the Council was authorized to give administrative advice and assistance to the Turkish Finance Ministry, under conditions to be determined by the financial commission.[27] Furthermore, the reorganized Council should review all transactions made by the attenuated portion thereof during the war. Any disbursements which were not in accordance with its powers and duties as defined in the Decree of Mouharrem or otherwise before the war were to be reimbursed to the Council by the Turkish Government as soon as, in the opin-

---

[25] "The designation, by the French Government, of MM. des Closières, Sallandrouze de Lamornaix, and Boissière, of the Ottoman Bank, as financial experts charged to aid our representatives, has allowed the commission [instituted for the defense of the French interests in Turkey] the opportunity of coöperating in the closest possible manner with the French representatives in drafting the financial clauses of the treaty." *Annuaire de l'Association Nationale des Porteurs Francais de Valeurs Mobilières*, 1915-20, p. 146.

[26] *Parliamentary Papers*, No. Cmd. 964, Treaty Series No. 11, 1920, Articles 231-260; also available in *The Treaties of Peace, 1919-23* (2 volumes, Carnegie Foundation, N. Y., 1924), Volume II, pp. 864 *et seq.*

[27] *Infra*, pp. 195-6.

ion of the financial commission, such payment was possible. The new Council was to have the power of reviewing any action taken by its predecessor during the war, and to annul any obligation which in its opinion was prejudicial to the interests of the bondholders and which was not in accord with the powers of the Council. The Allied governments were to decide by majority vote and after having consulted the bondholders whether the newly-formed Council should, upon the expiration of its members' terms, be maintained or replaced by the financial commission.

Under such a régime the future actions of the Council would no doubt coincide with the desires of Allied holders of Ottoman government bonds. Not only was the reconstituted Council envisaged as functioning unrestricted by obligations to the Turkish Government; but also, composed solely of nationals of the Allied powers, it would be unhampered in the future by the presence of potentially hostile elements. Nor, indeed, would the financial tutelage of Turkey henceforth be shared by other powers possessing interests at variance with those of Allied nationals. Also, by virtue of the treaty the Council possessed the power to review actions taken during the war; thus conceivably the entire financial policy of the period 1915-18 could be overturned to the advantage of Allied bondholders.[28] Moreover, the Turkish Government was to be held accountable for the reimbursement of sums disbursed by the old Council in contravention of its powers. An Allied financial commission was to decide when such repayment was to be made; and, as concerns the meaning of the organic statutes of the Public Debt, the exclusion from the Council of nationals of the Central powers and the existence of an Allied-constituted commission assured an interpretation as favorable to Allied desires as that reached during the war had been consonant with Turco-German aims.

But the dictators of the Treaty of Sèvres were not content to refashion in their own interests the unofficial international control of Turkish finance which had been set up in 1881. Upon the newly-shaped foundation of the Council the Allies sought to erect a rigidly-buttressed fiscal superstructure the nature and powers of which still further coincided with Allied objectives.

---

[28] Cf. *supra*, pp. 185 *et seq.*

As has already been indicated, side by side with the new Council was to function an international financial commission. But only secondarily was it international; primarily the proposed organ was Allied both in composition and in scope. According to the preamble of the financial clauses of the Treaty of Sèvres, "the Allied powers, desiring to afford some measure of relief and assistance to Turkey," proposed to institute a body composed of official representatives of the governments of the British Empire, France, and Italy. And this body was to hold the whip hand over Turkish fiscal policy and administration.

Note first the rights of the commission in the field of Turkish domestic economy. The annual budget was to be submitted in the first instance to the financial commission, and was to be presented to parliament in the form approved by the commission. Nor was this the extent of its rights in this respect. No modification introduced by parliament was to become operative without the approval of the commission. Neither the Turkish parliament nor the Turkish Finance Ministry was to possess ultimate rights over the execution of the budget and the financial laws and regulations; such supervision was confided to the commission. To it was also accorded an absolute veto on internal borrowing; and, in agreement with the Council of the Ottoman Public Debt and the Imperial Ottoman Bank, the commission was to undertake the regulation and improvement of Turkish currency. At the commission's disposal were to be placed all Turkish resources, except those ceded or already ear-marked for the service of the public debt. Finally, the commission was to receive all the rights of the Turkish Government under the Decree of Mouharrem and subsequent decrees.

Even where Turkish financial administration touched foreigners the word of the commission was final. Its veto on internal borrowing also extended to the negotiation of foreign loans. No new concession was to be granted by the Turkish Government either to a Turkish subject or otherwise without the commission's consent. This was likewise necessary for any changes in customs schedules; and Turkish customs were to be administered by a director-general who was appointed and removable by, and responsible to, the financial commission. Wide were the powers delegated by the treaty in respect of war claims. The commission was to adjudicate on and provide for payment of all claims in respect of personal damage suffered by Allied nationals in Turkey during the war.[29]

It is hardly necessary to comment at length upon the state of economic vassalage to which Turkey would have been reduced by the Treaty of Sèvres. Here was a situation of a nature to satisfy the most zealous advocate of financial control over "backward" countries. The essential elements of official fiscal surveillance—the sanctioning by a diplomatic act of the future conditions of service of the public debt and the official character of the executive—were to be achieved by the eventual merger of the Public Debt into the international financial commission. Such is the significance attributed to these clauses of the Sèvres settlement by Sir Adam Block in his Special Report for 1921-22:

> An international financial commission assumes the rights and attributions of the Turkish Government in regard to the Debt Council, which in due course will be merged with the commission. That is to say, an official international body controlling Ottoman finances under a solemn treaty will take the place of an institution whose delegates are appointed by unofficial syndicates representing the bondholders.

Moreover, this international body, officially representing the Allied powers, would have been supreme in every phase of Turkish economy. Not a single item of the economic order in Turkey as forecast by the Sèvres Treaty would have remained within the sole jurisdiction of the Turkish Government. Currency improvement, economic regeneration, tax reform, government financing both domestic and foreign, tariff policy, concessions, all resources of the country (even those not assigned to meet charges on the foreign debt): all fell within the domain mapped out for the international financial commission. By this ring of economic servitudes Turkey would have become effectively shackled to the

---

29 Although Turkey had by Article 231 accepted responsibility for the payment of reparations to the Allies, the latter had, in turn, waived these claims. This policy was not so altruistic as it seems at first sight, for, by Article 236, Turkey accepted the principle that expenses of Allied forces of occupation since October 30, 1918, and indemnity on account of claims for damages suffered by Allied nationals in respect of their persons or property in Turkey during the war, were to be considered first and second charges respectively on the resources under the control of the financial commission.

Allied powers. Such, it seems, is the only rational interpretation to be placed upon their phrase, "to afford some measure of relief and assistance to Turkey."

ANGORA SEVERS THE SHACKLES

The policy pursued by the Public Debt subsequent to the occupation of Constantinople by Allied forces was in harmony with the principles finally incorporated into the Treaty of Sèvres. Following the expulsion of the German and Austrian members in December, 1918, the Council, under the alternate presidency of Sir Adam Block and the new French delegate, Sallandrouze de Lamornaix, attempted to establish relations with the agencies of the P. D. A. in the interior in order that normal activities might be undertaken once more. Its object was to consolidate the position of the Council. Although the operations of the war had created chaos in the Empire, the lines of communication between headquarters in Constantinople and the head offices in the provinces had been maintained. These lines were not ruptured by the change in the composition of the Council. The organization of the P. D. A. remained practically intact, except in those parts of the Empire that were occupied by Allied forces. In these places, the Council attempted to continue to receive the revenues, but if this were impossible, uttered protests concerning its rights, pending a definitive settlement. The helplessness of the Ottoman Government, and the ability of the Debt to call on the Allied High Commissioners in case of need, both contributed to stimulate the hopes that the future would find the Public Debt even more firmly intrenched than before the war.

The assistance of the Allied political authorities was not of a nature, however, to overcome certain formidable handicaps. Owing to the depreciation in the Turkish pound, it was impossible to pay, at pre-war rates, the coupons held by Allied subjects and passed during the period of hostilities. However, out of the available receipts to the end of February, 1920, centralized by the Council in London, two payments of one shilling three pence in April, 1921, and nine pence per eight shilling coupon in June, 1922, were made on the eleven coupons matured from March, 1915, to March, 1920. In addition to these payments it was also possible out of the receipts collected since March, 1920, to make payments of six pence per eight shilling coupon on account in respect of the coupons maturing from September, 1920, to September, 1922, inclusive.[30]

The depreciation of the Turkish pound was hardly the most serious obstacle which blocked the path of the Council. Of far greater gravity was the increase in strength of the nationalist movement. Article VI of the Turkish Nationalist Pact (January 28, 1920) states in part:

> It is a fundamental condition of our life and continued existence that we . . . should enjoy complete independence and liberty . . . in order that our national and economic development should be rendered possible. . . . For this reason we are opposed to restrictions to our development in . . . financial and other matters.

Even before the signature of this document on the above date by the members of the Chamber of Deputies in Constantinople, the incipient nationalist uprising under Mustapha Kemal had followed a policy of collecting for its own use the revenues of the country as they successively came under its control.

In December, 1919, the Council had already realized the nature of the situation in the interior, and, in order to protect itself, had notified the Ottoman Bank, the National Bank of Turkey, the *Deutsche Bank*, and the various railway companies, of the alienation by nationalist forces of the revenues of the Council. On January 15, 1920, a protest was sent to the Allied High Commissioners, who responded on February 29 to the effect that

> the Ottoman Government will be held responsible for the losses to the Administration caused by these actions.

The attention of the Sultan's Treasury was called to the situation, and on April 1, 1920, that department of the Constantinople Government enjoined in the future the action of the Kemalists in seizing the revenues of the Council. On May 1, the French High Commissioner notified the Council that

> he has consistently protested through official channels against the violations of the rights of the Debt.[31]

These injunctions of the Sultan's Government (which was still the *de jure* although hardly the *de facto* government of the coun-

[30] *Report of the Council of Foreign Bondholders* (London) 1924, pp. 409-10.

[31] *Procès-Verbaux*, December 10, 1919, January 15, February 29, March 2, April 1, and May 1, 1920.

try) and the threats of the High Commissioners had little effect on the policy of the Nationalist Government. As that movement spread its control over Anatolia, it continued to increase its collections at the expense of the Council. The years 1921 and 1922 were repetitions of the two preceding ones: steady increases of the powers and collections of the new government, and a corresponding diminution of the revenues and prestige of the Debt. Consolidated in its position by the military and diplomatic victories of September and October, 1922, the Angora Government on October 16, 1922, notified the Council that

> inasmuch as the Government of the Grand National Assembly is alone competent to undertake negotiations and conclude contracts relating to taxes imposed by the state, all treaties, conventions, contracts, official decisions, or official concessions which have been or shall be concluded or entered into by the Government at Constantinople, without the approval of the Angora Government, are null and void. As a consequence, the following are not recognized: neither the loans nor other contracts concluded on the proposals of the Administration at Constantinople, nor payments relating thereto made, for the account of the Treasury, by privileged financial institutions to any administration whatsoever, but made without the adhesion of the Grand National Assembly.

Thus the Council was notified of the intention of the Kemalist Government to be the *de facto* and ultimately the *de jure* government of the country. A Direction of the Public Debt was instituted at Angora; the agencies formerly under the control of the Council gradually became centralized around the executive at Angora. In April, 1923, the new Government collected for its own account the customs surtax in Constantinople; a year later the remaining revenues under the control of the Debt were seized.[32]

In the meantime, important happenings took place outside of Ottoman territory. Due to the initiative of the Allied delegates on the Council, effected through the medium of the Allied High Commissioners in Constantinople, the treaties of peace with Germany and Austria contained clauses calling for the transfer to the Bank of England and the Bank of France of the gold deposited in German and Austrian banks as security for the first issue of Turkish paper money. Moreover, when those treaties

---

[32] *Ibid.*, October 16, 1922; *Report of the Council of Foreign Bondholders* (London) 1924, pp. 411-12.

went into effect, the Allied bondholders' syndicates brought suit to procure for their use the amounts deposited by the Council in German and Austrian banks during the war. The award of the Franco-German mixed arbitral tribunal was unfavorable to the French syndicate in respect to their right to these deposits, holding that

> the right of possession belongs to the Council alone, that Council not being an Allied subject.

On being notified of this decision, the suits instituted by the English and Belgian syndicates were withdrawn, but the Italian bearers fought their case to a finish, only to receive a similar adverse judgment.[33]

Overshadowing these facts in importance, however, was the Lausanne conference of 1922-23 between the Allied powers and Turkey, and the treaty which on July 24, 1923, emerged from these negotiations. Allied subjects on the Council of the Public Debt Administration had had a finger in drafting the financial clauses of the Sèvres Treaty; but, when that settlement, although signed, was never ratified, their efforts went for naught. Again, at the Lausanne proceedings the British, the French, and the Italian, delegates were important factors in the determination of the Allied viewpoint.

The Allied powers, Great Britain, France, and Italy, fought valiantly at this conference to salvage some of the points of the Treaty of Sèvres which pertained to the future of the Council. The Turks, however, knew their desires and contested every Allied argument. An early draft of the financial clauses, drawn up by a sub-committee of the Third Commission, included an article confirming the Decree of Mouharrem and the Supplementary Decree. The Allies were insistent on its inclusion. M. Barrère, temporary chairman of the Third Commission, on November 28, 1922, set forth their point of view:

---

[33] *Procès-Verbaux,* August 25, 1919, and January 27, 1921; *Compte-Rendu,* 1923-24, pp. 48-50. The Council accepted the reimbursement of the Ltqs. 1,150,000 which was the object of these suits in the mixed arbitral tribunals. *Ibid.* This sum was all that remained of the Ltqs. 8,471,381 deposited by the Council in Germany during the war, the remainder having been converted into marks, whose value was effaced by their depreciation.

> The Allies could not consent to any discussion regarding the maintenance of the Ottoman Public Debt with all its attributions and guarantees. The Debt was an institution the status of which had been defined by the Decree of Mouharrem, and officially communicated to the powers. That status was thus placed under their guarantee.[34]

The Turks categorically refused to accept this argument, and maintained a viewpoint which in the end prevailed. On January 13, 1923, Hassan Bey made the statement that

> the Turkish Government was ready to make a declaration [that no change would be introduced into the situation created by the Decree of Mouharrem] to the Council of the Debt before the end of the Conference. The bondholders' syndicates would be informed of it. It is impossible to confirm the Decree of Mouharrem by a treaty, since that Decree was an internal matter and the Council of the Debt was a private institution.

On February 4, the day the first conference broke up, Ismet Pasha, the chief Turkish delegate, confirmed this point of view:

> We are prepared . . . to make a declaration to the bondholders of the Public Debt regarding the Decree of Mouharrem, which defines the position of the Public Debt Administration. We are convinced that the former acts of the Ottoman Government, which have never ceased to inspire the bondholders with full confidence, will constitute a sufficient confirmation of this declaration. . . .[35]

By its silence the Treaty of Lausanne (July 24, 1923) is evidence of the acceptance of the Turkish contention. No statement is contained confirming the Decrees. Nor indeed did the Turkish Government ever make the declaration referred to. In this matter, as in most others relating to the future of the Administration of the Public Debt, the Allies attempted to gain a strategic advantage by assuming the initiative. A draft statement was prepared by the Allied representatives, but the Turkish delegation wished to make reservations, in this statement, on the question of the currency of the coupons in arrears.[36] This question of the

---

34 *Parliamentary Papers*, No. Cmd. 1814 (1923), p. 553.

35 *Ibid.*, pp. 572, 839.

36 On April 23, 1928, the Council of Foreign Bondholders (London) informed the author to this effect. The Turkish reservation was not accepted, and eventually the Allied representatives made a declaration to the effect that their governments would take up the matter if Turkey failed

currency was a vexed one and defied solution during the Lausanne negotiations and, indeed, until the conclusion of the Draft Contract of 1928. In having prepared the statement and in having made its proclamation by the Turks contingent upon their acceptance of a point of view on the currency matter with which they could not agree, the Allies placed themselves in an unfavorable position for subsequent bargaining and practically released the Turks from the obligation of making the desired declaration. That such was the case is afforded proof by the actual setting aside of the Decree of Mouharrem by the Turkish Government and its creditors, and the substitution therefor of the Draft Contract, an instrument infinitely less desirable for the bondholders.

Bearing in mind the acceptance of the Turkish point of view in regard to the confirmation of the Decrees it is not surprising to learn that in the provisions of the Lausanne Treaty itself the rights of the bondholders under the Decree of Mouharrem are overturned. The position of the bondholders in respect of their right of ownership of the ceded revenues is essentially modified by the Lausanne settlement, inasmuch as in the territories detached from Turkey as the result of the Balkan Wars or the Great War, new guarantees must be given to the Debt Council in place of the ceded revenues formerly collected therein. These territories shall contribute separately and severally to the annuities and to the Ottoman public debt in the proportion which exists between the average revenue of each territory and the average total revenue of the Ottoman Empire in the years 1910-11 and 1911-12. The Council of the Debt is entrusted with the preparation of the tables indicating the respective annuities, and any disputes which such distribution may give rise to shall be decided by an arbitrator to be named by the Council of the League of Nations. For the distribution of the capital a commission shall meet in Paris within one month of the definite distribution of the annuities. The commission is to be composed of one representative each of the Turkish Government, of the Ottoman public debt, of the debt other than the Unified Debt and the Turkish Lottery Bonds, as well as a representative which each of the interested states shall have the right to nominate. The same arbitrator as above shall

to make a direct agreement with its creditors. The bargaining between the Turks and the bondholders on this point seems to have resulted in the Draft Contract of February, 1928. See *infra*, pp. 204 *et seq.*

be invited to decide questions upon which the commission may be unable to agree.[37]

The Lausanne Treaty came into force on August 6, 1924. At the end of that year the Council announced the contributive annuities due by the states concerned, and appeals from this decision were heard by an arbitrator, M. Eugène Borel, whose award was made on April 18, 1925. With certain modifications necessitated by the settlement of the differences between Great Britain and Turkey over the delimitation of the Mosul boundary, M. Borel's award, communicated by the Council on April 30, 1925, to the debtor states, contains the definitive partition of the annuities. According to this division, the Turkish Republic is responsible for sixty-seven percent of the annuity of the pre-war Ottoman public debt. The distribution of the capital was then fixed by a commission instituted by the Treaty of Lausanne, which defined Turkey's responsibility for seventy percent of the capital. Among the other debtor states, Greece with eleven percent and Syria and the Lebanon with eight percent have the greatest responsibilities. The remaining fourteen percent is divided among the other states in whose favor territory was detached from the Ottoman Empire during the Balkan Wars and the Great War.[38]

M. Borel also announced his decision on a question which had been debated by the Turkish Government and the bondholders' representatives, namely, the currency in which the service and capital on the debt was to be resumed. The Turkish contention upheld the thesis that this payment should be made in paper francs, while the Council, relying on the argument that the loans had been contracted in Turkish gold pounds, felt that the repayment should be forthcoming on a gold basis.

The arbitrator decided that the Treaty of Lausanne did not intend to regulate that question, nor was it within the province of the Council or the competence of the arbitrator to decide this point. The judgment brought out the fact that the proceedings of the Lausanne conference show plainly that the negotiators

---

[37] Articles XLVIII, LI, XLVII, and XLIX respectively. Articles LIII and LV fix the date from which the annuities are due, and provide that the annuities already due at the date of the coming into force of the treaty shall be paid without interest in twenty equal annuities.

[38] *Report of the Council of Foreign Bondholders* (London) 1927, pp. 412-14, and *Compte-Rendu*, 1923-24, pp. 52-3.

excluded the idea that the treaty should decide the question; moreover, the contracting parties, by their statements in this connection, intended to leave intact the rights of the bondholders and the debtor states respectively.[39] The question was thus left open for decision by direct negotiation between the interested parties. The recent negotiations with the Turkish Government indicate that the bondholders' contention seems to have been accepted in principle, at least as far as the Turkish portion of the debt is concerned. The Draft Contract of February, 1928, fixes the annuities in Turkish gold pounds. On the other hand, the rising scale of charges recognizes the inability of Turkey to make complete payment on a gold basis. Moreover, Turkey has in fact obtained a forced moratorium of four years, since, according to the Treaty of Lausanne, she should have furnished her contribution as from 1924.

A New Contract to Replace the 1881 Decree

The Draft Contract of February, 1928,[40] represents the results of over two years of negotiation between the Turkish delegation and the bondholders' representatives. Although the Treaty of Lausanne traced the outlines of the situation in which the Council would supposedly function in the future, Turkish feeling was opposed to the Council's winning back the privileged status under the Decrees. Accordingly, in the early stages of the debates this point was left untouched. The bases of an agreement on the financial aspects of the situation, however, were reached in August, 1927. Sixty-seven percent of the annuity of the pre-war Ottoman debt is to be paid by the Turkish Republic; this responsibility had been decreed by M. Borel in his award of April 18, 1925. For the first seven years, beginning June, 1928, Turkey is to pay thirty-eight percent of her share of the annuity. This percentage will rise by stages to one hundred percent in 1951. In distributing the above thirty-eight percent, preferential treatment is to be accorded the Unified Debt, which will receive forty-eight percent of its contractual interest, as compared with thirty-five percent for the other loans. The items of the future

---

39 *Ibid.*, p. 53.

40 A summary appears in the *Report of the Council of Foreign Bondholders* (London) 1927, pp. 432-5.

position of the Council and of the guarantees for the payment of this portion of the service were undecided at this time, and it was not until February, 1928, that a tentative agreement was reached.

The divergent points of view maintained by the Turkish delegation and the Council as to its future position were complicated by the proposals of certain French and German financial interests for the creation of a new committee representing the bondholders of loans outside the Decree of Mouharrem, and a joint general council to deal with matters pertaining to both categories of debt. It was proposed that the national representation on the new committee should be proportional to what were assumed to be the present amounts of the respective national holdings. On this basis, the proposed joint council would contain a "Hors Décret" majority, and this body, in practice, would exercise functions and powers properly belonging to the existing Council.

The British and Italian representatives, Sir Adam Block and Commandant Nogara, supported by their respective syndicates, protested in vigorous terms against the proposed virtual effacement of the lawful custodian of the interests of the unified bondholders. Sir Adam based his argument on the terms of the Decree of Mouharrem which had set up the Council as an autonomous body, and also on the fact that under the Treaty of Lausanne the Council was charged to receive the annuities of the various states responsible for the service of the total debt, as well as with the custody of the securities to be provided for that service. In his opinion the creation of any new body which would infringe upon the duties, rights, or attributes of the Council would not only create confusion, but would constitute a modification of the Treaty of Lausanne. This modification would necessitate the unanimous consent of the signatory powers.[41]

The threatened alteration of the Lausanne Treaty did in fact bring the negotiations to the attention of the foreign offices of the signatory governments. The French and German interests, representing, it was maintained, ninety percent of the Turkish external debt, enlisted the aid of the French Foreign Office in protesting against the intractable attitude of the British and Italian delegates. It was reported that these latter were on the point of

[41] *Ibid.*, pp. 25-9.

undertaking separate negotiations with the Turkish Government, a policy which must have been adopted with the object of weakening the position of the proponents of the idea of a new "Hors Décret" directing body.[42] With the question thus introduced into the political realm, a compromise was effected in February, 1928, which, it was hoped, would safeguard the attributions of the existing Debt Council in respect of the Unified Bonds, the Lottery Bonds, and the arrears, leaving the new body to make decisions in questions which concern "Hors Décret" loans only. Joint sessions of the two bodies are proposed for the purpose of dealing with questions arising outside "the ordinary course of business," and also concerning both categories of loans. The administration and execution of the new contract is confided to the present Debt Council, which will hereafter sit in Paris.

The proposed new functions of the Council as thus outlined are not to be compared with the attributes formerly possessed by that body under the original Decrees. The ceded and assigned revenues will disappear, and the Turkish Government will substitute the receipts of the Constantinople customs, which will be paid to the Ottoman Bank for account of the Council. These revenues are at present more than sufficient to cover the annuity, but in case of insufficiency, the deficit is to be made up by direct payments from the Turkish Treasury. Concerning the control over the revenue collection, no information is available except that the new Debt Council will have the right to a "modified control." [43]

The ratification of the Draft Contract of February, 1928, by the Turkish Government and by the syndicates would strike a fatal blow at the position and prerogatives of the Council under the Decree of Mouharrem. In fact, the new contract would replace the Decrees. The power and prestige attained through thirty-five years of administration, but compromised during the years subsequent to 1914, would finally become so attenuated as to be hardly recognizable. No longer do the ceded revenues belong to the bondholders; in the future they cannot rely on the Decree of Mouharrem. They will have to count on a new con-

[42] *New York Times*, December 17 and 21, 1927; *Journal des Débats*, February 10, 1928.

[43] *Report of the Council of Foreign Bondholders* (London) 1927, p. 434.

tract, a fact which undoubtedly weakens their position and deprives them of the guarantees which they have hitherto enjoyed. The creation of a parallel organism for the control of "Hors Décret" loans, and the adoption of the principle of proportional representation for the composition of this body, relegates the previous Council to the position originally forecast by the Decree of Mouharrem. The "Hors Décret" loans are, from the standpoint of bonds still unredeemed, twice as important as the Unified Debt and the Lottery Bonds. This preponderance is bound to make itself felt in the direction of the policies initiated by the proposed general council. Moreover, the service of any new loans, if confided to an outside organization, would undoubtedly be entrusted to the new "Hors Décret" committee, an action which would still further diminish the importance of the old Council.

The significant consideration is that the successor organizations of the Administration of the Ottoman Public Debt will no longer be "imperium in imperio", as was that former entity. The Turkish Government regains the control and administration of the revenues to be used in discharging the service on its portion of the pre-war debt. With its transfer to Paris, whatever modified control the new Council may enjoy over the Constantinople customs can be little more than nominal. The provincial agencies which formerly reported to the Council at Constantinople will retain their present position as agencies of the Treasury at Angora. The old Council's function of collecting the customs surtax has disappeared with the abolition of the Capitulations. If the Draft Contract, when ratified, is rigorously respected by the Turkish Government, the future function of the old Council and of the new Committee will be little more than that of a transfer body. The Turkish Government will have regained its sovereign financial rights.[44]

[44] On December 1, 1928, the Turkish Grand National Assembly ratified a government proposal embodying the terms of the Draft Contract. The ratification was subject, however, to two conditions: reservations of the rights of the Turkish Government in the matter of the Lottery Bonds, and also reservation of its rights in the matter of the reserve funds still held by the Council. These questions still remain to be settled.

The representatives of the bondholders' syndicates decided that this action of the Turkish Assembly fulfilled the provisions of ratification, and the Turkish Treasury, in March, 1929, paid the first instalment on the coupons due under the terms of the definitive settlement.

Chapter IX

THE TECHNIQUE OF FINANCIAL IMPERIALISM

It was no accident that the heyday of the Administration of the Ottoman Public Debt coincided with a period of enormous industrial, commercial, and financial expansion in Europe. Prior to the origin of the Public Debt the Ottoman Empire had attracted substantial amounts of capital which had been created by the substitution in England and in Europe of the factory system for the handicraft system of production. Subsequently, the new commercial revolution (world-wide application of steam to land and marine transportation) occasioned additional production of exportable capital, part of which was invested within the Sultan's domains. The rôle of the Debt in this later period was that of the link between European financial sources and Turkish economic potentialities. But an added factor, imperialism, was present after 1880, a factor which caused acute international rivalry and the final dismemberment of the Ottoman Empire. This discussion of the work of the Council may perhaps well lead to an interpretation of its relation to European imperialism.

The isolated mid-nineteenth century attempts to satisfy demands for foreign markets, for raw materials, and for opportunities to invest "surplus" funds, were undertaken during a period of governmental non-interference. In another place we have pointed out the difficulty experienced by the owners of the many millions of pounds sterling invested in Ottoman securities in interesting European governments in safeguarding these investments. Their failure to stimulate government interest was duplicated in the case of owners of corporate obligations of foreign-directed enterprises in the Ottoman Empire.

These same governments, however, during the '80's and '90's were converted to the doctrine of neo-mercantilism. The amorphous economic factors isolated in the mid-nineteenth century were brought together by the logic of economic nationalism. The structure was reared on a foundation of ideas readily understood by the mass of the population. Thus fear and self-preservation, stimulated by the arguments of preventive self-defence and surplus population, provided excellent bases for an active national policy seeking both the control of raw materials essential in case of war, and opportunities for "expansion." Finally, the keystone of the structure was national honor and prestige, to be defended from attack at all costs. This was surmounted by a figure symbolizing national altruism, "the white man's burden," the *mission civilisatrice,* or *kultur.*[1] While expediency still played an important rôle in the policy of European governments in the Ottoman Empire, imperialist belief had become strong enough to bring official pressure to bear to support "national" projects, or to obstruct them, if deemed injurious to "national" interests.

Of the economic causes which impelled European nations to imperialistic expansion, the most important to this discussion is "surplus" capital. Profitable investment of surplus industrial earnings in enterprises in Europe became increasingly difficult in a market which capitalists considered all but "saturated." Eager for a return on their money in excess of the two or three percent procurable in similar projects in Europe, French financiers, following the policy of their predecessors of mid-Victorian days, envisaged profitable possibilities in loaning to the Ottoman Government. Impelled by the same desire, English promoters constructed port and harbor works, and opened up Turkish mines. Appearing on the field in the last decade of the century, a powerful German combination, under the leadership of the *Deutsche Bank* in Berlin, conceived and all but achieved the construction of the Bagdad railway, bringing in its wake schools and factories, hospitals and harbor works, all the recognized paraphernalia of imperialist expansion. The economic pulse of the entire Near East was quickened by the advent of the German promoter, engineer, industrial manager, and culturist.

FRANCE POINTS THE WAY

Two of the cardinal principles in French foreign policy since 1880 have been, first, governmental control of foreign loan issues in France, and second, an increasing conviction of the oneness of private and national interests abroad. Since that date, an absolute

[1] See Moon, *op. cit.,* particularly Chapters III, IV, and XI; also Earle, *op. cit., passim.*

adherence to the first of these principles, and a general application of the second, have been among the directing forces in the foreign policy of the Third Republic. The first was embodied in an executive decree of 1880. Agitation over large losses in repudiated foreign obligations caused the promulgation of an order on February 6, Article V of which gives to the Minister of Finance the right "to prohibit the negotiation of a foreign loan in France." [2]

The character of the second principle, and its general acceptance by French statesmen, may be indicated by quotations from several of its adherents. Difficulties in regard to Portuguese railway bonds issued in France gave Casimir-Périer in 1894 an opportunity to express the viewpoint of the Government in this matter. Speaking in the Senate as President of the Council, he said:

> In the matter of foreign policy, it is not only the honor of France, but also the interests of her nationals that the Government must defend. It will never fail in performing that double duty.[3]

These statements were approved by the Senate.

Again, in 1901, when the French Government seized the Mytilene customs houses in order to satisfy certain claims of its citi-

---

[2] *The Economist* (London) 1913, p. 334, quoted in Edwards, G. W., *Investing in Foreign Securities* (New York, 1926), p. 274. Writers have divided on the question as to whether this decree extended to foreign government bonds. Thus, Becker, H., *Emprunts d'États étrangers en France* (Paris, 1880), p. 17, thinks that it does not. This view is shared by Saint Maurice, *Les instruments modernes de la politique étrangère* (2 volumes, Paris, 1912). But Politis, N., *Les emprunts d'états en droit international* (Paris, 1897), considered that the decree did include the obligations of foreign governments, and practice has demonstrated the validity of this interpretation. The 1880 decree came as the result of a long agitation. On January 24, 1877, the French Chamber passed a motion for the appointment of a commission of inquiry for the investigation of foreign loans negotiated in France since 1852. The commission was named, but, due to an early adjournment, and to other factors, made no report. Its failure to act was perhaps influenced by the report of an analogous select committee of the House of Commons, which, following scandals connected with several foreign loans, submitted a report in 1875 in which the Committee was of the opinion that "the best remedy against the return of such faults consists not so much in legislative measures as in measures designed to enlighten the public on the situation. . . ." Cited in Becker, *op. cit.*, p. 6; see also *Journal Officiel, Débats Parlementaires, Chambre des Députés*, January 24, 1877.

[3] Quoted Deville, *op. cit.*, p. 49.

zens against the Ottoman Government, M. Delcassé, the Foreign Minister, spoke thus:

> A government that completely understands its duties gives proper consideration to the increasing importance of economic interests. . . . Since I took charge of the foreign policy of France three years ago . . . I have defended the material interests of my compatriots with the same firmness as the moral interests of my country.

The Chamber approved, by a vote of 305-77, the policy of the Government and the opinions of its foreign minister.[4]

Six years later, on the eve of the Second Hague Conference, M. Pichon, the Foreign Minister, explained the policy of the Government in instructing the French delegates to that conference. Diplomacy, he said, could not be called upon to defend every loan made by French citizens beyond French borders. Different situations demanded different treatment. But, M. Pichon concluded,

> it is impossible systematically and in all cases to avoid coercive measures in international relations in order to satisfy pecuniary claims, particularly when these claims rest on the execution of treaties, on incontestable rights, and on interests relating to commerce, industry, and the prosperity of states, interests that are found to be injured by governments unfaithful to their promises or careless in executing contracts.[5]

On December 28, 1909, M. Pichon, in the debate on the budget for his ministry, made the statement that

> as minister of foreign affairs, I utilize my country's outposts of action and of influence wherever I find them.[6]

Thus do railways, ports, mines, and industries become agencies of foreign policy! In 1926, M. Caillaux, Minister of Finance, was extremely frank in his explanation of the Government's policy:

---

[4] *Journal Officiel, Débats Parlementaires, Chambre des Députés,* November 4, 1901, p. 2025. For a more extended statement of the incident, see *infra,* p. 212, and note.

[5] *Journal Officiel, Débats Parlementaires, Chambre des Députés,* June 7, 1907, p. 1230.

[6] *Ibid.,* December 28, 1909.

France lent to Turkey on the security of Turkish customs, not on confidence in the Treasury. It was realizable security, for whence could the Turkish customs be seized except from the outside?

French authors and writers in the press expressed opinions approving the general course outlined in these quotations. The outcome of the Franco-Turk incident of 1901 mentioned above was received by the press as a vindication of legitimate French rights and interests, although the extremes to which the Government had resorted received some criticism.[8] One writer, Reynaud

[7] *Le Temps*, July 10, 1926. Even as early as 1881, a group of French holders of Ottoman bonds invoked the argument of "national interest" as a reason for abandoning their opposition to association with the group represented at the 1881 proceedings by M. Valfrey. The interests of the former group were thus placed under the care of M. Valfey. *Procès-Verbaux et Annexes de la Commission de 1881*, p. 52.

[8] See the London *Times* and *Daily News*, *Fremdenblatt*, *Gazette de Francfort*, November 6 to 14, 1901; *Le Temps*, November 13, 1901; *L'Asie Française*, September, 1901, p. 232; *ibid.*, October, 1901, pp. 306-7; *ibid.*, November, 1901, pp. 319-22. For favorable criticism of the alleged excessive rate of interest demanded on the Lorando and the Tubini credits, see Moncharville, "Le Conflit Franco-Turc de 1901," in *Revue Général de Droit International*, Volume IX (1902), note p. 685; for unfavorable criticism, see Leroy-Beaulieu, P., "Neuf Pour Cent," in *L'Économiste Français*, Volume II (October 12, 1901), p. 497.

This affair was the climax of a series of attempts by France to settle four outstanding differences with Turkey: the status of the Constantinople Port Company, the Lorando and the Tubini credits, and a claim of a French reclamation company in Ada Bazaar. French demands were satisfied by occupying the Mytilene customs, by the seizure and endorsement of customs bills of an amount sufficient to satisfy the pecuniary claims, and by the delivery to the French Embassy of the edicts necessary to satisfy the other demands. Relations were ruptured between August 22 and November 11, 1901.

French prestige, as well as French money, was at stake. M. Delcassé wrote to the French Ambassador, M. Constans, that "the repurchase [by the Ottoman Government] of the quay company's rights, the price of which is now being debated . . . does not concern solely the pecuniary interests, which the Company could settle to its advantage without the Government; it also raises questions of an entirely different nature that concern the situation on the Bosporus of France itself. . . . You have been the first to realize the compromising blow which French prestige would suffer by dispossessing the quay company of its rights. . . ." French pride was also injured in the matter of pecuniary claims, inasmuch as the German Consul had stated in 1886 that all credits to German subjects since 1875 had been satisfied, and he thought it was the same for the English and Austrians.

The Turkish policy of refusing at first to accede to the French demands caused further concessions to be claimed by the *Quai d'Orsay*. Thus, the Porte, by its intractable attitude, had "pushed" France into the expense of the naval expedition to Mytilene, and was compelled to grant official recognition of the legal existence of lay and parochial schools, and hospitals, in Turkey, the *firman* necessary for the construction, enlarging, and repair of certain of these, and the delivery of the investiture of the Chaldean Patriarchate. *Livre Jaune, Affaires de Turquie* (1900-1).

Lacroze, believed that this

> demonstration made a great impression on the Sultan. If he might have cherished some idea of shaking off the foreign yoke that was beginning to weigh heavily on his shoulders, and of regaining the old administrative liberty of his predecessors which allowed them to devote themselves to all kinds of follies, he must now feel, as a result of this act of authority, that it was still wiser to continue to be served by foreign assistance in the restoration of his finances.[9]

An eminent economist, Paul Leroy-Beaulieu, was convinced that

> the state whose protection and whose intervention in another state is implored by its nationals must protect them from spoliation. . . .[10]

A French international lawyer, H. Imbert, thus expounds the doctrine:

> In the investments of their nationals in foreign government bonds, modern states look for another useful instrument [of foreign policy]. More and more they can be seen struggling to direct the free and personal choice of the subscribers towards the attainment of a collective interest. To accomplish this object they intervene more or less unofficially in the negotiations which precede the loans; they add the weight of their moral guarantee and of their support, and sometimes of their credit itself, to the chances of success of those who purchase these obligations. In a word, they use foreign government loans as an instrument of colonial expansion, of foreign policy, of partition [of territory], or of sharing [economic] influence [consortium].[11]

Another author, speaking of financial control in backward countries, offers this opinion:

> . . . The equality of rights between nations has ceased, to be replaced by relations between client and patron. Constellations of states are formed in which the weakest ones move in the orbits of the strongest, like satellites about plan-

---

[9] Reynaud Lacroze, *op. cit.*, pp. 95-8.

[10] Leroy-Beaulieu, P., "Neuf Pour Cent," *loc. cit.* But he did not advise going beyond this. See his unfavorable criticism of the Franco-Turk affair in the same article.

[11] Imbert, H., *op. cit.*, p. 8.

> ets. As the need of financial ties between the controller and the one controlled becomes evident, . . . the bait of material interest makes participation in this [financial] tutelage desirable. This is why the powers, possessing world-wide policies, strive to intervene in all financial control, in order that supremacy [in financial influence] may not be gained by a rival.[12]

In this statement one can imagine the Ottoman Empire as the financial satellite of the European powers, dependent upon them for financial aid to develop resources, and with the Council of the Ottoman Public Debt as an equalizing force between the influences exerted by the different powers.

While it may be admitted that under certain conditions it is proper for nations to interfere in the affairs of their neighbors for the satisfaction of pecuniary claims, there are protagonists of a doctrine who would utilize such opportunities to go much farther. In 1912 appeared a comprehensive work, *Les instruments modernes de la politique étrangère,* in which the doctrine of financial imperialism is set forth in detail. Its author, Count St. Maurice, emphasizes the importance of the step of obtaining the quotation of a loan on the stock exchange. This juncture, in the opinion of this author, is

> the time for the minister of foreign affairs to obtain commercial or political advantages for his compatriots in exchange for their contribution to the proposed loan.

As the result of adroit manipulation of the security of a loan (for example, the signature of the borrowing state, the customs houses, concessions, monopolies, etc.),

> a political protectorate succeeds the economic protectorate, and the debtor country sooner or later becomes the prey of its creditors. In this peaceful fashion are the modern conquests of the great powers prepared and executed.

Indeed, this author maintains that

> intervention [to satisfy pecuniary claims] ought to serve France and her citizens at the same time. To the latter it must be the sanction for the execution of a loan contract; to

[12] Deville, *op. cit.*, p. 79.

the former it must give a foothold in the country, and an opportunity to obtain commercial advantages or a grasp on the local administration.[13]

The financial history of the constitutional monarchy established by the Young Turks in 1908-9 furnishes an example of the technique of this operation. During the summer of 1910, Djavid Bey, Young Turk Minister of Finance, went to Paris for the purpose of negotiating a loan. His initial *pourparlers* with French financiers were unsuccessful, but finally he signed a contract with the *Crédit Mobilier* of Paris. At this point the French Government stepped in, and imposed four conditions on which the Ministry of Finance would allow the quotation of the loan on the Paris Bourse: first, a "real guarantee for the loan"; second, certain reforms were to be realized which would end the recurring budget deficits; third, if the proceeds of the loan were to be used in purchasing materials from foreign countries, French industry must receive its share; finally, a long outstanding political dispute was to be settled. The Sublime Porte considered Algerian and Tunisian residents in Turkey as Ottoman subjects; in the future they were to be recognized as French in nationality.

As it happened, the second of the two financial requirements had been embodied in a project for the reorganization of the Turkish Treasury and the installation of a system of bookkeeping prepared in 1909 by M. Charles Laurent, an eminent French financial expert whom the Turkish Government had invited to Constantinople to advise in financial reorganization. This project, approved by the Turkish Government, had been submitted to the Chamber of Deputies in Constantinople, and had been rejected. Thus Djavid Bey was not in a position to accept the second of the French requirements. Nor was he disposed to accept the other conditions. The degree of control which France was to be allowed to exercise over Turkish finance, however, proved to be the point on which no agreement could be reached. The Turkish Finance Minister made a proposal that two French citizens should

---

[13] Saint Maurice, *op. cit.*, pp. 4, 89, 15, 19. In another place, where this author refers specifically to Turkey, he says: "a financial protectorate has superseded the religious protectorate which has so long guaranteed French influence in the Orient!" *Ibid.*, Volume II, preface, p. viii. See also F. Charmes, *Revue des Deux Mondes*, October 1, 1910, pp. 715-20; and René Pinon, "L'Europe et la Jeune Turquie," *ibid.*, February 15, 1911, pp. 405-6.

be chosen by the two Governments jointly, one to supervise the movement of funds in the Turkish Finance Ministry, the other to be president of the *Cour des Comptes.* The French Government accepted this proposal, but stipulated that these two functionaries should have very clearly defined powers, for otherwise their control would be nominal instead of real. The qualifying clause in the French acceptance was absolutely inadmissable to the Turkish Government, and on this point the negotiations broke down, not to be resumed. The Turks contended that the French demands amounted to placing Turkey under the financial tutelage of France, and, as such, could under no circumstances be countenanced.[14]

[14] Delaygue, *op. cit.*, pp. 269 *et seq.* The loan was later floated by an Austro-German syndicate. See Earle, *op. cit.*, pp. 224-6; and Moon, *op. cit.*, p. 253. Concerning the check on the negotiations in Paris, the London *Times*, October 20, 1910, thought that "the opposition of Djavid Bey to the French proposals is unexplainable. In view of the financial interest of France in Turkey, it is its duty to make its voice heard in a decisive manner, when Turkey proposes to increase her obligations to French capitalists. It is only in insisting that a large part of the capital of the loan be used for expenses for public utilities that France could hope to put Turkish finances in a more healthy condition. It could not be said that the French conditions are excessive in view of the large interests that France has in Turkey." In its London correspondence, *L'Économiste Européen*, of November 4, 1910, p. 439, mentioned that "the English press has been unanimous in approving the policy followed in this matter by the French Government. . . . It is impossible to refrain from emphasizing this manifestation of the *entente cordiale* to which this financial operation has given rise, and the friendly sentiments of the English people towards France, of which the whole British press has in this connection been the interpreter." Reasoned French opinion took the same stand as the *Times*. *Le Temps*, on October 23, felt that "France has to defend the past, present, and future interests of her capital. The attitude of her government has been worthy of praise. Without meddling in any way in the defence of legitimate, but special, interests, MM. Pichon and Cochery, in agreement with M. Briand, have taken their stand on purely national ground. They have wished to avoid allowing this middling loan of 150 millions becoming a disastrous precedent which would disarm us in the future in protecting our interests. This is an excellent policy, wise and prudent, and one for which the public will be grateful." See also *ibid.*, July 24, and September 21 and 26, 1910. But the financial editor took a different stand. While he admitted the legitimacy of having the government under certain conditions give unofficial advice to bankers, "to wish to make out of it a direct financial negotiator in dealing with foreign borrowing governments is to misunderstand its rôle completely and the limits of its responsibilities. In fact, this amounts to the assumption of a dangerous attitude towards national capital, because ordinary investors are easily accustomed to consider official intervention in these matters as material guarantees, which they would not hesitate to invoke in case of need." *Ibid.*, October 23, 1910. M. Cruppi, former French Minister of Commerce, contributes an interesting note in the Vienna correspondence of *Le Temps,* October

It would be difficult to isolate a more typical example of the fusion of finance and politics. It is illuminating as an indication of the psychological attitude dominating high financial and political circles. Recrimination against the meddling of the French Government bounded from Constantinople to Paris, and was countered by the charge that the Turks, if they desired to utilize the assets of a foreign country, should be willing to accept "legitimate" proposals for their expenditure.[15]

Driving Forces of Economic Penetration

The injection of the imperialist spirit into the complicated situation in the Ottoman Empire changed that area from what had been regarded a profitable field for investment and speculation into a cockpit of international rivalry. Of course, even prior to the conversion of western Europe to imperialism, Turkey had witnessed a contest of varying degrees of intensity between nationals of western European nations for the privilege of floating Ottoman Government loans, and of building the short lines of railway undertaken by the promoters of that period. But these enterprises were individual undertakings; the favorite form of investment was in government securities; there had been no widespread and all-embracing idea of endowing the Empire with industries on the western model. Industrial and rail securities were less important than government bonds. In the operation of under-

30, 1910. See also Charmes, *loc. cit.*, and Pinon, *loc. cit.* Even *L'Asie Française* commended the action of MM. Pichon and Cochery in refusing to make the success of the negotiations contingent upon the reorganization of the Turkish Treasury by the Ottoman Bank. "They [MM. Pichon and Cochery] have already done more for that establishment than prudence and appreciation of services rendered would allow." October, 1910, p. 415. See also *ibid.*, August and September, 1910.

15 "In the first place, the state has the duty to defend French savings from exposure to a catastrophe, and, secondly, that they will not serve political or military ends contrary to our interests or to those of our friends. . . . French capital is an element of our strength, and it must be used in the direction of our [foreign] policy." Pinon, *loc. cit.* Cf. the following extract from the Report of the Committee of Union and Progress to the General Congress of the Party, September 28, 1916: "After each loan France endeavored to obtain some financial or political advantage. Unwilling to renounce her influence, she increased constantly her outposts of culture in Syria and Palestine, sections which she had given over to herself as a zone of influence. In them she propagated the French language, endeavored to 'Frenchify' the region, and disturbed its tranquillity by corrupting and stirring up the native population by fallacious promises." Cited in Mandelstam, A., *Le sort de l'Empire Ottoman* (Paris, 1917), p. 130.

writing the latter category of loans there was considered to be sufficient spoil for the nationals of all western European nations desiring to participate. Furthermore the failure to obtain a loan contract or a concession was not yet considered as involving national prestige; financial competition was a concern primarily of the interested establishments. Industrial developments were still talked of as such, and little consideration of national honor was present if a particular industrial group had unsuccessful or unfortunate dealings with the Turkish Government.

Beginning with the modern imperialist era—starting roughly in the 1880's—zealous advocates of the imperialist doctrine discovered that there already existed in Turkey certain agencies which could be turned to splendid account. The Imperial Ottoman Bank was one such agency. This bank had been established in 1856 under a royal charter by a group of London bankers. Under the original terms of its organization this institution was in no way an Ottoman state bank, although from its beginning it engaged in the business of loaning to the Ottoman Treasury. But the attempt to introduce western financial methods through the medium of this institution had been unsuccessful in stemming the flood of financial difficulties which beat against the Ottoman Government at that time. After the disastrous Mirés loan in 1860,[16] and in response to agitation instigated by certain officials high in the Ottoman Government, a reorganization took place in 1863. To the original group of English capitalists was added a number of Paris financiers, persons identified with the French world of high finance. A charter was obtained from the Ottoman Government granting to the Bank the exclusive privilege of issuing notes against gold reserve, and creating it the general receiving and disbursing agent of the Government for Constantinople and its suburbs. In succeeding years the main office in Constantinople opened branches in most of the important Turkish cities and towns in the interior of the country and along the seacoast. In 1875, the area in which the Bank acted as the depository and payer of the Government was extended to include the localities wherein the Bank maintained its branches.[17]

---

[16] *Supra*, pp. 33-4.

[17] The text of the important 1875 charter is in *Parliamentary Papers*, No. C. 1210 (1875). See the criticism of an English contributor to the London *Times*, of November 4, 1874, *supra*, pp. 68-9, and note.

Under the 1856 charter the direction of the Bank's activities was vested in a board constituted entirely of Englishmen, but, with the reorganization in 1863, control was placed in the hands of a joint Anglo-French directorate. Ten of the twenty members of this board were French and resided in Paris; the remainder were English and resided in London. While for a time this equality of responsibility and initiative was real, and although the provisions of the 1863 charter in this respect have not been altered, much of the capital stock held in England eventually migrated across the Channel and took up a permanent abode in France. Even after this migration nominal control of the activities of the Bank was shared equally by the two groups of directors. Actually, however, this change in the ownership of the stock transformed the nominal equality of control into French predominance. Through its London and Paris offices the Bank transferred the funds owed abroad by the Ottoman Treasury. Since the bulk of Ottoman Government bonds has always been held by French citizens,[18] the Paris office has been more important than the London office in the matter of transfer of funds. This fact, together with the majority of the stock being in France, has contributed markedly to the French character of the institution.[19]

A comparison of the scope of its activities prior and subsequent to 1890 shows that about that date the importance of the Ottoman Bank as an economic factor in the Empire greatly increased. Operations during its first thirty-five years were confined almost entirely to dealings with the Government. It had little commercial business; neither was it identified with public works enterprises. In conformity with the spirit of the times, however, and, it may be ventured, because of the increasing importance of French influence in its management, the last decade of the nineteenth century witnessed a remarkable enlargement and extension of the interests of the Bank. In 1884 it had combined with a German,

[18] Thus the percentage of bonds in French hands which in 1885 had been approximately forty, by 1914 had increased to fifty-eight. *Procès-Verbal*, February 17, 1902, *Annex*, and Poulgy, *op. cit.*, p. 160.

[19] The nominal equality of control has been used by the Bank and its subsidiary enterprises as an argument against the existence of any French predominance. In Turkey, however, there has been little doubt as to which committee, Paris or London, was the more influential. Figures indicating the ratio between the amount of stock held in France and the amount in England are not available.

and an Austrian, group, to take over from the Public Debt Administration the exploitation of the tobacco monopoly.[20] By virtue of its support in 1896 there was accorded to a French group the concession for the exploitation of the Heraclea coal mines, the most important coal-bearing area in Turkey. Through interlocking directorates the Ottoman Bank was represented in the three most important French railway enterprises in Turkey, the Damascus-Hama, the Smyrna-Cassaba, and the Salonica Junction-Constantinople lines. In 1899 the Ottoman Bank combined with the Smyrna-Cassaba railway to sign with the *Deutsche Bank* and the Anatolian Railway an agreement providing for the participation of the Ottoman Bank in the capital stock of the proposed Bagdad Railway Company.

The Ottoman Bank likewise played an important rôle in the negotiation of the secret Franco-German agreement of February 15, 1914, defining French and German spheres of influence for railway construction in the Ottoman Empire, and settling the outstanding disputes between French and German railway and financial interests. Of the three most important seacoast towns in Turkey before the Great War, the ports and quays of two—Constantinople and Beirut—were in the hands of companies in the establishment of which the Ottoman Bank had played an important rôle. Similarly, the Constantinople water, trams, and electric light companies have drawn members of their administrative boards from the board of directors of the Ottoman Bank.[21]

The only other institution which rivalled the influence of the Ottoman Bank was the *Deutsche Bank,* of Berlin. The entrance of the Ottoman Bank into the public utility field very nearly coincided with the granting, in 1888, of the first German railway concession to the *Deutsche Bank's* representative, Dr. Alfred Kaulla.

---

20 *Supra,* Chapter VI, pp. 113-14.

21 Much of this information has been obtained from a brochure, *Les intérêts financières de la France dans l'Empire Ottoman,* prepared by the Ottoman Bank in July, 1919, for *Le groupement des intérêts français dans l'Empire Ottoman.* Its publication was undertaken for propaganda purposes in connection with the drafting of the Treaty of Sèvres. The *Groupement* mentioned above comprises the French syndicate which names the French Council member of the Ottoman Debt, and thirty-six railways, public utility enterprises, banks, industrial organizations, etc. The Ottoman Bank heads the list. For the negotiation of the 1899 agreement with the *Deutsche Bank* and the 1914 convention, see Earle, *op. cit.,* pp. 59-60 and 247-52; a summary of the 1914 convention is on p. 248.

From that time on, it was a question which one of these foreign institutions would ultimately be able to occupy the dominant position in the extension of foreign economic influence in the Ottoman Empire. Although enjoying a privileged position in the financial realm, the Ottoman Bank was troubled by the initiative and energy displayed by its German rival.[22] The original German concession of 1888 for taking over and operating the Haidar Pasha-Ismidt line, and its extension to Angora, was followed in the same year by a loan of thirty million marks from the *Deutsche Bank*. This was the first indication of its intention to dispute the quasi-monopoly of public loans which France, through the medium of the Ottoman Bank and the financial establishments grouped around it, had enjoyed since the voluntary removal of English financial establishments had occurred shortly after the satisfaction of English political aims in the Near East by the revision, in 1878, of the Treaty of San Stefano. With the concession of 1903, and the development of the "Bagdad policy" of Germany, the activities of the *Deutsche Bank* were grouped around this enterprise. As the important French-directed railways drew their financial strength from the nebula of banks clustered around the Ottoman Bank, so the German-conceived lines derived their energy from the *Deutsche Bank*. The ports and harbors developed by French initiative with the collaboration of the Ottoman Bank had their counterpart in the construction of the port at Haidar Pasha—the railhead of the Bagdad line opposite Constantinople—by the Haidar Pasha Port Company, a subsidiary of the *Deutsche Bank*.

The *Deutsche Bank* and the Ottoman Bank were the most important driving forces of European economic penetration in Turkey. Either under their supervision or as a result of their policies can be enumerated the financial operations, the energetic policy of railroad construction, the exploitation of mines, public utility concessions, commercial and industrial establishments, and the construction of harbor works in the main ports of the Empire.

---

22 By the *Comité de l'Asie Française* the Turkish Empire was considered a privileged area for French enterprise and this organization resented any newcomers in the field. Thus, in 1914, when the Russians demanded representation on the Public Debt Council, and the Germans requested concessions for their consent, *L'Asie Française* said that this "gives us a new example of the manner in which the Germans profit from every opportunity in order to enlarge their own position, compromising, as a result, those of old-established powers possessing interests superior to the ones which are defended with such roughness by the *Wilhelmstrasse*." June, 1914.

THE CHANNEL OF PENETRATION

In one way or another the Administration of the Ottoman Public Debt was affiliated with the most important of these undertakings. In another place the obligations of the Debt under the railway and loan contracts have been dealt with.[23] It was found that in the collection of pledges the agents of the P. D. A. were in reality the agents of foreign-directed railway companies, or of foreign banks. The assigned tithes in the specified provinces were adjudicated only if an agent of the Public Debt was present. He had an effective voice in all the various proceedings connected with the adjudication. His was the responsibility of making sure that the promissory notes which the successful bidders were bound to furnish were properly endorsed to the account of the Council. In the main offices of the Debt at Constantinople the receipts from the provincial agencies were centralized until the close of the fiscal period, at which time the proceeds were turned over to the respective railway companies or financial establishments. It has also been pointed out that the Debt was not content to play a passive rôle in discharging this function. Behind the forces of the Ottoman Bank or the Anatolian Railway would be ranged the unanimous Council, in case the Government was dilatory in the adjudication of the tithes, or made an administrative change affecting the provincial subdivisions in which pledges had been made, or contested the figures or accounts of the establishments in question. The activities of the Council in the defence of the financial interests of the *Deutsche Bank*, the Ottoman Bank, and the other foreign financial houses, justified the confidence reposed in the Debt. It was in truth the permanent guardian of the interests of foreign nationals in the Ottoman Empire.

If uncertainty exists concerning the reasons which prompted such a zealous policy, it may be dispelled by revealing the interests of the members of the Council outside the activities of the Debt itself. Sir Vincent Caillard, British and Dutch delegate for over ten years, shared with Dr. Kaulla, the representative of the *Deutsche Bank*, the preliminary concession in 1888 for the extension of the Haidar Pasha-Ismidt railway. It was Sir Vincent who originally suggested that the Council assume the rôle of collecting

---

[23] *Supra*, Chapter V.

the guarantees pledged by the Government to foreign concessionaires and financiers. Sir Edgar Vincent, who was the first representative of the British and Dutch interests, and who resigned in 1883 to be succeeded by Sir Vincent Caillard, was again a member of the Council ten years later, but this time as the representative of the Ottoman Bank. When the Anatolian Railway Company was organized in 1889, two members of the Council, Sir Vincent Caillard and Herr Goescher, were elected to the board of directors. When the Bagdad company was formed in 1903, four of the twenty-seven members of the board were drawn from the Council: Dr. Testa, Commandant Berger, and Hamdy Bey, the German, French, and Ottoman representatives respectively, and Count D'Arnoux, the director-general. Commandant Berger was, moreover, the dominating personality in the councils of the Damascus-Hama, the Smyrna-Cassaba, and the Salonica Junction-Constantinople railways. In 1902 he was elected vice president of the *Régie des Tabacs,* while, at the same time, Dr. Testa was likewise elected to this board. M. Sallandrouze de Lamornaix, French delegate from 1918 to 1921, was simultaneously inspector-general of finances of the *Régie* and a member of the Damascus-Hama board, and of the Smyrna-Cassaba board.

Sir Adam Block was a director of the Constantinople Company of Ports and Harbors, a director of Sir Ernest Cassel's National Bank of Turkey, and president of the British Chamber of Commerce in Constantinople.[24] M. Arsène Henry, French delegate in 1909, was a member of the board of the French company working the lead and lignite mines in Balia-Karaidin; one of his colleagues was M. Léon Pissard, one-time director-general of the P. D. A. M. Henry was likewise a member of the administrative boards of the port companies of Constantinople and Beirut. In the former is found also the name of M. Steeg, who was on two different occasions the delegate of the Ottoman Bank on the Council. The present representative of French interests, M. des Closières, is

[24] By virtue of his numerous positions, Commandant Berger is said to have "reigned" in Constantinople. Sir Adam Block has been called "the permanent ambassador of British interests in Turkey." For an amusing and undoubtedly accurate characterization of native and foreign notables in the Empire, see Fazy, Ed., *Les Turcs d'aujourd'hui ou le grand karagheuz* (Paris, 1898), particularly Sir Edgar Vincent, p. 145; Dr. Testa, p. 160; Sir Vincent Caillard, Marquis Guiccioli, Dr. Lindau, Count d'Arnoux, p. 144; and Hamdy Bey, pp. 98-108.

director of *l'Association Nationale des Porteurs Français de Valeurs Mobilières.* On the directing board of the Haidar Pasha Port Company was always to be found the German delegate on the Public Debt.[25]

Not all of the foreign enterprises in the Ottoman Empire were represented in the Public Debt, nor did the P. D. A. collect pledged revenues for all of them. But the important railway enterprises and the powerful banks possessed the necessary indirect representation through interlocking directorates, and the *Deutsche Bank* and the Ottoman Bank, the latter with direct and the former with indirect representation, acted as the financial fountain-heads of many of the less important foreign enterprises. The Public Debt was not only the financial safeguard of foreign capital; it was also an effective partner, always on the ground, thoroughly conversant with the intricacies of the domestic situation in Turkey, and ever ready to pick up the cudgels in the defence of foreign interests.[26]

The "Unofficial" Composition of the Council

Of no less significance than the close inter-relation with the *Deutsche* and Ottoman Banks and their commercial and industrial progeny, is the previous training and the semi-official viewpoint which the members of the Council brought with them upon election to that body. This point has received scant attention from writers, but, coupled with the semi-official sanction by their respective governments with which delegates to the Council were endowed, these two attributes indicate strongly the quasi-official character of the Council.

The original group which assembled in Constantinople in 1881 as representatives of the syndicates responding to the invitation of the Ottoman Government was composed entirely of men who

---

25 See also *supra*, pp. 133-4.

26 Moreover, it has been stated that, in 1911, British, French, and Russian influence in the Council was exerted in a manner unfavorable to the request of the Ottoman Government for a further increase in Turkish import duties from eleven to fourteen percent. De Siebert, B., *Entente Diplomacy and the World* (New York, 1921), pp. 463-4. The funds realized from this increase were intended for construction purposes in connection with the extension of the Bagdad railway beyond Bagdad to the Persian Gulf. The minutes of the Council contain no evidence of this alleged obstruction, indicating that officially at least the matter was not considered by the Council. The Turkish request was shelved by official British opposition but agreed upon in 1914. See Earle, *op. cit.*, p. 111.

had seen government service in their respective countries. The representative of the British and Dutch interests, Robert (later Sir Robert) Bourke, had been privy councilor, a member of parliament, and, to accept the appointment as delegate of the British and Dutch bondholders, he resigned his position in the British Foreign Office as a permanent under-secretary. Likewise the French delegate, M. Valfrey, was formerly sub-director of the political section of the French Foreign Office. Baron de Mayr, the Austro-Hungarian representative, was at one time envoy extraordinary and minister plenipotentiary of the Austro-Hungarian Government in Washington. Herr Primker was legal councilor to the German Government. Commander Mancardi, who represented the very small Italian interest, was, nevertheless, a former deputy, and had been director-general of the Italian public debt.

Similar government training was possessed by the members who later composed the Council. Sir Vincent Caillard, the British and Dutch representative from 1883 to 1898, although young at the time of his appointment to the Council, had nevertheless profited by considerable experience in government circles. In 1879 he had been appointed as assistant commissioner for Great Britain on the Montenegrin frontier; a year later he was special attaché on the staff of Sir Beauchamp Seymour. Two years' connection with the British intelligence office was followed by service on the staff of the British commander in the Egyptian campaign, whence he was appointed to the Council of the Ottoman Public Debt. His successor, Major Fitz Gerald Law, held his appointment for two years only, resigning to accept appointment as finance member on the Indian Legislative Council. Henry (later Sir Henry) Babington-Smith, who was appointed in March, 1902, had been an official in the Treasury in London, and later private secretary to the Viceroy of India. His resignation in September, 1903, was caused by his acceptance of a position in the Civil Service. Sir Adam Block, who succeeded Sir Henry, was destined to remain on the Council longer than any other of its members. Appointed in September, 1903, he served continuously (with the exception of the war years) until February, 1928. His early career was spent in the consular service in Beirut, Damascus, and Constantinople. In 1890 he was appointed consul in the latter city; four years later he was promoted to the rank of first dragoman, whence he advanced to the post of secretary of legation in 1902. He occupied this position on the British diplomatic mission to Constantinople when he was appointed British and Dutch delegate on the Council.

Next to Sir Adam the member of the Council who served longest was Commandant Léon Berger, French representative from 1887 until his death in 1909. Immediately prior to his appointment, Commandant Berger had been connected with the French Embassy in Constantinople as military attaché. His successors were trained in the school of diplomacy. M. Arsène Henry, although he was French delegate for but a few months in 1909, had advanced through the diplomatic ranks until he was appointed ambassador to Sweden in 1907. For nine years after his resignation in 1909, French interests were in the hands of M. de la Boulinière, whose previous experience included appointments as attaché in Washington, the Hague, Rio de Janeiro, and St. Petersburg, chargé d'affaires at Tangier, Lisbon, and Constantinople, and minister plenipotentiary at Cettinje, Sofia, and Cairo. He resigned on account of ill health in November, 1918, to be succeeded by M. Charles Sallandrouze de Lamornaix, the personal representative in the Near East of Count George Vitali, French financier and railway promoter. Since 1921, the French representative has been M. Fernand des Closières, a Parisian capitalist, who has been active in *l'Association Nationale des Porteurs Français de Valeurs Mobilières.*

The incumbents of the post of German representative were schooled in governmental methods to as great an extent as their British and French colleagues. Herr Primker, the first who held the appointment, had represented German interests during the negotiations which resulted in the Decree of Mouharrem. Strange as it may seem, his successor was Herr Goescher, who had filled the post of legal adviser to the Sublime Porte during the debt negotiations of 1881! These two early incumbents held office for a total of only seven years, but they were followed by a series of personalities every one of whom had occupied a position in the German government service. Herman Gerlich was Consul General in Calcutta at the time of his appointment as representative of German interests. He was succeeded in 1892 by Dr. Rudolf Lindau, formerly special attaché of the German Embassay in

Paris and legal councilor of the German Foreign Office. Upon his retirement in 1902, Dr. Lindau was followed by Dr. Karl Testa, first dragoman in the German Embassy in Constantinople. Dr. Charles Bunz, German Minister in Mexico, was appointed to fill the post made vacant by Dr. Testa's death in January, 1911. Dr. Rudolphe Pritsch followed Dr. Bunz; he had been Consul General at Antwerp. His successor in 1917 was Dr. Johann Zahn, whose previous experience also included some time as legal adviser to the Foreign Office in Berlin. It seems to have been an established precedent that the German representative should be drawn from the ranks of the German diplomatic service.

Between them, the British and Dutch, the French, and the German delegates represented some four-fifths of the loans included under the Decrees, and an even greater percentage of loans "Hors Décret." Perhaps this explains the practice of appointing delegates of proved capacity and experience in government affairs. But the minority interest represented by the Italian, Austro-Hungarian, and Ottoman delegates, possessed as its spokesmen persons of equally wide official experience. Commander Mancardi, who had been the Italian representative during the 1881 negotiations, continued for more than ten years as the Italian delegate on the Council. The experience of Marquis Guiccioli, whose appointment extended from 1894 until 1905, seems to have been considered as equivalent to that obtained in government service, for his post on his resignation from the Council was that of Italian Ambassador at Belgrade, whence he was advanced to the ambassadorship at Tokio.

From 1897 until 1917, Austro-Hungarian interests were ably handled by a former member of the consular service, Chevalier de Janko, whose predecessor, de Herwalt, and successor, Count Wickenburg, had likewise seen government service.

The best known of the Ottoman delegates, and the one who held the appointment longer than any of his compatriots, was the versatile Hamdy Bey, painter, financier, diplomat, archæologist, and agriculturist, who served on the Council from 1888 until his death in 1910. Of his two successors, Hussein Djahid Bey was a noted Turkish journalist and litterateur, able protagonist of the Committee of Union and Progress, and supporter of the Turco-German alliance during the Great War, while Mehmet Djavid Bey, who succeeded him in 1922, was the most able of recent Turkish finance ministers.

From this enumeration of the outstanding members of the Public Debt, and their training and experience before appointment, two conclusions can be drawn. With few exceptions the appointees had received long and responsible training either in the diplomatic or consular sections of the foreign services of their respective governments; and in the few instances where this was not the case, the persons appointed were financiers, promoters, or business men, drawn from classes of society deeply interested in the development of enterprises abroad, and naturally in sympathy with a policy of active government defence of these foreign interests. Under any circumstances, the Council would be composed of individuals thoroughly conversant with the technique of granting official protection to special interests, or, on the other hand, equally familiar with the most effective means of commanding such defence. At the same time, it can be safely ventured that the larger interests of their respective governments would receive solicitous attention to the degree that each member was able to accord.

In such circumstances it is not surprising to learn that appointments to the Council of the Ottoman Public Debt were accompanied with unofficial approval by the respective governments. This existed in the form of a modified prior veto on nominations made by the respective national syndicates and nominating bodies. The German technique is probably the most illuminating in this connection, and it has its roots in an early precedent. It was at the desire of the German Minister of Foreign Affairs, who deemed it wise that Germany be represented, that the banking house of S. Bleichröder responded in 1880 to the invitation of the Ottoman Government, and sent Councilor Primker to Constantinople.[27]

As the sole member of the German syndicate, the House of Bleichröder until 1895 kept within its own hands the nomination of the German delegate. At that time, however, the interests of the *Deutsche Bank* began steadily to increase, and a private agreement was concluded between the House of Bleichröder, the *Deutsche Bank*, and the German Government, defining the method of nom-

27 Countess Baumgarten vs. Gerson de Bleichröder, Berlin Landesgericht, February 2, 1893, cited in Wuarin, A., *Essai sur les emprunts d'états et la protection des droits des porteurs de fonds étrangers* (Geneva, 1907), pp. 223-39.

inating and confirming the German delegate. The nomination was made by the president of the Prussian State Bank; the election was made by the House of Bleichröder, but only after previous unofficial consultation with the *Deutsche Bank*, and joint unofficial submission of the nomination to the Foreign Office.[28] This was the opportunity for the Government to place its unofficial sanction on the nomination.

Due to the prestige inherent in the office of president of the Prussian State Bank, and the opportunities for intimate contact with the Government, unofficial approval was signified by merely taking notice of the nomination, and the subsequent election by the House of Bleichröder was little more than the formalizing of the process. It is impossible to determine whether a nomination once made was ever refused approval by the Government, and thus whether a conflict of interest ever arose. From the fact that after 1892 all the German delegates were formerly permanent officials in the foreign office or career men in the diplomatic service, it can be concluded that a tacit approval by the Government was present before a nomination was made. The subsequent submission of the nomination to the foreign office was really little more than a formality.[29]

Elsewhere the practice has been not dissimilar. In England the nomination has been made by the Council of the Corporation of Foreign Bondholders, and the Government notified of this nomination. Here the action of the Government seems to be limited to acknowledging the receipt of the communication. But the position occupied by the Council of the Corporation as a result of being constituted by a special act of Parliament, and the usual inclusion of one or more privy councilors among its membership, assures it

---

[28] The author found some difference of opinion in Berlin concerning the form of this agreement. Dr. Weigelt, of the *Deutsche Bank*, and Dr. Breslauer, of the House of Bleichröder, are of the opinion that it was written, while Dr. Ziemcke, of the Foreign Office, thought it was oral. It was impossible to verify either opinion. Of the existence of some form of understanding there can be no doubt.

[29] The appointement was described by Dr. Breslauer as a "political act." Dr. Ziemcke would not concede this, but Dr. Boetzkes, of the German Bank for Industrial Obligations, and secretary-general of the Council during the war, considered that there was a certain political significance in the appointment. In general, the German Government seems to have been interested mainly in having persons designated who were in sympathy with German foreign policy in the Near East. The actual appointments seem to confirm this statement.

of opinion which, if it cannot be termed unofficial in character, is none the less of value concerning the acceptability to the Government of a proposed nominee. Again practice furnishes evidence of a preliminary approval when it is recalled that the majority of British delegates have been drawn from the government service.[30]

The nomination of the French, Italian, and Austro-Hungarian delegates resembled more closely the process followed in London than the method evolved in Berlin. The French syndicate was composed of six of the largest Parisian banking houses; the Austrian syndicate, likewise, was constituted by two leading Vienna banks; only in Italy, where no local issuing financial establishments had participated in floating Ottoman bonds, was it necessary to employ an outside agency, the Rome Chamber of Commerce.

In fact, however, all of these bodies were in the closest touch with high officials of their respective governments.[31] In Paris, certain board members of the constituent banks were likewise members of the governing council of the Bank of France;[32] in Vienna the most intimate relationships existed between the Credit Anstalt and the Austrian Government; while in Rome, on one occasion at least, the president of the Chamber of Commerce was Italian Ambassador to France and a former Minister of Foreign Affairs.[33] Although the Ottoman Bank was one of the members of the French syndicate, it also nominated a delegate of its own to the Council, a privilege which gave rise to the contention that France had two delegates.[34] Perhaps this complaint of the German delegate contains some truth, since that institution has been con-

30 Private information from the Council of Foreign Bondholders. "The organization coöperates very closely with the British Government, as is indicated by the statement in the report of *Foreign Relations of the United States* (1913), p. 52, that 'the Council of Foreign Bondholders cannot consider any proposal unless submitted and approved by the British Foreign Office.'" Edwards, *op. cit.*, p. 294.

31 Dr. Breslauer, of the House of Bleichröder, informed the author that these governments played as much part in the approving of the respective delegates as the German Government in the corresponding situation in Germany.

32 As, for example, Georges Heine, Baron R. Hottinguer, Baron de Neuflize, who, in 1919, were members of the Paris Committee of the Ottoman Bank and were also regents of the Bank of France.

33 Signor Tittoni, in 1911.

34 In 1914 Germany made this contention. See *infra*, pp. 231 *et seq.*

sidered more influential in Turkey than the French Ambassador to the Sublime Porte.[35]

However non-political the Council may have seemed in theory, in practice the political possibilities of its position became increasingly apparent. That such was the case is manifest by the demand of Russia in 1913 for representation in the Council. The Turkish request for an increase in customs duties from eleven to fourteen percent, originally presented in 1911 and sidetracked by British opposition, had been renewed two years later. On this occasion British consent was obtained, in exchange for Ottoman recognition of Great Britain's special position in the Persian Gulf region, and certain other concessions forming the basis of the Anglo-Turkish conventions of July 29, and October 21, 1913.[36] Having thus satisfied British demands, Turkey turned to Russia.

Here, however, additional obstacles were in the path. Russia's realization of the weakness of her "economic" position in the Ottoman Empire is clearly shown by the contents of a dispatch of October 19, 1913, from Baron de Giers, Russian Ambassador at Constantinople, to the Russian Foreign Minister. In order to develop Russia's "historical tasks" in Turkey, the Baron deemed it essential that Russian participation in oil and spirits concessions be assured, a step which, together with the establishment of a branch in Constantinople of the Salonica Bank and

> the simultaneous participation of our representative on the Council [of the Debt], would, for the first time, open up the possibility of constructing on a solid foundation our economic influence in Turkey.[37]

Only upon the satisfaction of these conditions did the Russian Ambassador consider that the consent of his government to the customs increase could be obtained.

---

[35] "Is not the Ottoman Bank, where a former ambassador of France reigns, a more important instrument of influence than even the ambassador of the French Republic to the Sublime Porte?" St. Maurice, *op. cit.*, Volume II, p. viii.

[36] Earle, *op. cit.*, pp. 255-6.

[37] Stieve, F., (ed.), *Der Diplomatische Schriftwechsel Isvolskis 1911-14* (4 volumes, Berlin, 1924), Volume III, p. 316. The idea of a Russian syndicate which would have the right to nominate a delegate to the Public Debt (the syndicate in reality, however, being founded upon Turkish bonds held by French bankers, who were to effect a nominal transfer to Russian hands) had been suggested to the Russian Embassy in Paris by M. Pichon, French Foreign Minister. *Ibid.*, Volume III, p. 316.

Although Germany had consented in 1910 not to oppose the Turkish request, the revival of the negotiations in 1913 witnessed German interest in the matter from a new angle. Turkey and Russia might come to terms regarding the Russian request for representation in the Council, but, since such an increase in the Council's membership would involve a change in the Decree of Mouharrem, the consent of the nominating syndicates to such a change would become an essential factor in the negotiations. The turn of the discussion in this direction not only emphasizes the increasing power of the Council in the political life of Turkey, but also shows the close contact maintained between the German Government and the German syndicate.

The official German consent to the election of a Russian delegate could be bought only by acceptance of certain definite conditions. The voice of Baron von Wangenheim, German Ambassador at Constantinople, dominated the tone of these requirements. In a dispatch of October 20, 1913, he developed his reasons for believing that the function of the Debt had changed since the early days when its activities were still circumscribed by the Decree of Mouharrem; in the Ambassador's opinion France had two delegates sitting in the Council, one elected by the French syndicate and one representing the Ottoman Bank. For these reasons, Germany should be allowed a second delegate and should be allowed the presidency of the Council every third year.[38]

After an exchange of notes between Germany and Austria, and between Germany and Russia, the formal presentation of these demands was embodied in a note of January 19, 1914, from the Foreign Minister, von Jagow, to the Russian Ambassador in Berlin. Only upon the fulfillment of three conditions "would the German syndicate consent to a change in the Decree of Mouharrem": (1) The entrance of a Russian delegate must be compensated by a second German; (2) German participation in the Council's presidency; (3) Financial questions arising out of the distribution of the Ottoman debt among the Balkan states as a result of the Balkan Wars must be finally settled before any change in the existing situation might be effected.[39] These requiremnts of

[38] Von Wangenheim to Zimmerman, *Die Grosse Politik*, Volume XXXVII, pp. 873-6. For a lengthy attempt to refute the German argument, see *L'Asie Française*, June, 1914.

[39] *Die Grosse Politik*, Volume XXXVII, p. 890.

the German Government were supported by the Austrian Government. Not only would Austrian consent to the Russian proposal be conditioned by acceptance of the German demands, but also Russia was to recognize the legality of the claim for the foundation of an Albanian state bank by an Austro-Hungarian-Italian consortium.[40]

Turkish consent to the Russian claim for representation in the Council seems to have been granted,[41] but the significance of this development was submerged by the political events of the summer of 1914. The widening breach between Austria and Serbia prevented the consummation of the Anglo-Turkish agreements of the year previous; moreover, the important point concerning the modification of the Council's composition never progressed to the stage where a statement of the position of the other syndicates was requested. The attitude of the British, French, and Italian syndicates may easily be imagined.

Nevertheless, the incident manifests in no uncertain manner the definite extension of the economic position of the Council into the political sphere.[42]

Nationalism and Imperialism: Conflict and Compromise

European imperialism means domination—whether political or economic—of non-European peoples by European nations. In view of the importance attributed to the Public Debt in the diplomatic contest just sketched; of the unofficial approval by European governments of the appointments of members to the Council; of the official viewpoint and training brought to the Council by appointees upon the assumption of their duties; of the Council's responsibilities to the *Deutsche Bank* and to the Ottoman Bank; of the system of interlocking directorates employed by these banks and their associated enterprises in dealing with the Debt; and, finally, in view of the *zeitgeist,* the spirit of extending western

[40] *Ibid.*, Volume XXXVII, p. 871, January 24, 1914.

[41] Poulgy, *op. cit.*, p. 97.

[42] "The Council of the Ottoman Public Debt is not at present, as it was at the beginning, a representation of bondholders administering the ceded revenues, but it has become little by little an international economic and financial organization in which the Russians have the right to the same place as the other nations there represented. The rôle played by the Council of the Debt, or rather the Turco-German-Austrian fraction, during the war, is the best proof" of its new position. Mandelstam, *op. cit.*, p. 122.

domination over non-western peoples, it must now be apparent that the Administration of the Ottoman Public Debt was an instrumentality of European imperialism. Turkish nationalism at least has so regarded it. Since 1918 the contest between these two forces has been centered in the Public Debt.

It is obvious on the face of the situation that the Council as a body and its members as individuals were devoted to the principles of the economic system—capitalism—which gave rise to modern economic empire-building. By the very nature of its function the Debt accepted the tenet that "surplus" funds seek employment in those habitable areas which, other things being equal, produce greatest returns. The *raison d'être* of the Council was to provide greater security for foreign capital than that afforded by Ottoman institutions. This object harmonized with the principle that the fruits of capitalism invested in so-called backward countries must, if native agencies provide inadequate security, be protected by European-constituted agencies. For the scattered sums of "surplus" capital which had been mobilized in Europe and subsequently had been placed in government or corporate securities in the Ottoman Empire the Public Debt was the first line of defense.

Together with its adhesion to the principles underlying the capitalistic order is to be noted the Council's alliance with the idea that official backing should be accorded the foreign business interests of a government's nationals. Imperialist doctrine is predicated upon such a belief. When one recalls the official training and semi-official viewpoint of Council members the prevalence of this idea becomes evident. It was translated into action by the process of "reminding" the Ottoman Government of the existence of political sanctions. The plausibility of the "reminder" was doubly patent, since not only were Council members schooled in the technique of commanding government action in behalf of the interests under their protection; but also directors of the nominating syndicates in Europe were in intimate touch with foreign offices. Association with foreign-directed corporate enterprises in the Ottoman Empire through the medium of interlocking directorates assured these undertakings of the active support of Council members. And in 1907, by virtue of its rôle under the customs convention of that year, the quality of the Debt's relation to official

Europe underwent a subtle transmutation which, rightly or wrongly, created in both European and Turkish circles the impression that henceforth the Council was the agent of the powers.

In integrating the forces which made for European domination in the Ottoman Empire the Public Debt functioned equally well for the interested circles of the countries of all its members. The Council discharged its duties to the *Deutsche Bank* with the same good faith and efficiency as it did those to the Ottoman Bank. Its obligations to institutions—banks and railway companies—were real and tangible. The support by the Council or by a part of it of any policy advantageous to the powers as a whole or to a single power was not envisaged in the enumeration of its duties, and any such support must have come personally from a delegate or from the Council unofficially. Such self-imposed duties, nowhere defined, were of a nature to increase and consolidate private interests to which the Council could not be held officially accountable.

It was, however, these personal and unofficial activities which built up enterprises that filled in the gaps between essential pillars of national policy. Was the Bagdad railway such a pillar of German policy? Towards it the Council possessed and discharged definite obligations. But the Haidar Pasha Port Company, towards which the Council had no official obligations, certainly benefited from the presence among its board members of Dr. Karl Testa. Did French influence depend in any way upon the Syrian railways or upon the preëminent position of the Ottoman Bank? Again, towards them the Council functioned under the terms of definite contracts. But the Beirut Port Company and the Balia-Karaidin mines must have enjoyed added prestige because the name of M. Arsène Henry appeared among those on their boards. Primary elements in French and German policy were safeguarded by the Debt; but secondary enterprises as well were favored by the personal prestige and influence of Council delegates. In neither case can it be assumed that the French and German governments were unaware of the official and unofficial backing received from the Debt Council.

None the less, the primary effect of the activities of the Public Debt was the furtherance of European imperialism as distinct from the extension of British, French, or German imperialism. Turkish nationalism opposed certain European beliefs and desires more than their expression by individual nations.

Certain elements necessarily stamped the result of the Debt's activities with such an imprint. The Council drew its membership from five different countries. These members were delegates of unofficial bondholders' syndicates. Being composed of diverse nationalities the Council, as far as economic rivalry among European powers in Turkey was concerned, represented five conflicting forces. Thus no single power obtained a preponderance of influence in the Empire's finances. In reality this rivalry was modified by the inability of Italy and the limited capacity of Austria to export capital to Turkey in appreciable amounts. The contest for control was thus narrowed down to two groups of competitors. In general, Austrian, German, and Italian interests clustered about the *Deutsche Bank*, and French and British interests about the Ottoman Bank. As regards the Ottoman Empire itself the Debt as constituted by the Decree of Mouharrem was the acceptance of foreign financial control in its least distasteful form.

Despite these qualifications the Debt associated itself with attempts to realize aims which, if successful, would have proved more advantageous to certain states of Europe than to Europe as a whole. The Administration of the Ottoman Public Debt not only embodied the principles of European imperialism; but also, in coöperation with Germany and Austria during the World War and with the Allied powers after 1919 the Debt strove to achieve imperialist aims.

From 1914 to 1918 the success of the Council in dominating the economic life of Turkey through the German and Austrian delegates was a demonstrable fact. That situation pictured the Council as released from forces motivated by Allied interests, and as free to devote itself to the consummation in Turkey of the aims envisaged by imperialist groups in Germany and Austria. Had the Central powers won the war the significant position of the Public Debt in the subsequent consolidation of Austro-German influence in Turkey may be imagined from the rôle exercised during that struggle.

But the actual march of events caused it to strive for the accomplishment in Turkey of Allied rather than Austro-German aims. According to the terms of the Treaty of Sèvres domination of Turkish economic life through the channels of the Council and the international financial commission would have been complete. The

Public Debt was capable of being turned to the achievement of imperialist objects for the Allies as well as for the Central powers. The unique *sine qua non* seemed to be exclusive control of the Council.

But, of course, both Allied and German plans were ultimately set aside. The fortunes of war removed German domination from the realm of permanent fulfillment. Turkish nationalism has registered a signal if qualified victory over both Allied and European imperialism.

It is perhaps obvious that such principles and aims were repugnant to the ideas underlying Turkish nationalism. This force had as its ideal the building of a sovereign, independent state. Such an achievement could not countenance the existence in Turkey of foreign supremacy or interference. As such the Public Debt held no place in the plans of Turkish nationalists. To accomplish Turkish political and financial independence the National Pact of 1920 was framed. Although it recognized that the conditions of settlement of proved Turkish debts were not contrary to the principles set forth in the Pact, this document opposed unqualifiedly restrictions inimical to Turkish development in financial matters. Between the aims of the National Pact and the aims of the Treaty of Sèvres there was complete incompatibility. Realization of the former meant independence; of the latter, submission to Allied control.

Thus because it symbolized the subordination of Nationalist objectives to European claims Turkish circles viewed the continuance of the Public Debt with disfavor. Such a policy was adopted despite the marked benefits which accrued to the Ottoman Empire from the functioning of the Debt. To the Government and to the population of the country it was an example of European administrative efficiency and integrity. Inhabitants of the country undoubtedly benefited by the foreign-built railroads and public utilities with which the Council maintained such close contact. Much of the intrigue and dishonesty which had accompanied European lending to Turkey prior to 1881 was abolished. Turkish credit in Europe was enhanced and the Government accomplished its financing on more favorable terms. Increased material prosperity came to the population in many sections of the Empire. But back of these beneficial results was foreign financial control. This situation was repulsive to Turkish pride. So irrational are human beings that touched pride often demands that the body politic be divested even of an agency conferring certain material benefits.

Recent history probably offers no more striking instance of the conflict between western political concepts than Turkish nationalism arrayed against European imperialism. The fact of nationality, transformed according to western logic into the sentiment of nationalism, is seen in operation against the fact of national capitalism, evolved into the idea of European imperialism. The conflict manifested itself clearly in the Turkish Nationalist policy towards the Debt.

At Lausanne the Turkish viewpoint prevailed. The obdurate attitude of the Turkish delegates during subsequent negotiations resulted in further lopping-off of the prerogatives of the Council. In the 1928 Draft Contract the culmination of the Turkish policy is plainly visible.

But republican Turkey has not been completely successful in abolishing foreign financial control. The ratification of the Draft Contract will sanction a regime which still retains certain remnants of the old situation. The serious attenuation of the functions of the once-powerful Public Debt is, however, ample evidence of the far-reaching Turkish victory.

As the safeguard of European capital in the Ottoman Empire the Debt was a success; as a permanent bulwark of European imperialism against Turkish nationalism it proved of doubtful value. Among the remote hills of Anatolia the force of nationalism converted Ottoman subserviency into Turkish independence. The Treaty of Lausanne restored to the Turkish Republic its economic rights. The entrance into force of the Draft Contract between Turkey and its creditors will signify the end of foreign financial control.

INDEX

VITA

The author, Donald C. Blaisdell, was born on August 12, 1899, at Chautauqua, Chautauqua County, New York.

He was granted the degree of Bachelor of Science by the Pennsylvania State College in June, 1920, and the degree of Master of Arts by Columbia University in June, 1926.

From 1922 to 1925 he was an instructor on the staff of Robert College, Constantinople. During the academic years 1925-26 and 1926-27 he pursued post-graduate work in international law and relations and European governments under the Faculty of Political Science in Columbia University. During 1927-28 he spent eight months in Europe and the Near East for the purpose of consulting sources and collecting material to be used in the writing of the present volume. His second year of graduate work was made possible by the grant of a Gilder fellowship from Columbia University, and the collection of material in Europe in 1927-28 was accomplished while holding a Cutting travelling fellowship from the same institution.

He is at present (April, 1929) an instructor in government in Columbia University.

(9001)

Bei Fragen zur Produktsicherheit wenden Sie sich bitte an:
If you have any questions regarding product safety,
please contact:

Walter de Gruyter GmbH
Genthiner Straße 13
10785 Berlin
productsafety@degruyterbrill.com